CIRCUS OF
NIGHTMARES

Death is the Ultimate Illusion

CONRAD JONES

Circus of Nightmares

ISBN; 9798713049478

Prologue

2015

The queue for the ghost train dwindled. Rain hammered down, intensifying as they neared the boarding platform. Katrina was wet and tired and wanted to go home. Her partner Leo had said they would go home when the circus show had finished but he went back on his word and insisted they ride on the ghost train before they left. It was as famous as the circus and a must for fans of the show. The Circus of Nightmares had been such an adrenalin rush. She hadn't laughed and screamed so much in her life. It had teetered along between hilarious and horrific, the crowd never knowing what was real and what was illusion and special effects. The entire show was riveting and made her breathless until the very last second. She was both disappointed and relieved when the lights came on at the end. Leaving the big top was such an anti-climax. When the circus finished, they went straight into the beer tent to talk about the show and got caught in conversation about it with some other locals. After an hour, they were drunk and tired and the fairground was winding down, readying to close. That was when he insisted, they ride the ghost train. Leo was munching his third hotdog of the night much to Katrina's disgust. He was supposed to be watching his weight. They both were but there was only one of them trying. His beer belly was growing. He was in total denial despite her constant cajoling. It was a pattern reflected in everything they did. She put all the effort in, Leo put zero effort into anything.

As they neared the boarding platform, a staff member put the closed chain across the queueing lane behind them. He was dressed in a scary clown costume. Her eyes met his and he winked. She tried to avert her gaze but couldn't. The clown grinned to reveal crooked teeth. He licked his lips and Katrina looked away. She was frightened. When she looked back, he was gone.

'We're the last to ride,' Leo said with a mouthful of sausage. He stuffed the last of his hotdog into his mouth as the couple in front of them climbed onto an empty car. The muffled screams of the riders who had gone before them could be heard. A car burst through the exit doors and a loud horn blared. A couple in their fifties clung to each other, him laughing but shaken, her almost hysterical. Tears streamed down her face. She looked to be genuinely terrified.

'Look how frightened she is,' Leo laughed. 'I told you this is the best ghost train of all time. The freaks are real just like the circus. They have performers in there to make it real.'

'I know,' Katrina said. 'You've been banging on about all day.' She wasn't sure she wanted to go on it at all. 'You go and I'll wait here for you.'

'Are you mad?' Leo asked. 'This is the last night. They may never come back this way. You will regret it if you don't go on it now.'

'It's not my thing,' Katrina said. 'I can't even watch a zombie film without wetting myself. Watching the circus was bad enough.'

'You loved it.'

'It was entertaining but I've had enough of being frightened for one night.' She shook her head. 'It's not for me. You go.'

'Come on. Don't be a spoilsport. The reviews are outstanding. This will be so cool. Don't make me go in there alone, I'll be scared. The ghoulies might get me,' Leo said, turning his hands into claws. An empty car arrived and the attendant released the safety bar. He gestured for them to get in without speaking to them. Katrina felt him staring at her. He undressed her with his eyes and made her feel uncomfortable. 'Cheers mate,' Leo said, oblivious to the leering clown. 'I'm buzzing here. I've been dying to go on this for years.'

'You've been dying to get on it, soon, you'll be dying to get off it,' the clown said, grinning. There was no mirth in his smile. 'You won't enjoy this one bit,' he added, pressing the button. 'Have fun. We will.' Katrina felt cold fear run through her. She tried to undo the belt but it was fixed. The car lurched forward and crashed through the entrance doors. Leo and Katrina screamed in the darkness as the ride began.

Circus of Nightmares

Exactly four and a half minutes later, the car burst through the exit doors and the claxon blared. The seat next to Leo was empty. His arm was broken and he cried out for help but no one heard him but the clown. He tried to reach for his phone but his fingers were shaking so much, he dropped it into the footwell. The car didn't stop. The clown pushed it back onto the track and it latched onto the drive chain and hurtled towards the entrance doors again. Leo screamed as the doors opened and the car entered the ghost train for the second time.

CHAPTER 1

Present Day

Sunday

It wasn't a memorable day when Edward's Circus arrived on the Newry Beach at Holyhead. There was nothing extraordinary about a fair being there apart from the fact it shouldn't have been there. The circus arrived under the cover of darkness and by the next morning it was fully erected, accompanied by a travelling fairground, which filled most of the three grassed areas between the houses and the promenade. It covered the size of two football pitches. There were over forty rides. It was an impressive company of attractions. A ghost train, waltzers, dodgem cars, a roller coaster and a funhouse and house of horrors were supported by the usual rifle ranges, hook-a-duck type stalls and food vendors. The jewels in the crown were the circus big top and the Ferris Wheel. It could be seen from miles away. One of the biggest in Europe. The circus big top was at the centre of the attractions. The huge marquee was black and white striped; its towers topped with triangular black banners, which waved on the sea breeze. The travellers' living quarters flanked the rides; campervans and caravans formed a ring around the fairground and an articulated lorry dropped its sides and became the ticket office, the entrance and exit. The fairground was encircled with barriers for security, one way in and one way out. Red and gold letters glowed in lights. Edward's Circus of Nightmares and a tag line. *The Circus with a Difference.*

The residents who overlooked the Newry Beach hated the fairground coming to town and opposed it every year. This time, there had been no warning of its arrival. There were no posters pasted on telegraph poles, no leaflets put through their letterboxes and no advertising banners fixed to the railings of the busy junctions on the island. There was no prior warning at all and worse still, the addition of the circus. An extremely popular circus at that. One minute the Newry was a wide promenade with sloping grassy areas running down to the sea with ornamental flowerbeds and Victorian shelters where tourists could sit and eat ice cream, the next it was a substantial fairground. Overlooked by the mountain and protected from the stormy sea by the breakwater, which was over a mile long. It was home to the marina where a flotilla of yachts anchored. It was no place for a circus, especially this one.

The Circus of Nightmares was an internet sensation with a cult following. Its performers entertained thousands with the most dangerous stunts and illusions possible. It would attract visitors from all over the island and beyond. Some welcome, most unwelcome. It would be busy and it would be noisy. The sound of banging music and the flashing lights would go on into the night. It was an annoyance of monumental scale at the best of times but arriving unannounced and without permission was totally unacceptable for some of the locals. Most of them moaned and did nothing but some were incensed.

Local resident Malcom Orange was one of those incensed. He was on the town council committee and they assessed requests to trade and granted permission for licences on the island and no application for a circus or travelling fair had been processed for over a year. The most regular visiting circus was Pender's and their behaviour had ruined it for other travelling shows. The last time Pender's circus was given permission to trade in Trearddur Bay, their employees refused to pay for their meals at The Imperial Palace Chinese restaurant. Tables were turned over and a wine fridge emptied, the contents stolen and the police were called. The staff and customers were traumatised but the police made no arrests. It was deemed to be more trouble than it was worth. The travellers would be bailed on minor charges and would never return to appear in court anyway. It was a massive waste of money and resources. Following that incident, the decision was made to boycott such travelling businesses from trading on the island for the foreseeable future. That suited Malcolm down to the ground. His house overlooked the Newry. He could see the sea from his settee and the lighthouse and breakwater from his kitchen and bedrooms. At least, he could before the circus arrived. His view was his pride and joy and they had stolen it from him overnight.

They had erected their fairground in front of his windows. The big top was completely blocking his view of the sea from the ground floor. He could still see the lighthouse from the bedrooms if he stood on tiptoes. It was an outrage and there was already the smell of hot dogs on the breeze. His garden would be full of popcorn cartons, drink holders and hamburger wrappers by teatime and the cheeky buggers didn't even have permission to be there. Someone was winging it. He'd seen it before. They set up without a license, trade for as long as they can before the local authorities could physically get the bailiffs and police to move them, by which time they were ready to move on anyway. They were fly-by-night operators and pirates who flouted the rules because they could. Malcolm wasn't having it. They were not going to get away with it here. Not right in front of his living room window. Not on his watch. He dressed and searched for his winter jacket. It made him look bigger. He thought about taking a walking stick and selected a bone handled cane but decided it could be seen as a weapon or a weakness and placed it back in the stand with a clatter.

'What on earth are you doing?' his wife Jane asked. She was wrapped in a bathrobe, her silver-grey hair hanging wet on her shoulders. She could see Malcolm was annoyed, which was nothing new. He was always annoyed about something. It was his permanent state. 'Please don't tell me you're going to tell the circus owners they shouldn't be there?'

'Someone needs to stand up to them, Jane,' Malcolm said. He zipped up his coat and put on his Russian style hat and gloves. His reflection in the mirror showed a portly middle-aged man with thinning hair and a grey beard. 'They don't have a licence and I intend to tell them that they cannot trade without one.'

'Have you lost your mind?'

'No. I am not sitting here allowing them to break the law when and where they choose, especially not in front of my living room window,' Malcolm said, nodding. 'Someone has to take a stand.'

'And who nominated you?' Jane asked, irritated. 'Unless you're Batman or some other crime-fighting superhero and you've done a marvellous job of keeping it a secret from me for all these years, you shouldn't go there and confront them if you value your health.'

'What on earth do you mean?'

'I mean they're ruffians with no respect of the law let alone what you think of it. What you think is insignificant to people like that. Unless you truly are a caped crusader, you could end up being hurt, Malcolm. Please do not go there and cause a fuss.'

'They don't have a licence and I'm not afraid of them,' Malcolm ignored her jibe.

'They don't have a licence, let's analyse that.'

'Here we go,' Malcolm rolled his eyes. 'Let's analyse it. We have to analyse everything in this house.'

'Don't be facetious. It doesn't suit you.' She wagged a finger at him. 'Think about it clearly. Do you think they've overlooked applying for a licence by accident?' Jane asked, sarcastically. She shrugged. 'Answers on a postcard please. Do you think they've overlooked it by accident?'

'Of course not.'

'Good, because they know they don't have an effing licence,' she said, shaking her head. 'The fact is they don't care that they don't have an effing licence. That's the way they operate.'

'Not here it's not,' Malcolm said. 'I'll tell them straight, to pack up and move on and if they don't, I'll have the police down here pronto.'

'And what do you think they will say to the police?' she said, tutting. 'The police have no powers to move them on and they know that too.'

'It's a disgrace,' Malcolm said. 'I will tell them so too.'

'You will just aggravate them, Malcolm,' she said, shaking her head. 'Have you lost your marbles?'

'No. I'm thinking very clearly. Someone needs to protest.'

'This is one protest that will end in tears.'

'I'm not letting it happen.'

'Oh, for god's sake. Have you taken your blood pressure tablets?' Jane asked, concerned.

'Yes.'

'I don't want you going there alone. You'll get a punch on the nose if you're not careful.'

'I'm going to give them a piece of my mind.'

'Oh, for god's sake. If you must go there and make a bloody fool of yourself, please don't go down there alone.' She gestured to the phone. 'Ask Glen to go with you. He is always banging on about having a brown belt in karate. Ask him to go with you. Don't go on your own.'

Malcolm nodded and picked up the phone. He didn't have a mobile. They were responsible for the decline in conversational skills and the root of all evil. He refused to have one, even though Jane had bought him one for Christmas five-years ago. It was still in the box. He dialled Glen's number.

'Hello,' Glen answered.

'It's Malcolm.'

'I know who it is,' Glen said. 'You're the only person who uses the landline. Don't tell me you've seen the circus?'

'Seen it?' Malcolm said. 'The cheeky buggers have put their big top right in front of my living room. All I can see is a chuffing big tent through my window. I can't sit on the settee and relax with that great stripy monstrosity there every time I look up. It's making my blood boil.'

'Close the curtains,' Glen laughed.

'It's not funny, Glen. They're taking the piss out of us.'

'That's just what they do.' Glen sighed. 'Have you called the police?'

9

'No. Not yet.' Malcolm paused. 'I'm going to have a word with the owners myself first and tell them I'm on the planning committee.'

'What will that achieve?' Glen asked. 'I mean seriously, what do you think they will say?'

'If I reason with them and explain what they're doing is illegal and that they need to pack up and move on, they might listen to sense.'

'You're dreaming.'

'I have to try but Jane is worried about me going on my own.'

'Jane is an incredibly wise woman,' Glen said. 'You don't want to be going down there and confronting them alone or otherwise. They're travelling folk, Malcolm, hearts of gold I'm sure but they don't take kindly to townies like us telling them what to do.'

'Maybe not but what's the worst that can happen?'

'They could kick you in the goolies, tell you to bugger off and mind your own business and laugh all the way to the bank.' Malcolm didn't laugh. Glen sighed again. 'Listen to me, Malcom. I wouldn't go there alone. You need to listen to Jane. She's right as usual.'

'Jane was wondering if you would come with me,' Malcolm said. 'Because you did karate.'

'I cannot use my karate. No one is in mortal danger, Malcolm.'

'My view is in mortal danger.'

'It's a martial art.'

'I know it is.'

'Well, as such, it can't be used willy-nilly.' Glen mumbled. 'Under normal circumstances, I would be right there with you,' Glen said, clearing his throat.

'These are not normal circumstances,' Malcolm complained. 'There is a circus tent in front of my window and I want it removed.' Glen remained silent. 'Are you coming with me as my bodyguard?'

'I've torn a muscle in my back. I wouldn't be much use to you at the moment.' The line went quiet again. 'You shouldn't approach them yourself. Call the police if you must but the truth is, there's nothing we can do about it except hope they do well for a few days and move on.'

'But the mess they left last time,' Malcolm moaned. 'I had litter in my garden for weeks.'

'Litter can be picked up, Malcolm. Leave well alone.' Glen warned. He knew Malcolm would be seething. 'They'll be gone before you know it.' There was an awkward silence. 'Anyway, I need to go. Tea won't make itself. You take care of yourself and say hello to Jane for me. Tata for now.' Glen hung up.

'Bloody coward,' Malcolm said, muttering when the line went dead. 'Brown belt in karate my arse. More like a yellow-belly belt. Karate indeed. He probably couldn't spell it if he tried.' Jane was drying her hair in the bedroom. 'Glen is a bloody coward, darling,' he called upstairs. The hairdryer whirred loudly. 'I said, Glen is a bloody coward.' There was no reply. 'I'm going to have a word with them.' Jane didn't hear him. 'I won't be long.'

Malcolm left the house and walked down the narrow pavement, which led to an opening in the stone walls that separated the Newry's grassed areas from the residential estate. It was a grey day but the sea was calm. An Irish ferry was heading into the harbour, passengers lined the rails watching its progress. He could see them taking photographs of the fairground, the mountain and the port. The travellers' caravans formed a barrier between the path and the fair. He could see the back of the big top and some of the workers milling around. Some were wearing costumes, obviously performers. Others were fairground employees. They were a scruffy bunch with tattoos everywhere; he didn't like people with tattoos. It was a pet hate. A prejudice he couldn't explain. He headed for a gap between two vans and a brindle pit bull launched itself at him from behind a large caravan. Only a sturdy chain kept it from reaching him. It reared up on hind legs, snapping his teeth and drooling. The snarling sounded unearthly. Malcolm stepped backwards and tripped over a binbag full of rubbish. He landed heavily on his bottom and felt his right-hand sink into something warm and sloppy. The smell of dog shit hit him like a slap on the nose.

'Oh my god,' he stammered, angrily. 'Dirty bloody do-as-you-likeys,' he hissed. It took him a few minutes to compose himself enough to stand. He tried to wipe the dog faeces from his fingers on the grass but it was a pointless task. It was under his fingernails. The smell was vile, making him want to puke. 'And this is why you're not welcome here,' he said to no one. The smell of candyfloss and onions was hanging in the air. The fairground was gearing up to open. 'You don't have a licence and you don't move your rubbish and you don't pick up your dog shit. I'll give them a piece of my mind,' he muttered, angrily. He made his way along the path, searching for a gap between the caravans, which wasn't guarded by a rabid terrier on steroids. Eventually, he reached an articulated lorry, which had converted into a funhouse. It dominated that side of the promenade. He navigated his way between the railings, ropes and power cables into the fairground and marched towards the first figures he could see. The men were fiddling with the engine of a Ford Transit, pouring oil into the block.

'Can you tell me who is in charge here?' They ignored him. 'Excuse me. I asked who is in charge?' They ignored him again but looked at each other. 'Excuse me. Do you speak English?' Malcolm asked unnecessarily loudly.

'Yes. We speak English,' one of them answered. His accent might have been German or Austrian.

'I need to know who is in charge,' Malcolm said, puffing his chest.

'Why do you want to know that?' one of them asked without looking at him.

'This is council business. I will discuss that with the manager.' The men ignored him. 'Can you tell me where to find him?' Malcolm said, tapping the man closest on the shoulder.

'Don't put your hands on me, understand?'

'Sorry. But it's important. I need to speak to the owner.'

'Who is asking?' the man answered. He turned to face Malcolm. His expression was aggressive.

'I'm asking. Malcolm Orange.' Malcolm stepped back. 'I'm a local resident and a member of the town council.'

'Town council indeed. If you've got any sense, you need to leave the way you came in,' the man said. 'The fair isn't open yet. Everyone is busy. Come back at twelve o'clock.'

'I need to talk to whoever is in charge before you open as you should not be opening at all,' Malcolm said, standing firm. 'And I won't be leaving until I have spoken to them.'

'You're going to get yourself into bother with that attitude.' The man picked up a wrench. He tapped the engine with it. 'Where we come from, aggression is met with aggression.'

'I mean no offence,' Malcolm said, backing away. 'But I would like to speak to whoever is in charge.'

'Suit yourself,' the man said, turning back to the engine. 'Don't say I didn't warn you.'

'Where will I find them?'

'You need to go to the big top,' the man said, pointing. 'Ask for Lottie.'

'Thank you,' Malcolm said, turning away. He headed towards the circus tent. The smell of burgers was wrestling with the smell of dog faeces. He couldn't get it out of his head, no matter how many times he wiped his hands on the grass. Manic laughter made him jump. It took several seconds to register it was recorded and coming from the funhouse. Another burst of laughter echoed across the fairground. A mechanical parrot squawked inside a glass cabinet filled with teddy bears. Its perch swung to and fro. Malcolm walked as quickly as he could. There was something eerie about the place. He reached the big top. The flaps were tied back creating a doorway a large van could fit

13

through. He looked inside. Tiered seating had been erected on three sides of the ring. The sound of chainsaws whirred loudly. He watched mesmerized as a man in a boiler suit juggled three of them. The blades gleamed as they span. He tossed them one at a time to a huge clown, who tossed them back in turn. Behind the jugglers, a fire-eater blew orange flames from his lips at another performer who became engulfed in flame and gyrated in a macabre dance. Seconds later, the flames were gone and the performer unharmed. A scantily clad female was spinning on a wheel, while a man in a ski-mask threw machetes at her; she giggled like a schoolgirl and shrieked with glee as each blade struck. Above him, a trapeze artist was practicing without a safety net. She was wearing a Lycra bra top and matching shorts, which didn't leave much to the imagination. Every inch of her skin was tattooed. He stared for longer than he was comfortable with, feeling guilty of the desire he felt. A circus with a difference, the signs said. Now he knew why. They were all mad.

'I hope you're not staring at my wife?' a man growled. His accent was thick and guttural. Probably Eastern European, Malcolm thought. He looked like he ate six-inch nails for breakfast. His neck was thicker than the average man's thigh. 'What are you doing here, pervert?'

'I'm not a pervert and I was not staring at anyone,' he protested. He blushed. 'I'm looking for Lottie. I was told he's in charge.'

'If you look at my wife again, I'll poke your eyes out of your head.'

'Leave him alone,' a female voice said from behind him. He turned to face her. Her long brown hair was plaited and touched by the sun at the ends. She was fixing a scrunchie to it as she spoke. Malcolm was taken aback. Her eyes were smiling and she was disarmingly attractive.

'He's a pervert, staring at Helga while she works.'

'I'll deal with it. Go and practice.' The man mountain snarled and walked away. 'Ignore Ivo,' the woman said. 'He's a little protective of Helga.'

'I wasn't staring at her,' Malcolm muttered.

'Of course, you weren't. Although I wouldn't blame you if you did. Helga is ridiculously hot, isn't she?' Lottie grinned. Malcolm opened his mouth but couldn't find his voice. 'No need to be embarrassed. How can I help you?'

'I'm looking for Lottie or whoever is in charge,' Malcolm said, irritated by his own hesitation. 'Can you point me in the right direction?'

'I'm Lottie,' she said, smiling. 'Lottie Edwards. Owner operator of this outfit.'

'Oh, I see.'

'You expected a man?' Lottie asked. Malcolm didn't answer but blushed. 'No problem. It's a popular misconception. How can I help you?'

'You could help by packing up and moving on,' Malcolm said.

'And why would we do that?'

'You don't have a licence to operate here or park here or even be here. This is public land owned by the people of Holyhead,' Malcolm said. 'And without permission, you're trading illegally.'

'And you are?' Lottie asked, half smiling. Her eyes assessed him. She looked through him.

'Malcolm Orange. I'm on the town council and this circus tent is right in front of my windows.'

'Okay, councillor Orange. Do you want us to relocate the big top because we can't do that now it's set?'

'No. I don't want you to relocate it.'

'Do you want money in compensation for your view?'

'No.' Malcolm was confused. 'I don't want your money.'

'What exactly do you want?'

'I want you to pack up and move on,' Malcolm said, feeling more confused. Lottie appeared to be friendly enough so far and she was incredibly attractive. It was difficult to be annoyed with her. 'You seem like a reasonable woman. You must appreciate you can't just turn up and operate wherever you choose without permission.'

'Yes. Of course, I do.'

'You do?'

'Yes. We're just passing through on the way to Ireland,' Lottie said. 'We have been touring Europe but we're ahead of schedule by three days so we arranged this stopover.'

'Sorry. I don't follow,' Malcolm said, shaking his head. 'You arranged what exactly?'

'Part of the original schedule was cancelled. I knew we would have time to spare before we crossed to Ireland, so I made a call and we have permission to operate here until Thursday and then we'll be on the ferry on Friday and away. Maybe it wasn't communicated to you. It was a lastminute arrangement but we have permission to be here.'

'Lastminute?' Malcolm asked confused.

'Yes. Our schedule is planned years in advance so this is what I would call lastminute,' Lottie said, smiling. 'Time is money in this game and we can't have the tent down any longer than is feasibly possible so, I made a few calls and arranged to stopover here for a few days. We have permission.'

'That's impossible. You have permission from who?' Malcolm said, flustered. 'I'm on the planning committee. I've seen no such applications made and certainly no permission granted in the last twelve months.'

'I can categorically tell you we have permission,' Lottie said. 'Wait a minute.' Lottie took out her mobile. Malcolm noticed how strong she looked. Her body was lean but toned. 'I have it here somewhere.' She scrolled through her messages. 'Here it is. Charles Milburn,' Lottie said, checking her phone. 'We had a long conversation about it and we agreed we would donate a percentage of the ticket takings to the local hospice and he said he would forward the paperwork on to us but I haven't heard from him and we've been travelling constantly, so I don't have a hard copy. He said we could pick it up when we arrived.'

'When did you speak to Charles?'

'Six weeks ago, was the last time, when we had a cancellation in London,' Lottie said, checking her phone again. 'It's all here on my phone.'

'This is most irregular.'

'It might be but we have his permission and he's in charge, isn't he, councillor Orange?'

'Charles was the chairman but he died last month,' Malcolm said, frowning.

'Oh, I'm so sorry to hear that,' Lottie said, frowning. 'He seemed like a lovely man. Definitely not a jobsworth like some people. What a shame.'

'You didn't know he was dead?'

'No. How would I?' Lottie asked. 'We've been travelling.'

'Charles wouldn't have done this. He couldn't give permission for this, certainly not over the telephone anyway.' Malcolm gestured to the fairground. 'This is a major operation and we're not prepared for it. It needs to be policed not to mention the waste you will create.'

'We will throw all the waste into the sea,' Lottie said. 'It's just over there. We threw a load in this morning.'

'I beg your pardon?' Malcolm said, horrified.

'I was joking,' Lottie said. She rolled her eyes. 'We have compactors. All our waste will be bagged and compacted ready for collection.'

'Yes, it may be compacted but we haven't arranged any pickups because we didn't know about it. Charles wouldn't have okayed this, last minute or not.'

'He did,' Lottie smiled. Her eyes narrowed. 'I can assure you Charles Milburn gave us permission.'

'He couldn't and wouldn't have given permission without the committee's agreement,' Malcolm said, adamant. 'Everything has to go to the vote.'

'He gave me permission,' Lottie said, sighing. 'Now. I'm a busy woman. I really need to get on as we're opening at lunchtime.'

'I absolutely forbid it.'

'You forbid it?' Lottie said, smiling. 'Bossy little man, aren't you, councillor.'

'You do not have permission,' Malcolm argued. 'This is a ruse.'

'Meaning what exactly?'

'His death was reported widely in the press. I think you've seen it on the news and taken advantage of it.'

'Are you calling me a liar?' Lottie's expression hardened. Several employees were approaching. They looked strong and they looked nasty. A clown came out of the big top. He stood six feet five at least. There was nothing amusing about it. It looked like something from a Stephen King novel. Several more joined it. Malcolm felt intimidated. Others gathered behind him, pushing and jostling. 'Don't upset the staff. That won't end well,' Lottie said, shrugging. 'We have permission to trade and we will be trading. And let's be clear that I'm not a liar.'

'I'm not calling you a liar.' Malcolm lowered his tone and picked his words carefully. 'I'm saying Charles didn't have the authority to grant you permission to trade,' Malcolm said, retreating a little. He looked around the bizarre collection of faces. A woman stared at him through yellow eyes. She had contact lenses, which made her pupils like those of a lizard. Her face was completely tattooed. She smiled to show her teeth were filed into fangs and her tongue was surgically split in two. Malcolm felt frightened. 'I don't believe he did give his permission and there's no way of checking, is there?' he said, shaking his head. 'We only have your word that this conversation with Charles ever took place.'

'So, you're not calling me a liar but you're insinuating I am one?' Lottie frowned.

'Who is calling you a liar, boss?' one of the clowns asked. He spat phlegm on the ground inches away from Malcolm's shoes. 'This little man?' A second clown barged into Malcolm's shoulder. The homemade tattoos on his neck looked childlike. One of his ears had been bitten off at the lobe. 'Are you calling the boss a liar?'

'I'm not calling anyone a liar,' Malcolm said, shaking his head. Fear made his blood run cold. More travellers arrived, crowding him. 'I'm not here for trouble,' he said, frightened. 'Maybe we should call the police to resolve this?'

'I think you should leave,' Lottie said. Her smile was gone. 'Before you offend someone.'

'I'm representing the town council,' Malcolm said, shaking his head. He began sweating profusely. 'And you don't have a licence to operate on this island. Charles Milburn would not and could not have given permission for you to set up here. You're leaving me no choice but to call the police.'

'Call them,' Lottie said. 'I'll tell them the same as I told you. We have permission from Charles Milburn. Today is Sunday. We'll be opening until Thursday and then we sail to Ireland on Friday.' Malcolm shook his head angrily. 'Please leave the pitch. We're getting ready to open.'

'I will not leave.'

'Leave for your own safety,' Lottie said, smiling coldly.

'You need to do as you've been asked,' the lizard woman said, her tongue flickered from her lips like a snake. She leaned in towards him. Malcom had seen enough. He was overwhelmed. 'Lottie has asked you nicely. So, be a good boy and fuck off before you get hurt,' she whispered in his ear.

'I will. I'm going now.' He nodded and wiped sweat from his brow. 'But I will be back,' Malcolm warned. 'This isn't the end of the matter.'

'Escort the councillor off the pitch,' Lottie said to her employees. 'Take him to the entrance gate and show him out. We wouldn't want any ill befalling him on his way home now, would we?' Malcolm turned and tried to walk away but his path was blocked. The giant clown barred his way. 'Hugo. Be nice now,' Lottie said. 'Don't upset Hugo. He's a little unpredictable. Sometimes, he doesn't know his own strength. He pulled a man's arm off in Leipzig. It was an accident but painful nonetheless.'

'Oh, god.' Malcolm felt dizzy. 'I don't feel very well. Could someone call me an ambulance?'

'Come with us and we'll take you to the road and call you an ambulance. Don't phone the police,' the big clown said, shaking his head. His voice was deep. 'Don't use your phone, please,' Hugo said, holding out his hand. His hand was the size of a garden spade. 'The police are not our favourite people. We don't want them here.'

'I don't have a phone,' Malcolm stammered. Beads of sweat formed on the back of his neck. His chest began to tighten. Voices were raised and angry, threatening and abusive. His breathing became laboured. 'I'll go but this isn't over,' he muttered. He felt like he was being crushed by an invisible hand. 'I'll be calling the police as soon as I get indoors,' Malcolm said, clutching his chest. Cold sweat ran down his forehead. 'Excuse me,' he gasped, trying to find a gap through the throng. 'I'm feeling a little breathless.'

'He doesn't look too good,' Lottie said. 'Carry him off the pitch.'

'Where to?'

'Anywhere but here,' she said. 'Take him to the road. There's a toilet block on the corner.'

'Call an ambulance,' Malcolm gasped. His chest constricted further. 'My heart,' he muttered.

'Get him off the pitch,' Lottie ordered. 'And don't hurt him.'

20

Malcolm was lifted from beneath the arms and carried quickly towards the exit.

'I need an ambulance. Please call an ambulance.' He was about to ask again when a blow to the back of the head knocked him to his knees. A second blow switched the lights off and he crumpled onto the damp grass.

Chapter 2

Michelle and Tiffany left the Albert Vaults and staggered up Newry Street towards the Newry Beach. They were both blond and petite. Michelle, affectionately known as Tinkershell because of how tiny she was, held Tiffany by the elbow to keep her upright. They'd been drinking gin and tonic and downing shots since dinnertime. It was Tiffany's birthday and the news that the circus was in town was just what they needed. Michelle was a fan of the Circus of Nightmares and followed them on social media. Their stunts and illusions were ground-breaking, always pushing the boundaries and blurring the lines between entertainment and horror. She had wanted to see the show for years. It was perfect timing. On Tiffany's last birthday, they had gone into every pub from one end of town to the other and back again. They had done the same the year before that too. And the year before that. It always ended up in tears and a kebab. Going to see the Circus of Nightmares would be the most exciting thing they'd done to celebrate a birthday for years. Chelle was giddy but Tiffany was drunk. They walked past the Empire and the sunbed shop. Tiff caught a reflection of herself in the window of a second-hand shop. She pouted and pulled her top down to expose a little more cleavage and hitched her miniskirt up and inch to show a little more thigh.

'Pack that in,' Chelle said. 'All that will attract is flies.'

'My milkshake brings all the boys to the yard,' Tiff sang and twerked. Her head began to spin and a wave of nausea hit her. 'I need to sit down for a minute, Chelle,' she hiccupped and sat on the low wall near the old library. 'Of all the places to be pissed, right in front of the copshop.' She looked up at the police station windows. 'Is anyone looking?'

'They're too busy to give a flying flute what you're doing. If you're going to be sick, don't do it on your shoes,' Chelle said, lighting a cigarette. 'You'll stink of sick all day. Be sick down the grid if you need to.'

'Don't be pissed off with me,' Tiff said. 'I'll be alright in a minute.'

'I told you not to take a drink off those blokes from the fair,' Chelle said. 'They were well dodgy. Only after one thing and one thing only.'

'I only had one drink from them.'

'You had three.'

'Did I?'

'Yes, and you know you did.'

'Don't peck my head. I just need a rest for a minute,' Tiff said. 'I can't do it like we used to, Chelle. I'm getting old.'

'You're nineteen for fuck's sake,' Chelle said, laughing. 'Not ninety.'

A van slowed down and stopped at the kerb. It belonged to the circus. The artwork on the panels was incredible. Full size clowns wielded chainsaws and flamethrowers and the name was emblazoned down the centre. Three men were sitting in the cab. The passenger wound down the window. It was the men from the pub.

'Hello ladies. We meet again. Do you need a lift to the fair?' he asked, eyeing them.

'We might not be going to the fair,' Chelle said. Tiff hiccupped again.

'Your friend said you were going to the circus. We'll give you a lift if you like?' he asked. His accent was foreign. Chelle couldn't place it. 'We work there. Your friend was talking to us in the pub. She looks like she needs a lift.'

'I'm fine thank you very much, cheeky arse,' Tiff said. Her head wobbled as she spoke. 'And she's not my friend, she's my sister.'

'Sisters?' the man said. 'Even better.' He nudged his friend. 'We're brothers and we like sisters, don't we?' His friend laughed and sneered at the women. 'Get in. We'll look after you.'

'We don't need looking after,' Chelle said. 'My mum told me never to get in a vehicle with a strange man and you three, look more than strange,' she said. 'So, if you don't mind, piss off and leave us alone.' Chelle raised her middle finger. 'On your way, sunshine.'

'No need to be nasty,' the man said, smiling. 'We bought your sister some shots for her birthday.'

'I know you did. That's why she's sitting on the wall wondering what her name is.'

'I know what my name is,' Tiff complained.

'We're just being friendly.'

'We don't need any friends,' Chelle said. She saw the Thomas brothers approaching. They were walking past the cinema coming from The Albert. The three brothers were about the same age as their dad. 'My boyfriend is here,' she said waving to the Thomas men. They waved back, laughing and joking, oblivious to their situation.

'You like older men?' the man asked, frowning.

'Don't you get the message?' Chelle said. 'Just piss off. We're not interested.'

'Everything alright, Chelle?' the eldest brother called.

The circus men looked around, closed the window and drove away. The passenger pointed at Chelle and pulled out his tongue. She flicked him the finger again.

'Who was that, Chelle?' one of the brothers asked. 'Were they bothering you?'

'Just a couple of chancers looking for an easy leg over,' she said. 'Tiff did shots with them. She's pissed. She looks like she's fair game to them.'

'Oh, bugger off,' Tiff said. 'So, what if I did a few shots. It doesn't mean I want anything else from them. Dickheads. I'm not that easy.'

'You two have always been easy,' the other brother said, laughing.

24

'I'll bash you around the head in a minute,' Chelle said. 'Then I'll tell my dad what you said.'

'He won't believe a word you say.'

'Funny. We'll walk up the road with you.'

'As long as you walk a few yards behind us. We don't want anyone thinking we're together.'

'Cheeky bugger,' Chelle giggled.

The group walked together, laughing and joking. They'd known each other most of their lives. The three men in the circus van sat watching from a distance. They didn't speak. There was no need to. It was easy to spot the vulnerable ones and there would be plenty over the next few days. There always was. Spotting the vulnerable ones had become an artform. The girl who had taken the shots with them wouldn't know what her name was in an hour. Her shots had a little something extra in them. Easy as taking candy from a baby.

Chapter 3

Jane Orange was sitting next to her husband's bed. He was attached to a heart monitor and had drips going into both hands. A nasogastric tube had been inserted. The doctors had stabilised him but his stats weren't responding as they should be. Malcolm had spoken only once and it was very briefly. The doctors were preparing to take him for an MRI scan. Jane was beside herself. They had been married for thirty-years and she adored him. They were soulmates. She was reminiscing in her mind. Malcolm was stubborn beyond belief. She was trying to rationalise what had happened to him but there was no sense to be made of it. She wished she had insisted he didn't go to the fairground but hindsight is a great gift. There was a knock on the door and two uniformed officers walked in.

'Mrs Orange?'

'Yes.'

'I'm sergeant Bob Dewhurst and this is sergeant April Byfelt,' Bob said. 'We believe your husband was assaulted?'

'Yes,' Jan said. 'He woke up for a few minutes and told me what happened to him.' She wiped a tear away. 'He went to the circus to talk to them about having a licence. He's getting old and can be a bit pedantic. They hit him. The bullies hit him because he couldn't hit them back. They punched him in the head and knocked him out. He has a lump the size of an egg on the back of his head.' She began to cry harder. 'I warned him not to go there alone. I would have gone with him but I had just got out of the shower and I was drying my hair and by the time I was dressed, he was already gone. The bloody fool. I told him not to go there alone.' She took a tissue from her bag and blew her nose. 'I followed him onto the Newry to find him and when I reached the road, I noticed someone waving at me from the public toilet block on the corner. It was Minnie Ellis from number thirty. A neighbour. They found Malcolm collapsed on the pavement and called an ambulance.'

'Okay,' April said, calming her. 'Take your time and go back to the beginning. Where did Malcolm go when he left home?' The door opened and a nurse and porter came in.

'We need to take your husband for a scan,' the nurse said. They detached the sensors and pushed the bed towards the door, leaving an empty space. 'We shouldn't be too long.'

'Should I be with him?' Jane asked, worried.

'There's no need. You can't go in anyway,' the nurse said, without stopping. 'He'll be back before you know it.' The door closed and an awkward silence fell.

'Don't worry, he's in good hands,' April said. 'You were telling us where Malcolm went to this morning.'

'To that bloody awful circus,' Jane said.

'On the Newry?' Bob asked.

'Yes. They turned up late last night and were set up by this morning. Malcolm is a councillor and he had a bee in his bonnet about them setting up without a permit. The big top is right in front of our living room window. It's blocking our view, which is what really wound him up. That was one thing but the main thing is he knows they don't have a licence. Malcolm overreacted. He's particular about things. Do you know what I mean?' She paused. 'Actually, he's way beyond particular. He's anal to be honest but he has a point.' She shrugged and blew her nose again. 'They just turned up last night and set up as if they owned the place. "*Do-as-they-likeys*," Malcolm calls them instead of pikeys. Because they do as they like all the time. I've told him not to call them names like that but his generation are stuck in their ways.'

'Yes. We get it,' April said, nodding. She glanced at Bob, who had a habit of being inappropriate. Bob smirked. 'So, he went to the circus to do what?'

'To tell them they didn't have a licence, of course,' Jane said. 'He went to tell them they needed to pack up and move on or he would call the police.'

'Oh, dear me. What on Earth was he thinking?' Bob asked.

'That's what I tried to tell him but he went anyway.'

'Did he go alone?'

'Yes.'

'Did he think they would pack up because he asked them to?' Bob asked, shaking his head.

'I told him they wouldn't and I told him he was likely to get a punch on the nose for his troubles but he didn't listen,' Jane said, sighing. 'His heart is bad. He shouldn't have any stress at all. I warned him. I wish I'd done more to stop him but he can be so bloody minded.'

'What did he say happened?'

'He said he got there and talked to the lady who runs it. Lottie, I think he said her name is,' Jane said. 'Anyway, she sent him packing and the fairground people bundled him towards the road when he started getting chest pains. He was asking for an ambulance but they ignored him and then a clown spoke to him. Someone punched him in the back of the head.'

'A clown?'

'Yes. That's what he said. A clown,' Jane said, nodding. 'A noticeably big clown, apparently. Then he woke up here.'

'Did he say anything else?' April asked.

'No. He drifted off. He was found outside the public toilets, so maybe he made his way there before he collapsed?'

'We'll have to speak to the fairground employees,' April said.

The door opened and a matron stepped in. She looked concerned. 'Mrs Orange. I'm afraid the doctors have found a bleed on the brain. They've taken your husband straight into theatre. Its vital they operate now.'

'Oh my god,' Jane muttered. Her hands were shaking. 'They did this. Those bloody awful pikeys. You need to arrest them.'

'We'll speak to them,' April said. 'Is there anyone we can call to sit with you?'

'My sister is on her way,' Jane said.

'We'll be in touch as soon as we have something to tell you,' Bob said. Jane nodded. They left the room and walked down the corridor. 'It doesn't sound good.' Bob shook his head. 'A bleed on the brain is never good.'

'Let's go and find a big clown,' April said.

'That shouldn't be difficult at a circus?'

'My thoughts exactly,' Bob muttered. 'How hard can it be?'

Chapter 4

Roy Jacobs watched as the last of the water drained away. The pumps began chugging mud and sludge, exposing everything that had sunk to the bottom of the pond over the many years it had been there. There was no way of knowing how long it had existed. It was marked on ordnance survey maps from their conception and was fed by several draining ditches from neighbouring farmland. The pond had taken three days to empty and filled sixteen tankers and thirteen skips. It had been used as a dumping ground for decades. Shopping trolleys, furniture, fridges, bicycles and an old Ford Escort had been removed during the operation to relocate it. It was set to be filled in and a car park for a German supermarket built on it. The ground workers on the project were being monitored by two environmental experts, making sure the damage to the ecosystem was minimal and the old pond was replaced by a new one, the same size. As part of the planning process, the developers had paid for a similar pond to be built a few hundred metres away although the monitors insisted none of the junk and refuse found in the pond should be transferred into the new one, which didn't seem fair. They had to dispose of the debris at their own cost. Only the newts and frogs would be relocated. The insects would find their own way, apparently, which sounded like bollocks to Roy but the world of construction was a different place nowadays. Environmental impact was a dirty word to the planners, even if it was the impact on a species of frog and his neighbours. Roy thought it was inconsequential to those in business but the world had changed. Conservation was king.

Draining the water down to the muddy bed had exposed an oil drum, which was within reach of the bank. It was rusted and dented at one end. The faded brand etched onto the metal was unreadable and covered in green pondweed. Roy gestured to the drum.

'Put a chain around it and we'll pull it out,' he said.

Two of his workers dressed in rubber waders, trudged across the pond bed through the mud. It was painstakingly slow work. When they reached it, they struggled to move the drum at all. It was buried deep in the clinging sludge. They wrestled with it and managed to lift one end and fastened a chain around it. It wasn't as tight as it could have been but it was the best they could do under the circumstances. Roy gave the signal and a JCB digger pulled it slowly from the mud. There was a loud sucking sound as it came free. The driver let the drum settle and shifted the balance slightly, then swung it towards the bank, where several labourers and Roy were waiting to check if it contained anything dangerous which couldn't be disposed of easily. If it was a corrosive chemical, the inspectors would have a meltdown and take a week to decide which way the drum should be carried, by who and where it should go. If it was empty, they could simply throw it in the scrap metal skip. Roy wanted it to be empty. The inspectors were beginning to drive him nuts. The drum was unstable and it swung back and too like a pendulum.

'That's heavier than it should be.' Roy shook his head.

'What does that mean,' one of the inspectors asked, taking a picture on his phone.

'It's not empty, Einstein,' Roy mumbled under his breath. 'Lower it here,' Roy shouted over the noise of the diesel engine. He'd been the foreman since the start of the job. The project manager was a ghost called Andrew Machin, who had been to the site twice since they broke ground eighteen months earlier and clearly didn't give a toss about it. Roy took it all in his stride. The machine whirred and stopped suddenly when the mechanical arm hit a tree branch above them. Roy had told Machin the trees should be removed before the pond was drained but Machin disagreed. There was a loud crack as the limb splintered from the trunk and the workers ran for cover as the huge branch fell to earth, barely missing them.

'Careful!' Roy shouted at the machine operator. The drum swung wildly from the chain. It became unbalanced and slipped free, hitting the ground with a clatter. The drum split and the lid burst open. Thick stinking sludge sprayed skyward and splattered Roy and the workers. One of them wiped the rotting goo from his face and vomited. The stink of decay engulfed them. 'What the hell is that?'

Roy felt the sludge on his cheek and nose and waited for it to burn his skin but no pain came. He wiped it off, relieved it wasn't acidic but recoiled at the stench. It wasn't any chemical he had encountered before.

'It reeks like a rotting fish,' another said, backing away. The contents of the drum were partially exposed. 'Look at that,' he said pointing inside the drum. Roy could make out the shape of a human. 'That's a woman.'

'Is she dead?' one of the workers called Greg asked.

'Of course, she's dead. You idiot,' Roy said, shaking his head.

The head and shoulders of a decomposed female were visible, protruding from the drum. Her skin was leathery and creased. The blond hair was long and matted. Her lips had receded exposing the teeth and gums, and her eyes were long gone, leaving deep black sockets. The remainder of the corpse remained stuffed inside. Roy took a closer look. It wasn't a manikin or dummy of some kind. It was human. He took out his phone and turned on the torch. He could make out the twisted limbs of another person.

'There's another body in there,' he said. One of the environmental inspectors was sick. The stench of decomposition was overpowering. 'So much for worrying about newts and frogs, eh matey.' Roy laughed. 'They're the least of our problems now. We've got a couple of murder victims to deal with.'

'How do you know they were murdered?' Greg asked.

'Someone explain to Greg how we know they were murdered please. Use a diagram if necessary. I haven't got the time,' Roy said. He took out his work phone and called the office. 'This is Roy at the Liverpool site. We've got a major problem at the pond,' he said. 'We've recovered a chemical drum from the pond bed and there are two bodies in it.' Roy listened to the startled response and a barrage of questions, which he answered as best he could. 'Give Machin a call and tell him he needs to get here sharpish. This will cheer the miserable bastard up and we need the police here too. Okay thanks.' He ended the call and looked at the decomposed bodies. Greg looked confused. It was clear no one had explained the situation to him. Roy patted him on the back. 'Listen to me, Greg. She didn't climb in there by herself and put the lid on and neither did her companion. Someone put them in that drum, sealed it and dumped it in the pond.'

'That's not good,' Greg said, shaking his head.

'No. It isn't,' Roy agreed. 'The police will be all over this like a rash. They'll want everything we've pulled out of there and they'll want to examine the pond bed. This is going to put us back weeks,' Roy added, lighting a cigarette. 'There will be a massive delay.'

'Is that all you think about?' the inspector said, wiping rotting human soup from his cheek. His jacket was covered in decomposing goo.

'Yes. We were under a completion clause. That's my bonus up the swanny,' Roy moaned.

Chapter 5

Kelly and Jack were walking along the beach at Rhosneiger. There were kite surfers whizzing across the bay at crazy speeds, jumping so high they looked like they would never come down, somersaulting and jiving until they splashed back down onto the waves. Ahead of them in the distance, Holyhead Mountain was outlined clearly against the blue horizon. The craggy rocks near the summit glowed silver grey against the heather. It was a crisp day; the sun was shining like summer but the snow-capped peaks of Snowdonia to their left, reminded them it was winter. Apart from the surfers, tourists were thin on the ground and most of the beachfront properties were empty for the winter months. It made little difference to the locals, who relished the peace and quite and traffic free roads. Kelly and Jack had been dating for a few months and things had become complicated. Kelly wasn't as interested in Jack, as Jack was in her. He wasn't the man she thought he was in the beginning. The cracks in his personality were starting to show. To make things worse, Kelly had a daughter, who was the most important person in her world and she didn't like Jack. That was a massive problem. It wasn't jealousy. She said she didn't feel relaxed around him. He made her feel uncomfortable. When Kelly pushed her for more details, she used the word creepy. Creepy was not the word any mother wanted to hear to describe their partner. It wasn't the starting point for a long-term relationship and Kelly had decided days ago that she was going to let him down gently as he was a decent enough guy and there was no need to part on bad terms. She was going to tell him earlier that day but he'd turned up at her flat in tears with flowers. He'd been to see his mum and dad and they'd told him his mum had terminal lung cancer. Her heart sank as she listened to him recount the conversation. Kelly felt so sad for him. He was close to his parents, especially his mum. There was no way she could add to his woes by finishing their relationship. Not today. It was too cruel. Kelly suggested they take a drive out and have a long walk on a beach. It didn't matter which beach. Any would do. They ended up at Rhosneiger. Jack had been quiet, which was understandable but he seemed to be brooding on something.

'What are you thinking about?' Kelly asked.

'Everything and nothing. I'm sorry I was upset earlier,' Jack said, squeezing her hand. He stopped walking and faced her, pulling her closer to him. Kelly felt awkward. She felt her body stiffen. Her feelings for him had changed. He kissed her and she wanted to gag and run away but she couldn't. She went through the motions but it didn't feel the same. She knew it didn't feel normal and he would pick up on her reluctance at some point. She didn't want to be cruel but she couldn't pretend to love him. It was an impossible situation. 'I know you'll help me get through this, Kelly,' he said, staring into her eyes. 'I feel so safe around you. It's like we were meant to be together. You know what I mean, don't you?' he asked. His eyes studied hers and she felt sure he could read her mind. She looked away and nodded. 'I want to be with you, Kelly.'

'You are,' she said, cringing inside.

'I mean with you properly,' Jack said, kissing her neck. It made her feel queasy. 'I want to be with you and Elle and look after you both, like a proper family. I can see us being happy together and if things work out, we could look at getting married.' Kelly died inside. She was going to speak but he put his finger on her lips. 'I know it's a bit soon to be talking about marriage but knowing my mum is going to die soon has made me think about life. We're not here for long. I think we should make the most of every day we have together. Let's think about living together and giving Elle a little brother or sister to play with,' he said, smiling. His eyes searched hers again. She was frozen to the spot. Her mind was screaming at her to tell him she didn't want to be with him. 'A baby would be good. Maybe we could have one of each.' Kelly wanted to cry. 'Don't say anything right now. I just want you to know how I feel, Kelly. I love you with all my heart. I'd do anything to be with you always,' he said, kissing her again. This time she recoiled slightly. It wasn't much but it was there. He sensed something. 'What's wrong?' he asked. 'Have I gone too far?' he asked, shaking his head. 'I didn't mean to ambush you. It's just finding out about my mum. It's made me think about things.' He looked at her. Kelly couldn't find the words she wanted to say. 'Say something for god's sake.'

'You've had a nasty shock, Jack,' Kelly said. 'Let's take one day at a time. It's been a lot for you to process.' He looked like a wounded puppy. 'It's lovely you feel like you do about me and Elle but whatever decisions I make for our future cannot be spontaneous spur of the moment things.'

'I understand that.'

'Do you?' Kelly asked. 'Elle is the most important human on the planet to me. My decisions will shape her life. I can't make them on the back of an emotional crisis in your life.' His eyes filled with tears. 'I don't want to sound cold but I have to keep my feet on the ground no matter what is happening in your life.' He didn't speak. 'I can't act on impulse. I'm a mother.'

'Sorry. I didn't mean to put pressure on you,' he looked offended. 'I didn't mean to rush things. That was stupid. I'm upset. I shouldn't have said what I said.'

'What is said, can't be unsaid.' Kelly stepped back from him. Her attention was drawn to one of the beachfront houses behind Jack. 'Look at that woman, there,' she gasped, putting her hands to her mouth. 'Oh my god!'

Jack turned around reluctantly. He followed where Kelly was pointing. A dark-haired woman was banging on the glass. She was on the middle floor of a three-storey house. There was a balcony and patio doors and she was desperately trying to get out. Her fists pounded against the glass. Kelly could see blood on her face and hands and it was smeared on the glass. They saw movement behind her. She was pulled away from the doors violently. Kelly and Jack looked at each other, stunned into silence for a moment.

'Call the police,' Kelly said. Jack hesitated. 'Call the police, now Jack!' Kelly shouted, running towards the property. She ran as fast as her legs would carry her across the sand. It was like running through mud. Her feet sank deep into the dryer patches of sand, making it difficult to gain a rhythm. She made slow progress towards the house. The woman appeared at the door again, hysterical. She pounded on the glass with her fists and then lurched backwards again. A few seconds later, she reappeared. Her head hit the glass with force and the patio door shattered into a thousand pieces. The momentum carried her forward. She hurtled across the balcony and hit the handrail at hip height. It appeared to Kelly like slow motion as her lower body stopped and her head and upper body carried on. She tumbled headfirst over the balcony rail and hurtled towards the ground. Kelly heard her scream as she fell and then the scream stopped suddenly as she connected with the concrete below.

'Did you see that?' Kelly said. Kelly looked up at the balcony. A figure stood stoic, hands by its sides, its eyes fixed on Kelly. The stare stopped her dead in her tracks. She was transfixed by the gaze. Ice cold terror ran through her veins.

'The police are on the way,' Jack shouted, catching up. 'Did you see her fall?'

Kelly looked at him but couldn't answer. When she looked back at the balcony, the figure was gone. There was no movement inside the house. Kelly ran towards the sand dunes, which were between the beach and the house. It was painfully slow. She reached the garden wall and looked over. The woman was lying on the concrete, bleeding from her ears and nose. Her eyes were open, staring lifeless at the sky. Kelly could tell she was dead. They couldn't help her. She heard a door slam at the front of the house and she ran towards a narrow path which connected the beach with the main road. Sharp grasses grew on either side of the sandy strip of dirt. They stuck to her clothing as she ran, like sandpaper on cotton.

'Kelly. What are you doing?' Jack shouted at her from the beach. He wasn't following her. Spineless little man, she thought. Her chest was heaving as she reached the side of the house. She could see two men running down the drive. They climbed into a white van, one in the passenger side, the other in the driver's side. The big man was the passenger, only half inside the van. His head was strange. Patches of hair dotted his scalp on one side. His scalp was red and angry. She stopped running. The big man turned and looked directly in her direction; his eyes burned into hers. She felt her stomach drop to her toes. Fear gripped her. The man put his finger to his lips. Shush, he mouthed to her. He climbed into the van but never took his eyes from hers. She wanted to take a picture of him and the van with her phone but she was frozen to the spot. The van pulled away and disappeared around the corner. Kelly had the uncontrollable urge to pee.

Chapter 6

The beer tent was getting busy. Most of the tables were full and the sounds of chatting and laughter filled the air. The fairground was in full swing and the claxons and sirens were blaring along the Newry. The atmosphere was charged with excitement. Most of the people were locals but there were lots of visitors too, drawn to Holyhead by the infamous Circus of Nightmares. The opportunity to see the show was too good to miss for fans of the online performances. It was pitched as a once in a lifetime chance to see the circus on the island. The tour dates for the next few years were already booked and published and would take the circus from Ireland, across Europe and into Russia before turning south to Ukraine, Romania, Bulgaria and Greece. There were no plans to return to North Wales at any point in the foreseeable future. It was pure luck and due to the cancellation of a London show which had made it possible at all. This was an impromptu stopover; Ireland was the true destination, so many fans had grasped the opportunity with both hands. It was too good to miss.

Chelle wasn't sure her sister Tiff was going to make it to the show. She was bladdered. More bladdered than she had ever seen her before. Tiff could usually handle her drink and Chelle was beginning to think there was more than alcohol in play. She'd been spiked. The fairground men had given her at least three shots but the effect they were having was unusually severe. She suspected they may have slipped a little something else into them. It was a cheap and dirty trick but it happened. Drugging someone to have sex with them was about as sick as it got but Chelle was well aware that it happened. She was also aware of several friends who had fallen foul of Rohypnol. It was a sad fact of modern society that both males and females had to be wary of being drugged on a night out. Luckily for Tiff, she was being looked after by her sister.

'I don't feel right, Chelle,' Tiff slurred. Her eyes were rolling.

'You're not right,' Chelle said. 'I think you've been spiked.'

'No way,' Tiff said. 'Really?'

'Yes. Really. I think the men who bought you shots, spiked you.'

'Bastards. No wonder I feel terrible.'

'We need to get you home,' Chelle said. 'I'll call a taxi.'

'I don't want to ruin your night. Get me some coffee,' Tiff said, shaking her head. 'I won't drink anymore. I'll sweat it out. Bastards. If I see them, they'll be in for a kick in the nuts. I don't want to go home. I really want to see the circus.'

'I can't see you staying awake.'

'Let's see how I am in a bit.'

'Do you want some food?' Chelle asked.

'I'm not sure. Do you think it might sober me up?'

'Have something to eat. That will help soak up the alcohol. It might help.'

'I feel a bit queasy but I'll try something,' Tiff said.

'What do you want?'

'Get me a couple of hotdogs and some chips.'

'A couple of hotdogs and some chips?' Chelle said, chuckling. 'There's nothing wrong with you, fat cow.'

'You said it might help,' Tiff said, laughing. The world was fading in and out. She had some lucid moments but the urge to sleep was overwhelming. Her skin felt numb, as if it wasn't attached to her. 'I'll have some coffee and food and I'll be right as rain. If not, I'll go home. I don't want to spoil it for you. I know how much you want to watch it. What time is it?'

'Half past four,' Chelle said. 'The show doesn't start until eight o'clock. You might be alright by then if we get some food down you.' Tiff nodded in agreement. 'Don't move from there,' Chelle said, standing up. She finished her gin and tonic in one gulp and put her coat on, hanging her handbag from her shoulder. 'I'll be back in five minutes.'

'I'll be fine,' Tiff said, nodding. Her eyelids felt like lead weights. 'Don't worry.'

'Can you keep an eye on this numpty for me,' Chelle said to the people on the next table. They were vaguely familiar and speaking Welsh, probably from the island. Maybe Llangefni or somewhere close to there. 'She's had a few too many. I'm getting her some coffee.' One of the women smiled and nodded.

'No problem. We've all been there. There're plenty of people around. She'll be safe there.'

'Thank you,' Chelle said. 'I won't be long.' She turned to Tiff. 'Don't move from there, understand?'

'Understood, sergeant major,' Tiff saluted. She smiled. 'I'll be right here when you get back. You can't get rid of me that easy.'

****

Llangefni market was busy. It wasn't as busy at it used to be but that was a sign of the times. People bought online more and more. Market traders were a dying breed. Sharon was browsing the stalls. She had just finished her show on Mon FM. It had been a good day, plenty of listeners, calling in to ask for requests and chat about the topic of the day, which was the proposed building of apartments and shops at the marina on Newry Beach. The developers were promising to renovate two iconic buildings in return for planning permission for their mammoth project. Porth-y-felin House and the old Soldier's Point Hotel were derelict and deemed as white elephants for decades as they fell into ruins. No one was sure what to do with them and the cost of renovation astronomical. It was a hot topic for debate and the show had gone well.

Across the road, a commotion outside the Market Vaults caught her attention. Two clowns were meandering through the light traffic, giving out balloons to the children. The pavements were packed with shoppers. One of the clowns had a megaphone and was informing people that the Circus of Nightmares was operating at Holyhead until Thursday. They were creating a lot of interest as they walked along the main road. She bought the blouse she wanted and then joined the crowd of onlookers as the clowns performed magic tricks for the crowds. Everything appeared to be wholesome and entertaining until one of the clowns started to juggle. The crowd cheered and applauded as he added more and more balls. The second clown appeared to be jealous of the attention he was getting. He took out two ornamental daggers that gleamed in the winter sun. They were encrusted with gems, which glistened as he started to twirl them. The crowd's attention was drawn to this more dangerous trick. He added a third dagger to his act and the crowd went wild. The blades twirled higher and higher, faster and faster and then the other clown kicked him up the backside with an oversized shoe. The performing clown caught all the daggers and put his hands on his hips, offended. The other pocked him in the eye. Holding his eye, the offended clown stuck one of the daggers into the other's chest. Blood spirted from him. Then he stuck a second dagger into him and then the third. The injured clown fell to floor dramatically, clutching his chest. Crimson sprayed skyward in a ridiculous fountain.

The crowd was stunned into silence. Children began to cry. Dozens of phone cameras filmed the drama. Someone shouted for the police to be called but before anyone could act, a van pulled up. It had a blue flashing light on the top. Two more clowns got out, wearing mock police uniforms. They ran to the injured clown and picked him up on a stretcher, dropping him several times. Eventually, the hapless clown was put into the back of the van. Then they all climbed into the back of the van and closed the doors. No one was in the cab. A siren began to wail. The crowd watched amazed as the driverless vehicle made a three-point turn and then sped off up the hill towards Bodffordd.

Chapter 7

Alan and Kim arrived at Station Road, Rhosneiger. The front of the detached property faced inland; the back overlooked the beach. A call to the emergency services had been made indicating a potential homicide had occurred. An ambulance and two uniformed units had made it to the scene before them. They parked the car and walked up the drive. Kim tied up her blond hair with a scrunchie and zipped up her wax jacket against the wind. Alan felt the cold on his scalp, his thinning grey hair offered little protection nowadays. The pea-sized growth on his forehead was purple. It became itchy in the cold. He pulled on a wool beanie hat, tucking his ears beneath it. His knee was painful and stiff today, reminding him retirement wasn't far away. It was time to think seriously about hanging up his handcuffs. His mother always said, old age doesn't come alone, she brings unwelcome friends with her. Now he knew what she meant. As they reached the front door, another uniformed unit arrived.

'We'll need cordons set up front and back,' Alan said to the officers as they exited their vehicle.

'No problem,' a female officer replied. 'Is it a fatality?'

'We've just arrived,' Alan answered. 'Let's treat it as one, just to be on the safe side and keep an eye out for the press.'

'Yes sir.'

Alan and Kim approached the house. The front door was open. They walked into a wide hallway, tiled with granite. The floor gleamed like black glass. Contemporary artwork adorned the walls alongside black and white photography. Most of it featured local beauty spots. It was an old house but it had been recently renovated. Someone had spent a lot of money on structural improvements and décor. The interior had been renovated to a high spec.

'Nice house,' Alan said, making his way down the hallway into a kitchen the size of a squash court. High-gloss units lined every wall and an island feature

43

dominated the centre. The fridge freezer was as wide as a double wardrobe. Through the window, he could see Bob Dewhurst at the back of the property. They headed across the kitchen to the back door, which was open. It led onto an external dining area, which was concreted; there was a lawn and garden beyond. It overlooked the dunes, the bay and Holyhead mountain beyond. 'Great view. Who owns the place?' he asked

'Doctor Gerard Telford and his wife, Elisha,' Kim said, without checking her phone. 'She's a dentist. They are registered as living in Kent but are currently working in Dubai. We can't get hold of them but we're trying.'

'A doctor and a dentist from Kent, who work in Dubai, need a beachfront property on Anglesey. That figures,' Alan said, assessing the kitchen as they passed through. 'Look at this kitchen. It probably cost more than my car,' he added.

'Your car is a twenty-year old BMW estate.'

'And your point is what?' Alan said, frowning.

'My jeans cost more than your car.'

'That's a bit harsh,' Alan said. He stepped outside and approached Bob. Two paramedics were covering up the bloody body of a female. It was clear the victim was beyond medical help. 'Do we know who she is?'

'Sort of,' Bob said. 'It's all a bit odd if you ask me.'

'Can you be a bit more cryptic,' Alan said. 'I nearly had a clue what you were talking about.'

'Sorry. I was thinking aloud. According to this passport, her name is Mary Adams,' Bob said, handing an evidence bag to Alan. 'The address is in a village south of Cork.'

'Where was the passport?' Alan asked, frowning.

'In her back pocket,' Bob said. 'Like I said, it's a bit odd. Why walk around with your passport in your pocket?'

'Maybe she's used it recently,' Kim said.

'She's from Southern Ireland?' Alan said. 'That's not so odd.'

'Take a look yourself.'

Alan approached the body. The woman was in her thirties, tanned with short dark hair. Her eyes were green like a cat and her teeth were perfect. Too perfect to be original. There was a deep gash down the centre of her forehead surrounded by bruising. Her neck was twisted at an unnatural angle. He noticed a tattoo on her left hand, just below the thumb.

'A crescent moon and a star tattoo,' Alan said, nodding. Her shoes were Prada and the rings on her fingers were expensive. White gold or platinum, definitely not silver. 'She was wealthy,' he added.

'Whoever owns this place is wealthy. Certainly, doesn't look to me like she's come straight from Cork.' Bob pointed to the passport. 'Odds on that's a fake.'

'What do women from Cork look like?' Alan asked frowning.

'Pale, and ginger,' Bob said.

'You're not stereotyping are you, Bob?' Kim asked, frowning.

'Heaven forbid,' Alan agreed.

'I'm just making an observation,' Bob said. 'You don't get a tan like that in Cork. It's freezing.'

'The owners work in Dubai,' Kim said. 'Maybe she visited them recently. It would explain the passport.'

'Who called it in?' Alan asked.

'The young couple over there,' Bob said, gesturing to their left. Alan hadn't noticed them. They were on the beach beyond the boundary wall. The male was smoking and slouched against a concrete bollard, which stopped vehicles driving onto the beach. The female was biting her nails and watching the police setting up a cordon. The space between them indicated there was an issue. Maybe a lovers' spat, Alan thought.

'Let's have a word with them before we go upstairs,' Alan said. 'I want to hear what they saw before we make any assumptions.'

'You're the boss,' Kim said. 'There's a gate there.'

They crossed the patio to an ornate iron gate, which led to a path between the houses and the beach. The young couple looked visibly shaken by what they had witnessed. The male lit another cigarette as they approached. He looked edgy and preoccupied.

'Thank you for waiting,' Alan said. 'An officer will take statements from you shortly. I'm DI Williams and this is DS Davies. What are your names?'

'I'm Kelly Williams,' Kelly said, taking the lead. She was naturally pretty. Not much makeup. 'No relation to you, I don't think,' she smiled, nervously.

'I doubt it to be honest. All my relations are in Scotland,' Alan said, shaking his head. 'The island relatives are no longer with us. Nice to meet you, Kelly.' He turned to her companion. 'And you are?'

'Jack Henderson,' he said. He inhaled deeply on his cigarette. Jack didn't look happy.

'Can you tell us what you saw?' Alan asked.

'We were walking on the beach, just over there,' Kelly said. 'I was facing the house and movement in the window caught my eye. I wasn't sure what I was seeing at first but then I realised it was a woman. She was banging on the patio doors.' She paused. 'There was blood on her hands and her face. It was all over the glass.'

'It was the weirdest thing I've ever seen,' Jack added. 'One minute she was there, the next she was gone.'

'What do you mean?' Alan asked.

'It was as if she was pulled back away from the glass but really hard,' Jack said. 'Like she was yanked backwards.'

'Someone was behind her,' Kelly said. 'At least one person, probably two. They yanked her away but a few seconds later, she came back, banging on the glass again. It was awful. I could see she was terrified. She was shouting for help, well, screaming actually and banging on the glass.'

'Could you hear her?' Kim asked.

'No. We were too far away.'

'And it was obvious that she was shouting for help?' Kim asked.

'Yes. I could see her lips,' Kelly said. 'And the expression on her face. She was terrified, trying to get away from someone. Whoever was behind her, obviously.'

'Did you see who she was trying to get away from?' Alan asked.

'Not straightaway,' Kelly said. She glanced at Jack and he looked away. 'The light was reflecting from the glass. I could see her but not who was behind her. Then she was pulled away again but when she came back this time, her head hit the glass and she crashed through it. It just disintegrated, shattered into pieces but she kept going.' Kelly wiped a tear from the corner of her eye. 'She stumbled into the balcony rail and for a moment I thought she would stop but the impetus carried her over the rail. It was like slow motion. She tumbled headfirst over the balcony. I heard her scream. Then she hit the floor and that was it.'

'I was calling you when she fell,' Jack added. 'She didn't try to stop herself from falling. She tipped upside down and fell. I heard her hit the concrete. Then she was quiet. We went to the wall and looked over to see if we could help her but she was still and her eyes were open. There was blood coming out of her ears and her mouth. We knew she was dead and we were worried about whoever was in the house. So, we just waited for the ambulance and your guys to arrive.' The couple looked at each other again. It was Kelly's turn to look away this time.

47

'Did you see who she was trying to get away from?' Alan asked Kelly. He studied her expression. She was in shock. He could see it in her eyes. But there was something else there too. 'After she fell, I mean.'

'There was a man there,' Kelly said.

'On the balcony?' Alan asked.

'No. He was inside.'

'What was he doing?'

'He was standing there staring at us.'

'Can you tell me what he looked like?'

'He was huge. As wide as he was tall,' Kelly said.

'Could you see his skin?' Alan asked.

'He was white. His face was mostly in the shadows but I could see his eyes. They were dark. Very dark,' Kelly said.

'What did he do?' Alan asked.

'Do?' Kelly asked, confused.

'Did he step onto the balcony or look to see if she was still alive?'

'No. He just stood there like a statue, staring,' Kelly said. 'Jack spoke to me and I looked away for a second. When I looked back, he was gone.'

'What colour was his hair?' Kim asked.

'I couldn't see his hair. He was too tall.' Kelly thought back. 'There was something odd about him.'

'Odd how?'

'I can't put my finger on it,' Kelly said. 'His face wasn't right somehow. Expressionless. There's something wrong with his skin.'

'Can you explain what you mean?' Kim asked. She sensed Kelly was holding back.

'I'm not sure what I'm trying to say,' Kelly said. 'If you watched someone smash through a glass door and fall off a balcony, you would be scared or startled or something but his expression was blank.' Kelly shrugged. She appeared frightened. 'He looked at me as if nothing had happened.'

'How old would you say he was?'

'I don't know,' Kelly said. 'He was too far away and there was too much shadow and it all happened so quickly.'

'Roughly?' Alan said.

'Not as old as you,' Kelly said. Alan smiled. 'Sorry. I didn't mean to be rude or anything.'

'Don't worry. No offence taken. After she fell, did you see anyone else, coming or going?' Alan asked. The couple swapped glances again. Kelly looked down at the floor.

'No. Sorry. We didn't see anyone,' Kelly said. Alan caught the lie but wasn't sure why she would lie. 'Do you know who she is?' Kelly asked.

'We can't say just yet,' Kim said. 'Why?'

'I was wondering if she was from the island,' Kelly said.

'We don't think so,' Alan said. He waved to a uniformed officer and they approached. 'This is Kelly Williams and this is Jack Henderson. We need a detailed statement from both of them please.' He turned back to the couple. 'Do you live together?' he asked. Jack looked away and blushed.

'No,' Kelly said. 'It's early days yet.'

'I see. Thank you for calling this in. We'll be in touch if we have any more questions. Please contact me directly if you think of anything else at all, no matter how insignificant you think it is,' Alan said.

'Okay. We will,' Kelly said, nodding. Her eyes told a different story. The couple walked away with the constable. Alan watched them leave. There was a cloud hanging over them. He could sense it. They would need to speak to them again.

'We need to take a look inside,' Alan said to Kim. 'We need to make sense of what happened to Mary Adams.'

They walked into the house and Bob gave them forensic suits and overshoes. Alan briefly studied the ground floor on the way to the stairs. It was separated into a games room with a pool table and cinema room and a reading room lined with bookshelves and a leather-topped desk. A door beneath the staircase drew his attention. He tried the handle but it was locked.

'Have you seen any keys?' Alan asked Bob.

'There was nothing on her body.' Bob shook his head. 'Maybe they're upstairs. We had a brief look around but I didn't notice any.' Alan knocked on the wall with his knuckles. It sounded hollow. 'It could be storage space under the staircase or steps to a cellar,' Bob said.

'These old houses all had cellars,' Alan said. 'We'll check for a key while we're upstairs. How long on the CSI unit?'

'Pamela Stone said they would be here within the hour,' Bob said. 'That was about forty minutes ago.'

'Okay.'

Alan climbed the stairs to a wide landing, which opened into the lounge. The patio doors were directly in front of them. Glass shards covered the laminate floor, glinting in the winter sunlight. Congealed blood pooled on the balcony and the interior floor. The furniture in the room was positioned to make the most of the view. All the seating faced the beach. There was a patio set on the balcony. Metal framed with a glass table-top and an umbrella stand although there was no sign of the umbrella. Stored away for the winter or blown away, he thought. Umbrellas don't fare well on Anglesey. The chairs were pushed under the table neatly. A thin layer of sand coated everything on the balcony, carried there on the wind. A single set of footprints in the sand led from the doors to the balcony. Drops of blood stained the sand.

'She was bleeding heavily before she hit the glass,' Alan said. He walked away from the patio doors to the other side of the room, which overlooked the road to the front of the house. It was fifteen metres at least. There was a blood trail from one side to the other. He spotted a circular dent in the wall. It was surrounded by blood spatter. He tapped the wall with his fingertips. 'Plasterboard. The indentation could have been made by someone's head?'

'Agreed,' Kim said. 'It's too big to be a fist and too wide to be a hammer or other blunt instrument.'

There were two glasses on a marble coffee table. They looked to be expensive crystal. Alan picked one up with a gloved hand and sniffed it.

'Whisky,' he said, looking around. In the far corner of the room, a bar had been built into the wall. Downlights illuminated it and louvre doors hid it from view when they were closed. He scanned the bottles of spirits. Everything was at the expensive end of the range. Single malts, Polish vodka, boutique gins that he had never heard of. None of it was from the supermarket. 'They have expensive taste.' There was no blood around the bar or that side of the room.

'What do you think happened?' Kim asked.

'There were two or three people in the room.'

'Why three? There are only two glasses.

'I'm surmising someone was driving,' Alan said. Kim nodded. 'They were sitting on the sofas, two that side, one on the other, drinking scotch. Something happened and one of them tried to leave. The others stopped her.'

'Mary Adams,' Kim said, nodding. 'Her head is smashed into the wall over there. She tried to escape, bleeding profusely from her head but she couldn't for some reason, so she ran to the patio doors either to look for help or to escape.' Alan tried to slide the doors open but they wouldn't budge. 'She couldn't open them because they were locked, so she tried to attract attention by banging on the glass.'

51

'I'm with you so far,' Alan agreed.

'According to our witness, she was pulled back into the room several times by someone, which might explain the amount of blood around that area.' Kim pointed to the pooling inside the room. 'She broke free and stumbled into the glass, which shattered. Her momentum carried her into the balcony rail but because it's low, below her waist, she tumbled over.'

'Maybe she couldn't see,' Alan said. 'She may have had blood in her eyes or the breaking glass frightened her and instinctively, she closed them.'

'The impact would have stunned her either way,' Kim said.

'I'm okay with all that,' Alan said. He moved a tea-towel that was on the bar next to some glasses. 'Here are the keys,' he said, picking them up to inspect them. 'What I want to know is who Mary Adams was drinking with and why they didn't wait around to see if she was dead.'

'Pissed off boyfriend? Maybe an argument which got out of hand,' Kim said.

'Why run if it was an argument?'

'Who knows? They clearly weren't good friends as they didn't call an ambulance,' Kim said. 'I'll get uniform to knock on doors and see if we can shine any light on who actually lives here. The place looks like a show home to me. What do you think?'

'I agree. It doesn't look lived in. Ask Bob to go and check the kitchen,' Alan said. 'See if there's anything in the fridge and cupboards. These whisky glasses are the only thing out of place from what I can see. Take the keys with you.' Kim went downstairs to speak to Bob and organise a door-to-door enquiry. Alan climbed the stairs to the top floor. Everything smelled new. A quick look around revealed four bedrooms, all ensuite, a small office and a huge bathroom. All the bedrooms were pristine and unmade. The bedding was stored in zip-lock containers in the wardrobes. Quilts, pillows, sheets, towels and dressing gowns all looked new and unused, ready and waiting for visitors to arrive. The bathrooms were stocked with soaps and lotions but everything was unopened. Mary Adams didn't live in the house. No one did.

'Alan!' Kim called from downstairs.

'What?' he said, reaching the landing. She sounded panicked, which wasn't like her.

'You'd better come and see this,' she called.

'What's wrong? he asked, descending to the middle floor. 'Is the house on fire?' No one replied. He reached the downstairs hallway. Kim and the other officers were gathered around the door beneath the stairs. 'What's all the fuss about?'

'There are dead people down there,' Kim said, calmly. Alan stopped in his tracks. The smell of decomposition drifted to him.

'Dead people, plural?' he asked.

'Yes.' Kim nodded. 'Three or four at least.'

Chapter 8

Detective Superintendent Anne Parry was based at the Matrix headquarters, Speke, Liverpool. The Matrix unit dealt with serious organised crime in the city and beyond. It was such a problem that Matrix warranted the building of their own headquarters. The successful criminal outfits on Merseyside had international operations that were beyond the reach of normal policing. Recently, Anne and her team had been key in bringing down several notorious criminal gangs. Being sent to the scene of a historic body dump was a distraction from her current workload but in this case, a necessary one. She arrived at the construction site on the outskirts of the city, where the gruesome find had been made. An extension to an established retail park near the airport was being built and the remains of two people uncovered in a chemical drum. The condition of the bodies indicated the crime was committed many years before, which meant the trail wouldn't just be cold, it would be virtually non-existent.

On the face of it, it wasn't the type of crime Matrix officers would investigate but due to the possible identity of one of the victims, the chief had insisted she take the lead until the facts were established. Whoever dumped the bodies in the pond, didn't intend for them to be recovered anytime soon. A hundred years from now maybe, when global warming had sucked all the moisture from the soil. No one expects a pond to be drained. The construction project was a stroke of luck for the police. It was about time she had some luck with the case, which she had all but forgotten about. The case had been unsolvable, so she pushed it to the back of her mind. There were too many serious crimes waiting to be solved to dwell on a dead duck.

She was accompanied by her detective inspector, Gill Robinson. They were both from the Huyton area of the city and had been partnered for over seven years; they had moved through the ranks together. Both detectives were cautiously optimistic that the bodies found during the reclamation of pond land, might be related to a historic misper case which they had worked on five years ago. Technically, it was still open but in reality, it was inactive. A young couple in their early twenties had vanished following a visit to a travelling circus. They hadn't been seen or heard of since and every avenue of enquiry had led to a dead end. Leo Jobson and Katrina Watkins simply disappeared from the face of the Earth.

Matrix was involved because Leo Jobson was the eldest son of a key figure in the organised crime world. His father, Len Jobson was a dangerous enforcer for the Quinn family. The Quinns were heavily involved in the distribution of class-A drugs across the UK and people trafficking across Europe. They had become experts at moving people and product together, in tandem with removing the competition in brutal fashion.

Initially, it was hoped the couple had taken off and gone on a bender but as the days turned into weeks and weeks turned into months with no phone or bank activity, it became clear something sinister had happened to them. Matrix was given the lead because of the organised crime connection but without any evidence, bodies or ransom demands, it was effectively a missing persons case. Len Jobson was adamant Leo had been kidnapped by rivals because of his link to the Quinn family. Initially, the search for them had been feverish. Dozens of local people from all over the North West travelled to the area to search for them. Following a television appeal, a tipoff indicated the couple had been seen in the back of a minibus in Betws-y-Coed, North Wales. The witness said she'd seen a young couple matching the description and that the female was crying. It was a spurious lead but the search was extended to the rivers, mountains and forests of Snowdonia and the surrounding areas but no trace was found. Despite all the searches and media attention, nothing came to fruition. Slowly but surely, resources were moved onto other cases and the investigation ground to a halt. Eventually, it was parked. The terrible truth was Katrina Watkins and Leo Jobson, a popular couple with large families had vanished without a trace. The discovery of the two bodies at the construction site was the first break they had had for five years. Anne couldn't help but feel nervous excitement mixed with a lingering sense of dread. Finding them would solve a mystery that had plagued her for years but it would also pick the scabs from old wounds. Some things were best left undiscovered.

Gill parked the Shogun as close to the cordon as she could. There was a refrigerated van from the mortuary and a CSI vehicle already on the scene. A small crowd of reporters and a larger crowd of onlookers were being corralled by uniformed officers. The journalists and police officers looked thoroughly dissatisfied by the situation, neither side was giving an inch. She lowered the window. There was a lot of shouting and balling coming from the crowd. She noticed some of them were crying. That wasn't good. They were not there out of random curiosity.

'The ghouls are here already,' Anne said, checking her appearance in the mirror. She was fifty and in good shape. Her hair was streaked blond and tied tight to her head. She pulled on a baseball cap and threaded her hair through the back. A pair of dark sunglasses completed the guise. She wasn't the most popular superintendent on Merseyside by a long way. Failure to find the couple had been laid squarely at her feet by the families. Gill was a more petite version of Anne. They could have been sisters.

'Unfortunately, they're not ghouls,' Gill said. Anne looked confused. 'I think they're family.'

'What?' Anne sighed and scanned the crowd for familiar faces. There were several. 'How the hell did they find out so quicky?'

'Facebook,' Gill said, struggling into her padded coat. She opened the door and climbed out. The wind blew in from the Mersey and she immediately wished she had put tights on under her jeans. 'One of the construction workers posted pictures of the bodies online before we were even alerted. People thought it was a hoax at first. They've been removed but it was too late to stop them being shared a few hundred times.'

'A few hundred times?'

'It doesn't take long. Rumours are rife on social media. Because they were found here in Speke, people in the area are guessing who the bodies belong to.'

'It doesn't take a genius to work it out.'

'There was a post saying some of the families were on their way.' Gill gestured to the crowd. 'Looking at them, I'd be surprised if they're not there already,' she added, pointing to the angry gathering.

'Jesus,' Anne said, getting out. 'There are two bodies but we don't know who they are yet. They're making huge assumptions. What is wrong with people?' she said, shaking her head. 'And why would you post photographs of dead people on the internet, for heaven's sake?'

'Likes and shares,' Gill said. 'The more you get, the more popular you feel. It's all about creating a response. The poster is famous for a while. A couple of dead bodies in an oil drum is like gold dust online, even if it is short lived.'

'I despair,' Anne said. 'We can't keep anything secret for more than a few minutes.' Some of the crowd noticed them arriving. A number of them broke away and jogged across the car park towards them. She recognised one of the women as Alice Watkins. Katrina's mother. She'd been extremely vocal about how crap their investigation had been. 'Oh, for god's sake!' Anne muttered. 'We've been spotted.'

'Are you in charge again?' Alice Watkins shouted. 'It will be another bloody shambles if you are.' She was holding a blown-up image of a young woman. It wasn't the best image of Katrina but it made a statement. 'Do you remember this face?' she shouted. 'This is my daughter. How have you still got a job?' Anne ignored her and walked on; her head bowed. 'You should be directing traffic but you'd probably fuck that up too.'

'Bloody charming,' Anne said, under her breath.

'Don't make things worse,' Gill said.

'Have you found my Katrina?' Alice asked.

'We don't know anything yet,' Gill said, trying to calm things. 'As soon as we know, you'll know.'

'Is Leo there?' an elderly man shouted. He looked angry. It was Len Jobson. He looked a hundred years older than the last time she'd seen him. His

57

Armani leather jacket was hanging on him. The broad shoulders he once had were gone. Anne thought he looked seriously ill. 'Come on, Anne. You're a reasonable woman. If you've found our kids, we have a right to know.'

'We don't know who it is yet, Len.' Anne half turned to face him.

'You have got a good idea who it is or you wouldn't be here,' Len said, stony faced. His eyes were dull like a shark. Anne didn't want to disrespect him. Len was a coldblooded killer responsible for some of the most terrible crimes she'd ever witnessed. 'We're not idiots.'

'We have just arrived, Len,' Anne said, walking away. 'I'll know more once we've seen the bodies.'

'We've always been straight with each other, Anne,' Len said. 'You're Matrix detectives and this is not your remit unless it's linked to organised crime.' Anne sighed. There was little point in lying. 'Is it possible my son is one of the dead bodies?'

'We don't know anything yet,' Gill said, ushering the DS to the safety of the cordon. 'Don't give that man anything until we're ready,' Gill whispered in her ear. Uniformed officers arrived and moved the grieving families back without too much turmoil. 'As soon as we know anything, we'll let the relevant families know,' Gill said to the crowd.

'You know who they are,' Alice shouted. 'If that's my daughter, I want to see her. We've got rights!'

'We will keep you posted,' Gill said.

'It's all over Facebook that my Katrina is in there,' Alice shouted. 'How can Facebook know where my daughter is before you do?' She tried to follow the detectives under the crime scene tape but the constables held her back. 'You're a disgrace!' she shouted. 'You couldn't find your nose on your face, useless bitch.' The press photographers made the most of the opportunity to capture the superintendent being barracked. Cameras and microphones were pointed at Alice Watkins and Len Jobson. The grieving parents. Questions were fired in their direction. It was journalistic opium.

'This is going to be a nightmare,' Anne said. They picked their way to the pond listening to the torrent of abuse. CSI had erected a tent over the drum and the remains. Officers in forensic suits were picking through the skips on site and another team were painstakingly sifting through the mud on the pond bed. It was a mammoth task. 'Let's see what we have, shall we?'

The detectives suited up and put facemasks on, then went into the tent. Pamela Stone and her photographer were examining the remains. The air was thick with decay.

'Hello Anne,' Pamela said. 'Gill. Nice to see you.'

'Hello Pamela. What can you tell us?' Ann asked. 'We need some answers. There are angry parents on the car park.'

'I've heard them,' Pamela said. 'It's impossible not to hear them.' She paused. 'Okay, let's get down to business. We have a male and a female. The male is fully clothed. He's white, twenties to thirties, short blond hair, full set of teeth in good condition. He has a tan line on his left wrist, which indicates he was wearing a watch before he died but no watch has been found. From the shape of his lower arm, he has a broken right radius and ulna. The breaks are clean as if he was hit hard across the wrist with something solid. And there's a depressed fracture to the back of the skull. Possibly caused by a lump hammer. A heavy one with a square face.'

'It's the shape of a brick,' Gill said.

'It is but we would generally find brick particles in the wound. This is clean which makes me say the instrument was metal, probably a large hammer.'

'Okay,' Gill said. 'Carry on.'

'His wrists and ankles are fastened with heavy duty zip ties. His cause of death is uncertain yet but it's probably the blow to the head.'

'Is the lump hammer the type used by a tradesman?' Anne asked. 'A joiner or bricklayer maybe?'

'No. It's too big and heavy. It would be used to demolish or hammer something big into the ground. Fencing maybe?'

'Maybe the type for knocking stakes into the ground?' Gill asked. 'Like a marquee.'

'I think I know what you mean,' Pamela said, looking up at her. She smiled sympathetically. 'It's possible but obviously, I can't say for sure. He has no ID on him but there's a tattoo on his forearm and another on his right calf.'

'It has to be Leo Jobson,' Anne said, excitedly. 'A compass on his arm and a Liverpool Football Club crest on his leg?'

'Yes. I'm sure that fits with your misper case?' Pamela asked. Anne nodded and sighed.

'The tattoos match,' Gill said, nodding her head. 'Part of me didn't want it to be them,' Gill said. 'I was hoping they were running a bar on a beach in Goa.'

'Sadly not. It must be a relief to find them after all this time,' Pamela said. The detectives nodded imperceptibly. It was a bittersweet moment. 'If that is Leo Jobson, then we want this to be Katrina Watkins,' she said pointing to the female body. 'The female has long blond hair. Her ears are pierced, once in the left ear, twice in the right. She has a nose ring in her left nostril, which is still there. And most importantly, she has a butterfly tattooed on her right thigh.' Anne nodded and looked at Gill. Gill agreed. It matched Katrina. 'She is naked and her wrists are fastened with the same zip ties. There are grooves in the radius and ulna bones, so she struggled. She has a couple of teeth missing at the front, which don't marry up with the pictures of your mispers but they may have been lost at the time of death. I can't be certain but the cause of death looks like strangulation. The bodies have been preserved to a certain extent because the drum was sealed and the temperature at the bottom of the pond was cool and stable. I need to get them back to the lab before they start to deteriorate. The air will get to them quickly and I want to preserve what we have. Dental records should confirm it's them but I think the tattoos are enough to confirm their identities. We all know who they are.'

'Yes. We'll have to prepare something to give to the families and press,' Anne agreed. She looked at Gill and she agreed.

'Anything on the drum yet?' Gill asked.

'Not yet. I haven't had chance to look at it in detail yet.' Pamela gestured to the drum. 'From the markings, it didn't contain oil or a chemical. I think it's some kind of axle grease. The type used on plant machines and heavy equipment. JCB's, tractors, forklift trucks, the underneath of HGV's and the like. Anything with moving parts that are exposed to the air.'

'Like trailers?' Gill asked. 'And fairground machinery?'

'Just like trailers and fairground machinery,' Pamela said. 'I believe the circus was the last place they were seen?'

'Yes,' Gill said. 'Would fairground rides use grease like this?'

'Yes. They operate outside in all weather and they're transported large distances by road, so everything would need to be greased to protect the moving parts from the elements while they're in transit,' Pamela said.

'Leo paid for two tickets for the Circus of Nightmares on his debit card. His phone was located by a mast close to where the fairground operated and that was the last time his bank account was used. We need to go back to the beginning on this one and speak to anyone we can find who was around at the time they went missing. Hopefully, the fairground employees.'

'What was said when they were questioned at the time?' Pamela asked.

'There was a time lag, which was critical to the case,' Anne said. 'It was four days until their disappearance was taken as out of the ordinary. One side of the family thought they were with the other or they'd jumped on a plane and gone on holiday without telling anyone. Leo had money. We think he was a low-level member of the Quinns although we could never prove it. It was Katrina's absence on social media which caused concern. They didn't respond to text messages or phone calls from friends and family. The family reported it to us six days after they were last seen by which time, the circus was in France and the fairground employees had dispersed, some with the circus and some with another fair in Ireland and some down south with a fair at a music festival. With hindsight, we didn't have a cat in hell's chance of tracing them via the fairground employees.'

'Their workforce is transient,' Gill said. 'They work for a few nights then they are gone for months working on another event in a different part of the country. We've questioned employees who were working on the fairground around that time. Some of them several times and we hit a blank each time. Not a single person we spoke to remembers working that night or seeing the couple.'

'They must see thousands of people over a weekend,' Pamela said.

'Exactly,' Gill agreed. 'Now, we know what happened to them but five years have gone by and they've been all over Europe and back several times since then. The chances of finding the original employees are zero but we have to be seen to be doing something.' Gill shrugged. 'I think it's a massive waste of our time and resources but it's time to revisit them. I follow the circus online and get an update of their whereabouts on my phone,' Gill added. 'The circus has been back in the country for over two weeks. It's just landed on Anglesey.'

'We've got to go to the island for our next job.' Pamela smiled. 'I've always wanted to see that circus. I hear it's quite special. I might buy a ticket.'

'It arrived yesterday, apparently,' Anne said. 'We might see you there. That's where we're heading now.' She took out her mobile. 'I need to talk to the chief and see how much of what we know he wants to release to the press and the families. We can tell them the bodies are probably Katrina and Leo but we need to keep the details under wraps for now.'

****

Kelly and Jack got into his car and sat in silence for a minute. She could smell cigarettes on him and the smell was disgusting. He must have smoked ten while they were giving the police their statements. One after another. His smoking hadn't bothered her as much before but today it did. It bothered her a lot. He took out his cigarettes and put one in his mouth.

'Don't light that,' Kelly said. 'They stink.'

'My nerves are shot,' Jack said. 'I smoke more when my nerves are bad. First the news about my mum and then a woman dies in front of us. What a day. No wonder I feel like smoking.'

'Wait until you get home,' Kelly said. She looked around nervously. 'You can drop me off by the Kings on Land's End. I'll cut through the lanes from there.'

'What do you mean?' Jack asked, surprised she wanted to go home without him.

'It's simple. Take me back to town and drop me off by the Kings,' Kelly said. He reached for her hand but she pulled it away. 'Leave me alone. Don't touch me please. I'm feeling very on edge, nervous and frightened and I don't need to be touched right now, thank you. Just take me to town.'

'Okay,' Jack said. 'Are you going to tell me what is really going on?'

'I've got no idea what you're talking about,' Kelly said. 'Just drive us away from here.'

'Why didn't you tell the police you saw them leaving the house?' Jack asked, starting the engine. 'I know you saw them. You must have. I heard the engine starting up.'

'Did you see anyone?' she asked, abruptly.

'No.'

'Then don't tell me what I saw,' she said. 'And the reason you don't know what I saw is because you were still in the sand dunes,' she said, angrily. 'I ran down the path to see if they were still there, you were hiding on the beach.'

'I wasn't hiding,' Jack protested. 'That's not fair. I was looking at the dead woman lying on the ground. It's not something I see every day and I was shocked.'

'Whatever.'

63

'I don't want to argue about it,' Jack said. Kelly folded her arms and looked out of the window. 'If you say you didn't see them, I believe you.'

'Just drive me back to town,' Kelly said.

Jack drove past the clock in the square and up the hill towards the expressway. He didn't see the van parked at the side of the road by the Y Morfa pub.

'Jack Henderson, plasterer. No job too big or too small,' the man read from the side of Jack's car. The van pulled out and followed them. 'I've got his mobile number. Google him.'

'Here he is. Jack Henderson, Holyhead. I've got a Facebook profile and I've got pictures of him standing with his pretty little girlfriend and he's tagged her into the picture.' There was pause while he followed the tag. 'Kelly Williams also from Holyhead and that pretty little thing must be her daughter. Spitting image of her but there are no pictures of Jack on her profile. He's not the kid's father.'

'What do you want me to do?'

'Follow them. I want to know where the lovely Kelly lives and have a chat with her about keeping her mouth shut.' He paused. 'Once we know where she lives, get rid of the van. Take it to the workshop and swap the plates back over to the originals.'

Chapter 9

Tiff opened her eyes and couldn't remember where she was or why she was there. Nausea hit her like a tidal wave and she vomited. She tried to miss her shoes but failed. Tomatoes and carrots splattered on her left foot and the grass even though she hadn't eaten either. The acidic gunk filled her senses and she heaved again. A claxon blared, bells rang and music thumped. The sound of voices drifted to her. She was cold.

'Are you okay, Tiff?' A male voice spoke. She recognised it but couldn't place it. Someone shook her gently. 'Tiff. Are you okay?'

'What time is it?' Tiff asked. She tried to focus on him. It was Wayne. Tiff had snogged him outside the Stanley a few weeks back. They were interrupted by a smoker going out for a cigarette, which was a blessing as he'd dated Chelle for a while. Bonking her ex would lead to a difficult conversation. It was a line they didn't cross. All exes were out of bounds. Another wave of nausea hit her and she gagged but there was nothing left inside.

'Nearly seven o'clock,' Wayne said. He passed her a bottle. 'Here. Have a drink of water. You look hammered.'

'Thanks.' Tiff was gutted. Wayne was fit. 'What time did you say it is?'

'Seven o'clock.'

'Seven?' Tiff asked. 'It was only half past four a minute ago.'

'Maybe in your world but not in this one, you headcase,' Wayne laughed.

Tiff took the water and sipped from it. The liquid soothed her throat. She was thirsty. The beer tent was much quieter than it had been. She looked around the tables nearby but they were empty. The crowds had moved on.

'Have you seen Chelle,' Tiff asked.

'No. Was she here with you?'

'She was. She went to get some food but that was ages ago,' Tiff said. 'What time did you say it was?'

'Seven o'clock.'

'I must have fallen asleep. We wanted to see the show,' Tiff mumbled. She was confused. Too much time had passed. Something wasn't right. 'She might have gone to the circus without me. Probably embarrassed by her little sister as usual, eh?'

'Nothing new there,' Wayne said. His brown hair was cut close to his scalp at the sides, longer on top and combed over. Stubble covered his chin. He was wearing one of those expensive jackets with a patch on the left arm. Her brain wasn't working properly. She couldn't remember the brand but they cost a ridiculous amount of money. 'How did you get in that state?' Wayne asked, shaking his head. 'You're a mess, Tiff.'

'Thank you very much,' Tiff said, offended slightly. She couldn't argue with him. She felt like shit. If she looked half as bad as she felt, she looked like a zombie. 'I did some shots in the Albert with some guys who work on the fair,' Tiff said. She finished the water off. 'Chelle reckoned they spiked me. Bastards.'

'What?' Wayne said, angrily. 'That's out of order. Can you remember them?'

'I can just about remember what my name is,' Tiff said. 'I feel wiped out. I will wait for Chelle and then go home. I need my bed.'

'Chelle wouldn't leave you here on your own in that state,' Kev said, concerned. 'The circus doesn't start for another hour. She's probably in a queue for food.'

'It must be a long queue,' Tiff mumbled. 'She went ages ago. I hope she's not pissed off with me.'

'Where was she going to get the food from?'

'I don't know. She went to get hotdogs and chips from somewhere,' Tiff said. 'How many stalls sell hotdogs?'

'All of them,' Wayne joked. 'Do you want me to get you a taxi?' He looked worried. 'They've made a temporary rank on the Newry. We can have a look for her at the burger vans on the way. It's best to get you home. I don't want to leave you on your own here.'

'Okay,' Tiff said. 'Can we look around the fairground for her?'

'Yes,' Wayne said. 'There's a lost child van too. They can put out a call for her on the Tannoy. If she's here, we'll find her.'

'Of course, she's here,' Tiff said. 'Where else would she be?'

'I don't know,' Wayne said. 'Let's take a look around. Are you okay to stand up?'

'Yes,' Tiff said. She stood and her legs were shaking. She felt as weak as a kitten. Wayne took her arm which felt nice and they walked out of the beer tent. The fresh air felt good and the sea breeze touched her skin, cooling her down instantly. Her blood began to pump faster clearing the haze from her mind. The faces in the crowd sharpened and the sounds became clearer. They passed three food vans but Chelle wasn't there. She couldn't understand why she hadn't come back for her. It was completely out of character. She fussed around Tiff like she was her daughter not her sister. Sometimes, she was too much, stifling Tiff but she meant well. Her overriding instinct was to protect her younger sister. She would never have left her alone, especially drunk. As her senses returned to her, Tiff began to feel frightened. Something was wrong.

Chapter 10

Alan took the stairs slowly. Strip lights burned brightly revealing a cellar which ran the length of the house and beyond. The far end was beneath the front garden. Kim was close behind him. From the top of the cellar stairs, they had seen three pairs of feet; the ankles tied together. From a few steps further down, they could see the bodies in their entirety. There was a male in his sixties and a female around the same age, bound and gagged. Their wrists were tied behind their back and they were seated on the cobblestone floor, slumped against the wall. Next to them was a much older female lying on her back. She wasn't bound but she was clearly dead. Her mouth was open and twisted into a silent scream. When he reached the bottom step, he could see an elderly male, probably in his eighties bound and gagged, seated against the opposite wall. His head was slumped, chin on his chest. The air was sour and dry. Every wall was covered with wine racks, which were full of bottles of red, white and rose. Hundreds of them in every direction.

'I can't see any sign of trauma,' Alan said. 'Judging by the smell, they've been down here a while.' He approached the younger victims. 'Look how drawn their faces are,' he said. 'They look like Auschwitz victims.'

'They starved to death?' Kim said.

'They look like they hadn't eaten or drank for a while,' he said. 'Except for this poor old dear.' He looked closely at the older lady. 'She was in good health when she died. There are bruises around her neck.'

'Look at their clothes. All designer labels. These people were wealthy. Hair, teeth and nails on the women are well maintained.' Kim checked the male's clothing. His pockets were empty. 'There's no ID on him.'

'We need to trace the owners rapidly. Doctor Telford has got some explaining to do,' Alan said. 'There's more to this property than meets the eye. It's like a show home. Everything in the place costs a fortune but is untouched.'

He studied all four victims. There was no sign of violence on three of the bodies. The bruising and abrasions on their arms were from the bindings. The pallor of their skin told him they'd been severely dehydrated before they died.

'It looks like they were restrained in the cellar and left to die.'

'Who they are and why they are here is what we need to know,' Alan said. It was a mystery they would need to solve before the investigation could gain traction. 'Ask Bob to chase up Pamela Stone, please. We need DNA running pronto.' Kim shouted up to the top of the stairs and Bob acknowledged the order. They carried on through the cellar.

'All four victims are wearing watches and jewellery,' Kim said. 'Rolex, Tag, Hublot. They're not cheap. Probably worth thousands.'

'Robbery wasn't the motive unless the attackers were disturbed in the process, left and never returned.'

'In which case, an anonymous call to the police would have prevented them dying,' Kim said. 'Even the most hardened criminals would have thought long and hard about leaving elderly victims to die in such a long and drawn-out fashion. The hunger and thirst would have driven them to distraction long before they died. No one would want that on their conscience.'

'Some people don't have a conscience,' Alan said. 'Like the guy who watched Mary Adams take a nosedive from the balcony and didn't even look to see if she was dead.' He stooped down and rubbed his chin. 'Simple curiosity would make most people want to see what had happened to her yet he didn't venture onto the balcony. Why was that?'

'Maybe he didn't want to be seen clearly,' Kim said. 'Kelly said he knew they were there because he looked straight at them.'

'They must have known what was in the basement,' Alan said. 'Is this what caused the argument?'

'What do you think happened?' Kim asked.

'I can honestly say, I haven't got a clue,' Alan said. He walked deeper into the cellar. The air was dry and ambient temperature. Perfect for storing wine, he thought. Not people. A staircase to his left caught his attention. 'Look at that,' he said, turning to Kim. They approached it. 'It must lead up to the garden at the side of the house.'

'So, the cellar can be accessed from outside?' Kim said.

'Yes, but on the blind side of the house that you can't see from the driveway. Probably an old coal hole. Handy if you're receiving a delivery of a few hundred bottles of wine,' Alan mused. He looked beyond the staircase at the cellar wall. There were no wine racks beyond it and the cellar was narrower. 'Or something else,' Alan said, walking to the far end of the cellar. There was a door to his left, hidden from view from the rest of the cellar. He tried the handle but it was locked. 'It smells like a zoo down here. Have you got the keys?'

'Yes,' Kim said, fishing them from her pocket. She handed them to Alan. Alan sifted through the keys until he found one that opened the lock. The door creaked open and he recoiled from the smell. The room beyond was in darkness but he sensed movement and he could smell human waste, urine and excrement. The stink was choking. He could feel fear emanating from within. There was a whimpering noise. 'Can you hear that?'

'Yes,' Kim said.

He reached inside and felt along the wall until he reached a light switch.

'Hey presto,' he said turning on the light. Nine frightened young women cowered against the walls. Their eyes were wide in terror. They blinked against the light. Kim stood next to him. The floor was littered with empty water bottles. 'Well, I wasn't expecting that.'

'Nor me,' Kim muttered.

'There's no need to be afraid,' Alan said to them. 'We're the police.'

Chapter 11

Tiff and Wayne made their way around the fairground, checking every food vendor along the way. Chelle wasn't there. They approached the lost child van, which was located at the centre of the fairground. It was decorated with balloons and manned by two young women and an overweight clown performed outside. The clown looked friendly; his makeup applied to make him look happy. His giant shoes and loping walk made him comical to watch. A badge on his lapel said his name was Gonzo. He had a large flower on his lapel which squirted onlookers with water. People passing stopped for selfies with him and their children. Gonzo was clearly loving his job and the kids loved him. Some of the lost kids didn't want to leave with their parents, staying with the clown was more fun. Tiff walked to the counter and was greeted with a warm smile.

'How can we help you?' the young lady asked. Her accent was Eastern European. 'I'm Greta and this is my associate Judy. Have you lost a child today?' Her words were clearly scripted and practiced well.

'Sort of,' Tiff said. 'I've lost my sister.'

'Oh no,' Greta said, reaching for her mug of coffee. She took a sip. 'Tell me what happened.'

'She went to buy some hotdogs but she never returned.'

'Okay,' Greta said. 'Let's start at the beginning. Have you checked all the hotdog vans?'

'Yes. We've just been around the fairground and checked them all but we didn't see her at any of them.'

'Okay. Don't worry. We'll find her. What time did you last see her?' Greta asked, filling in a form.

'Half past four,' Tiff said.

'Oh dear. That's a while ago,' Greta said, checking her watch. 'What is your sister's name?'

'Michelle Branning,' Tiff said. Greta wrote it down and handed the slip of paper to Judy. Judy grabbed a microphone and tested it by blowing on it.

'And how old is Michelle?' Greta asked.

'Twenty-one,' Tiff said, a little embarrassed.

'Twenty-one,' Greta repeated. She grimaced. 'Twenty-one-year-olds don't get lost at the fair.'

'This one did,' Tiff sighed.

'You said her name is, Michelle Branning?'

'Yes.'

'Was there anyone else with you?' Greta asked. She looked at Wayne. 'Maybe she went off with a guy. A boyfriend perhaps?'

'No. She didn't and he's not my boyfriend,' Tiff said. 'We were alone all day.'

'Michelle, Michelle,' Greta repeated to herself. She checked the lost property log. 'What was the name in the handbag that was handed in?' Greta asked Judy. Judy shrugged and made an announcement for Michelle Branning to make her way to the lost children station next to the waltzers. She repeated the message several times. 'Wait there a minute,' Greta said. She opened a locker behind her and retrieved a sealed plastic bag. Inside was a pink handbag. She brought it back to the counter. 'What type of handbag does Michelle have?'

'A pink Michael Kors bag, like that one,' Tiff said. Greta opened the bag and removed a purse. 'Her address is Ffordd Beibio, Holyhead,' Tiff said.

'The name and address match. This is your sister's bag,' Greta said. 'It has her purse in it and her phone was found on the floor next to it.'

'On the floor where?' Tiff asked. She was beginning to panic. 'Oh my god. Chelle wouldn't leave her bag and phone anywhere. She's glued to her phone. Where did you get it from?'

'It came to us as lost property. They were handed in by our cleaning staff at the toilet block behind the beer tent,' Greta said.

'That's where I last saw her,' Tiff said.

'At the toilets?'

'No. In the beer tent.'

'Oh. I see. So, you were both in the beer tent?'

'Yes. Then Chelle went to get some food.'

'Were you drinking at all today?'

'What?' Tiff asked.

'Have you been drinking at all today?' Greta's smile faded slightly. 'I have to ask.'

'Yes. Of course, we have,' Tiff said, feeling sick. 'It's my birthday.'

'Ah, you've been celebrating?'

'Yes.'

'So, you've been celebrating all day?' Greta said, writing on another form. 'And she's twenty-one.'

'Yes. She's twenty-one. She wasn't drunk, if that's what you're implying,' Tiff said.

'I wasn't implying anything,' Greta said, smiling. 'Just getting the facts straight. What time did you start drinking?'

'Don't go there. I'm not getting into an argument about it,' Tiff said. 'When was her bag handed in?'

73

'About five o'clock but I can't be sure when she actually left it,' Greta said. 'That was when it was handed in to me.' Judy listened carefully to the conversation and made the announcement again, instructing Michelle Branning to make her way to the lost child station. 'The cleaners may have been busy and brought it to me when they had a spare minute.'

'Where did you last see her?' Judy interrupted.

'We were in the beer tent.'

'You're sure she wasn't drunk when you last saw her?' Judy said, shaking her head. 'Most people in the beer tent are getting drunk or are already drunk.'

'No. She wasn't drunk for god's sake.' Tiff shook her head. Wayne nudged her with his elbow. 'What's your problem?'

'Calm down, Tiff,' he said. 'She's trying to help.'

'Okay. I'm sorry,' Tiff said. 'She might have had a few but she wasn't drunk. Do not write on your form that she was drunk.'

'Do you think she might have felt unwell and gone home without telling you?' Greta asked in a slightly patronising manner. 'Maybe she had her period or something?'

'Oh my god,' Tiff said. 'She's twenty-one, not twelve.'

'Exactly my point,' Greta said, smiling. 'She's an adult and she may have decided to go home and forgot her bag and phone in the toilet. It happens every day here. These lockers are full of people's belongings. They leave them and go home. People celebrate too much and feel unwell after the rides.'

'Without her handbag, her purse and her phone, not to mention me,' Tiff said, irritated. 'Not a chance. She would not leave her bag and phone in the toilet. Something must have happened to her.'

'We can put calls out for her and tell her to come to meet you. That's all we can do I'm afraid.'

'You can call the police.'

'And tell them what?' Greta said, shrugging. 'They don't like us calling them and wasting their time.' She shrugged. 'I would have to tell them we found a handbag and phone in the toilet block, which belongs to a twenty-one-year-old woman who has been drinking all day?'

'That sounds a bit shit when you put it like that, to be honest,' Tiff sighed. 'I know what you're thinking but she wasn't drunk and I'm worried about her.'

'We'll make a few more announcements for you to make sure she has the chance to hear them but it's not our responsibility to report missing adults to the police, especially if they've been drinking.' Greta moved away to greet another customer, who had actually lost her children. 'Feel free to wait here. I shouldn't really do this but if you show me some ID to prove you're her sister you can take her belongings with you.' Tiff showed her driving licence and Greta gave her the bag and phone. 'Excuse me but I'll have to deal with another customer. I suggest you call home to see if she's there. You never know, she might be there sleeping it off.'

'Thanks for your help,' Tiff said, begrudgingly. She typed the password into Chelle's phone and scrolled through her activity. 'She hasn't had any calls or texts since earlier. Where is she?'

'Give your mum a call,' Wayne said. 'The woman is right. She might have gone home.'

'Without her stuff and her little sister?' Tiff said. 'You know her as well as I do. Never in a million years.'

'You were in a right state. You didn't know what day it was,' Wayne said. 'What if someone dropped something in her drink too?'

'Don't say that,' Tiff said. She stifled a tear. 'I didn't think of that.'

'Did you see her drink anything?'

'Yes. She downed her gin and tonic before she left,' Tiff said, remembering through the fog. 'She did it one.' The implications struck home. 'What if there was something in her gin?'

'Let's not think negatively. What time did you say she went for food?'

'Half past four.'

'That's at least two and half hours before I found you in the beer tent,' Wayne said. 'The lady said her handbag was handed in about five o'clock. She's been parted from her stuff for over two hours. That's a long time.'

'Oh shit,' Tiff said. She took out her phone and scrolled to her home number. 'What if she's not there?' Tiff waited to press send. 'Mum will have a heart attack if I tell her she's missing and her bag and phone have been handed in. You know what mum is like. She thinks everyone with a cock is a serial killer. I don't want to panic her.' She had an idea. 'You call my house and ask mum if Chelle is in.'

'Your mum doesn't like me,' Wayne said.

'That's because you shagged Hayley Barnes behind Chelle's back,' Tiff said. Wayne shook his head and blushed. 'Sorry. Now isn't the time. Just say you're calling to ask her if she wants to go out to the circus.'

'Okay,' Wayne said. He scrolled through his contacts. Chelle home. The number rang and Frances Branning answered. Wayne asked if Chelle was home and Frances told him she had gone to the fair on the Newry with Tiff and she wasn't expecting them home until after the pubs were closed. He hung up and shook his head. 'She's not gone home,' Wayne said.

'Something bad has happened,' Tiff said. 'I can feel it in my bones.'

Chapter 12

Lottie finished putting on her makeup. Her hair was down, ringmaster outfit on. Top hat brushed and ready. Just her boots to put on, which could be a mission. They zipped up to above the knee and needed a decent range of flexibility to fasten. Taking charge of the show took practice. Timing was everything. Each illusion paved the way for the next. One mistake and it could all turn to dust. The ringmaster was essential but merely the host. Her communication with the crowd was the key to getting them involved and their involvement was essential to building the atmosphere. Getting into the role was second nature to her. She had been part of the circus since she was a child. It was all she had known. Her father, Ben and mother, Juliet had run it before her, and her grandfather and grandmother before them. It ran in her blood. Travelling was all she knew. It was a challenging life but rewarding too. There had been good times, shit times and terrible times and times when she wished she had gone to a proper school and had a career, partner and children, although they were rare. Lottie was a free spirit. Life on the road kept her young at heart. She had a thirst to explore and experience the world.

It was Lottie who plotted the change of course for the business years before. She saw the writing on the wall a long time before her parents did. If it had been left to them, the circus would have folded. Leaving the traditional show behind and moving into the digital world was her idea and without it, the circus would have remained in the mundane. If you've seen one circus, you've seen them all, she used to say. The circuses of old were designed to shock and stun audiences with the bizarre. Bearded ladies, two-headed animals, strong men who could bend metal with their bare hands, exotic animals and deformities were new to the majority of people in those days. Curiosity drew the crowds and Lottie knew they had to break the mould. She sought out the best tricks, mind-blowing illusions and shock-horror scenes and they mastered them. The Circus of Nightmares became a sensation with millions of views on social media and sell out shows across Europe. She was contacted daily by performers wanting to be a part of the show. Being able to select only the best acts was a great position to be in. The money was ridiculously good and because it was an international act, taxes avoidable. Lottie was a rich woman and she paid her employees what they were worth. Her troop had been hired from all over the world.

Her grandfather, Sidney had won the circus from his employer during a game of cards. It was shortly after World War II and Sidney was just one of millions of servicemen who returned from Europe to a broken society, poverty and rationing. Sidney had no trade and no work and unless you had a skill, it was impossible to get work. Even manual work was hard to find. Sidney had the skills he had learned in the army. His skills were with blades and a rifle. Following a conversation in a pub with a travelling magician, Sidney saw an opportunity. He joined a circus to earn a crust and developed an act, shooting apples from his wife's head and throwing knifes dangerously close to her. Miriam soon became skilled at feigning fear, pretending Sidney was pushing his luck, landing the knives too close to her. The crowds loved the danger aspect. It made the blood pump faster. What started as an experiment fast became the highlight of the show. Lion tamers were old hat. People wanted danger and Sidney could give that to them in bucket loads.

Three years flew by as society rebuilt. Sidney became friendly with the owner, Billy and the men often stayed up at night drinking and playing cards. The card games could be brutal. Grown men would go back to their caravans broke, a wage packet lost on the turn of a card. Travelling men's card games were organised by a strict code of conduct. You could only lose what you owned; there was absolutely no borrowing allowed. If you won, you won no matter what the bet, likewise, if you lost, you lost, no matter what the bet. One night, Billy was holding an ace flush but he'd run out of money. Sidney had a good hand and refused to fold. It was up to Billy to call his bet. He gambled the papers for the big top and the wagon which carried it, which was essentially all the circus consisted of. It was the performers that gravitated to it which made it a success or failure. Sidney accepted the bet and laid down a straight flush, ten to ace. Lottie had heard the story a million times. Billy lost everything he owned in one night of madness and despite their friendship, her grandfather showed no mercy. He took the big top and the truck and control of the circus.

Billy and his wife had no performance skills and were surplus to requirements. Sidney took everything and sent Billy, his wife and three children packing. Edwards' Circus was born. Rumour had it, Billy followed the circus for a while, demanding the chance to pay his debt another way but Sidney refused to budge and he took the show on the road, paying top wages for top performers. He even bought an elephant. One day, Billy Hart was found with his throat cut. His wife and children were taken in by elderly relatives down south and never heard of again.

Grandfather Sidney made a huge success of the circus, in demand all over the country, all year around. The Edwards family became travellers and entertainers from that point onwards. Lottie didn't embellish the past with sentimental nonsense about her ancestry. Sidney was a tyrant, a misogynist bully, liar, thief and murderer. They were his best qualities. Her memories of him were crystal clear. She was frightened of him. Her father hated him with a vengeance and there was a toxic history between them, yet the circus kept them together and passed from generation to generation. When Lottie began managing things from behind the scenes, her father was reluctant to embrace the change but while most circuses were folding and going out of business, the Circus of Nightmares was growing beyond all expectations. Their online presence and venture into the darker side of magic and illusion had made it a million pound a year business. Lottie was the driving force behind it and it was her life. She was the gel which held everything together. Getting ready for the next performance was as exciting now as it had always been. A knock on her trailer door disturbed her thoughts.

'Lottie. Are you in there?' It was Liz. Liz was the administrator and right-hand woman. She dealt with payroll, licences, MOT's, insurances and all the other crappy necessaries that Lottie hated. Lottie wouldn't be able to run the circus without her. Not legally. Even a circus had to play by the rules sometimes. 'Lottie. Are you there?'

'Of course, I am, Liz,' Lottie said. Then to herself. 'Where else would I be?'

'There are some police officers here,' Liz said, lowering her voice.

'Are they there with you?' Lottie called, teasing.

'Pardon?'

'Are the police there with you?'

'Yes.'

'Then why are you talking really quietly?' Lottie laughed. 'I'm sure they can hear you.'

'They can. Bugger off, Lottie,' Liz said. 'They want to talk to you.'

'Oh god,' Lottie said. It was a familiar scene played out at almost every venue. Park up, set up, make a cup of tea and wait for the police to arrive. 'The police want to talk to you, Lottie,' she mouthed to the mirror. She checked her appearance again. 'Here we go again.'

She applied her lip gloss and opened the door. Liz was standing next to two police sergeants. One male, one female. Despite the hour, it was dark now and the fairground was illuminated. It was beautiful.

'Thanks Liz,' Lottie said. 'Have you eaten yet?'

'Not yet. I've been busy,' Liz said.

'Get something to eat before you fall over with exhaustion,' Lottie said, grinning. She turned to the officers. 'Good afternoon, officers,' she said, beaming. Her smile disarmed most people. It had broken hearts too. 'How can I help you?'

'We're investigating a serious assault, which took place around lunchtime,' Bob said. 'Would you mind answering a few questions for us please?'

'Not at all. Come in,' Lottie said. She stood back from the door. Bob and April climbed the four steps into her trailer. They were taken aback by the interior. One end of it was fitted out with digital screens, which showed the interior of the circus and fairground from multiple angles.

'That's an impressive set up,' Bob said.

'It streams onto the internet,' Lottie said. 'Every show is streamed live. This is the build-up. Thousands tune in to watch the crowds take their seats. It's beyond me what the attraction is but they love it and we give them what they want.'

'I love your trailer,' April said. 'It's amazing what you can do.'

The furniture was leather and expensive and the floor was carpeted and covered in sheepskin rugs and goatskins. The fittings were high-gloss, glass and chrome, like a display from Ideal Homes. It was unlike any mobile home they had seen.

'I'm forgetting my manners. I'm Lottie Edwards. I own the operation and this is where I live. Take a seat.' She gestured to the living area.

'We'll stand, thank you,' Bob said, taking out a tablet. 'I'm sergeant Dewhurst and this is sergeant Byfelt.' He showed Lottie a picture on his tablet. 'This is Malcolm Orange. Do you recognise him?'

'Yes. I met him this morning. Lovely chap. How is he?' Lottie asked. The police officers looked surprised by the question. 'He didn't look very well when he left.'

'What time did you see him?' April asked.

'Sometime before we opened,' Lottie said. 'Sorry. I can't be more specific but I don't wear a watch. We work to a tight schedule. I know what time it is by what I'm doing.' She paused. The officers didn't look satisfied by her answer. 'It was before twelve, if that helps.'

'Can you tell us what happened?' Bob asked.

'Yes. No problem.' Lottie sat down on a tall stool next to a breakfast bar. She opened a bottle of water and took a sip. 'I was walking to the big top when I noticed a stranger chatting to one of our trapeze artists. He'd called in at the big top this morning for a chat about the operating licence for this week. There was a miscommunication with the chairman of the planning committee and he was unaware we would be trading this week.'

'A miscommunication?' Bob said, raising an eyebrow.

'Yes. I spoke to a lovely gentleman called Charles Milburn months ago about setting up here this week because we had a date in London cancelled. We try to minimise downtime. Our performers need to be paid regardless of how many shows we put on or how many people buy tickets. I don't like blanks in the diary. We had a blank and Charles helped me to fill it.'

'I can appreciate that. Charles Milburn died a while back,' Bob said.

'I was unaware of that. We made a verbal agreement that a percentage of the gate takings would be donated to St David's hospice in return for five days trading. It's a bribe in every sense of the word but Charles suggested it and I was happy to make a donation to a good cause in exchange for a permit. Money makes the world go around.' Bob didn't look convinced. Lottie held up her phone. 'Do you want to take a look?'

'No. It's not important,' Bob said. 'Not in this instance.'

'Really?' Lottie frowned. 'Malcolm thought it was important enough to come here and challenge us. I have all the calls to Charles on my phone and a couple of emails to back it up. Should we need them, which is unlikely. We sail for Ireland on Friday.'

'I'm sure someone might want to see them but that's not why we're here,' April said.

'No. Of course, it isn't.' Lottie supped from her water. 'You mentioned an assault?'

'Yes. A serious assault,' Bob said.

'Who was assaulted?' Lottie asked. She looked genuinely concerned. 'How terrible.'

'Malcolm Orange was assaulted,' Bob said, rolling his eyes.

'Oh no. The poor man.' Lottie bit her bottom lip. 'When?'

'When he was here,' Bob said, shaking his head. 'Malcolm Orange is in hospital. He has a bleed on the brain. He says he was punched in the back of his head by one of your employees.'

'That's terrible news but incorrect,' Lottie said. 'I hope he recovers but he's clearly suffering from concussion. He didn't look well when he left here. I asked some of the staff to escort him to the gate, which they did. They left him near the toilets at the bottom of Newry Street and gave him a cup of tea. He was out of breath but safe when they left him. And at no point was he punched.'

'They left him with a cup of tea?' Bob said, shaking his head.

'Yes. From the tea wagon. It's for employees only and is open most of the time. We start early and finish late.' Lottie smiled. 'We can always get a cup of tea.' Bob flushed red, frustrated. 'Would you like tea?'

'No thank you. You said he was escorted from the site?' April asked.

'Yes.'

'Escorted sounds like he was removed, forcibly?'

'Does it?' Lottie asked. 'I suppose it does. I did ask him to leave as we were getting ready to open but he refused, so I asked some of my staff to escort him off the pitch. Then he started sweating and holding his chest. He should have stayed at home.'

'Why was he asked to leave?'

'It was for his own safety.'

'Can you expand please?'

83

'Yes. He called me a liar,' Lottie said. She put her hands on her hips. 'He called me a liar in front of my staff. Twice actually. A lot of my employees are incredibly grateful to work here and they're fiercely loyal and Malcolm was quite rude. It was best for everyone that he left.'

'So, what happened?' Bob asked. Lottie looked confused. 'When he called you a liar. What happened?'

'Nothing much,' Lottie said. 'I expect he was embarrassed that he had come here making wild accusations about us trading without a licence only to find the chairman of the committee had granted permission months ago. He must have been very embarrassed, poor man. I think his pride took a knock.' Lottie paused. 'You know what they say about pride coming before a fall. That's so true, don't you think?'

'All that is interesting but can you tell us what happened?' April asked. She could sense Bob was losing his cool. It didn't take much to annoy him.

'I told you. Nothing. He seemed like such a nice chap really. Some people are spoiled by a bit of power, aren't they?' Lottie shrugged and smiled. 'So, we discussed the licence but he wasn't happy at all with my explanation. I told him we were terribly busy as we were getting ready to open. Then he took a funny turn, so I asked some of my employees to escort him from the pitch.'

'What do you mean by a funny turn?' Bob asked.

'He was sweating and breathing heavily and holding his chest,' Lottie said, putting her hand on her own chest to demonstrate. 'The poor man must have a heart condition. Anyway, at no point was he punched.'

'He says he was jostled and punched,' April said.

'He's mistaken. I'm certain I can gather a dozen or so witnesses who will be willing to verify my version of events over the version from a man who was clearly poorly and confused.' She smiled a winning smile, forever the showgirl. 'That is if you need me to?'

'Oh, I'm sure you can gather witnesses. So, you saw him leave the fairground?' Bob asked.

'Not personally,' Lottie said. 'As I said, we were getting ready to open. There's a lot to do, I'm sure you can imagine. This is a big operation with a lot of moving parts and over a hundred employees. The setup is vital to the smooth running of the operation.'

'Mr Orange has had a scan and he has an injury to the back of his skull,' April said. 'And he told his wife he was punched, possibly by a clown.'

'Was he completely lucid when he made this accusation or under the influence of medication?' Lottie asked. The police officers looked at each other. 'I didn't think so. He was probably barely conscious and confused. Possibly punched by a clown, really?' Lottie smiled and shook her head. 'We have over twenty clown performers. It certainly wouldn't stand up in court, would it?'

'We need to investigate regardless,' Bob said.

'He has heart problems,' Lottie said. 'My father suffered with a bad heart. I recognise the signs. Collapsed all the time at the most inopportune moments. He could have fallen and banged his head near the toilets. There are a lot of stone walls and railings there, aren't there?'

'He says a clown called Hugo punched him,' Bob said. 'A big clown.'

'Hugo is my older brother,' Lottie said. 'He's a gentle giant and wouldn't punch anybody. He also has a twin called Boris. They're identical,' she added. 'I asked Hugo to escort him because he's strong and could support him. I wonder if he has named Hugo because I said his name and that's the only name he can remember?'

'So, Hugo escorted him alone or did he have help?'

'Boris helped him. I wonder if Mr Orange would be able to distinguish between them. I mean, could he identify which twin was which?'

'I'm not following,' April said.

'The devil is in the detail,' Lottie said, shrugging. 'If he was punched from behind, how does he know who punched him from behind? Unless he has eyes in the back of his head, he's speculating at best, about an incident which didn't happen, I might add.' Lottie shrugged. 'The twins were either side of him. I think Mr Orange is confused. He's miffed he made a fool of himself and is trying to cause us problems.'

'We will need to speak to Hugo and Boris ourselves,' Bob said. 'Just to clarify things.'

'Not a chance. We have a show starting at eight o'clock and the twins are integral to the show,' Lottie said. 'Enough is enough. I've been cooperative and I've answered your questions, sergeant. If you want to ask me or any of my employees any further questions about this or anything else, get a warrant and we'll come to the station with our solicitor.' She smiled again. 'Let's do things properly, shall we?'

'You're clearly a very clever lady,' Bob said. 'I get the impression you have had to shield your employees from the police before.' Lottie smiled but didn't reply. 'We'll leave it at that for now. Thanks for your time.'

'It was my pleasure,' Lottie said. 'If you want tickets for the show, you'd better be quick. They're selling like hot cakes.' She opened the door and gestured towards it. The officers walked out, shoulders hunched and a little dejected. Bob was fuming but they'd been woefully unprepared to confront Lottie Edwards. 'Take care and thanks for calling,' Lottie said, closing the door. 'Or as my old grandad Sidney used to say, "go and fuck yourself", god rest his evil soul,' she said to herself. It began to rain, further dampening Bob's spirit.

'Well, we had our pants pulled down there,' April said as they walked towards the rides. The lights strobed and searched the night sky. 'Good and proper.'

'I don't want to talk about it,' Bob said, fastening his jacket against the rain. 'That young lady thinks we're the clowns. I feel like I've had my pants pulled down and been spanked with a cricket bat.'

'That's an image I didn't need in my head,' April said. 'Back to the station?'

'Back to the station,' Bob agreed.

Circus of Nightmares

Chapter 13

Alan watched the CSI team set about their work. Pamela Stone was on her way, delayed by a case in Liverpool. Kim had finished speaking to the young women, who were being held captive. They had been in the room for three days, although they weren't a hundred percent sure. The darkness and stress had confused them. Some of the women wouldn't speak and some wouldn't shut up. Alan felt it best they were interviewed briefly by the female officers. It was more than likely their captors had been male. He listened from a safe distance and picked up that all except one of the women were from Syria. The other was from Iraq. She was Kurdish. They had travelled across Turkey, through Europe as far as Calais. Two of them had walked the entire way to France. The others had taken trains, buses, hitchhiked, stolen bicycles and hidden underneath lorries to get there. Each one of them had a different tragic story of their journey. None of them had known the others before reaching France and they had all set off from their homeland with their husbands or boyfriends and extended families, including children. The fact there were no children with them now, summed up their plight. Each one had become separated from their families by tragic circumstances, some of the men were arrested, some were drowned crossing the Mediterranean, some were tricked by pirates and some were murdered by fellow travellers for what little they had.

At Calais, the women had begged and scavenged, sold themselves and been raped to get enough food and bedding to survive until they were approached individually by a man and woman from Ghana. The couple were very plausible and convinced them that if they could get money sent to them from their families electronically, they could arrange passage across the Channel, visas and employment in Ireland. They had arrived in the UK in the back of an articulated lorry bound for Ireland, hidden in a container load of fruit. The women had no idea where they were or why they had been taken to the house. Their English wasn't good enough to explain Wales wasn't England. The traffickers had swindled each and every one of them. Again.

'Pamela Stone is here,' Kim said.

'Good. I need a laugh,' Alan said. Kim frowned. 'I'm not saying you're not a laugh.' He paused. 'Just that she's more of a laugh. Especially when it comes to cause of death. What do you think she will say Mary Adams died of?'

'The sudden stop?'

'Good one,' Alan said. 'Did you get anything from the women?' They were being taken away to be checked over at hospital. Their traumatic journeys were visible by the sadness in their eyes. He wondered where they would be taken to and where they would eventually turn up.

'It was all sadly predictable, to be honest. People fucking over other people for a profit. Nothing of any use,' Kim said, shaking her head. 'They were told if they paid a deposit, they would be given jobs when they got to Ireland and that they could pay off the remainder of their debt for carriage into the UK. Twenty-grand each. They had to pay ten in advance in France.'

'Bargain,' Alan said. 'Things at Holyhead port are vastly different since Brexit. Most hauliers are drowning in paperwork at the docks and the inspections are thorough. Customs are checking loads they didn't have to check before. Smuggling is going to be much more difficult from now on. I reckon the driver bottled it and unloaded them here. That or the traffickers got wind of something and pulled the plug at the last minute. They dumped them here until they could work out what to do with them.'

'I think you could be right.' Kim held up her phone. It had a profile picture on the screen. 'Who do you think that is?' she asked.

'Vaguely familiar,' Alan said. 'I haven't got my glasses. Help me out.'

'That is the Linkedin profile for Doctor Gerard Telford,' Kim said.

'The owner?'

'Yes.'

'Where did you get that from?'

'I ran a Google search and this is the only photograph of him online. That is a much older Doctor Telford over there.' Alan walked over to the bodies. He looked from the phone to the corpse.

'He looks better on that photograph and about fifteen years younger,' Alan said. He looked at the dead man and studied his face. 'That is him,' he agreed. 'No wonder we can't find them. They're here. We need to assume that is Elisha Telford for now.'

'I agree. There are no photographs of her online which is unusual,' Kim said. 'They deleted their online footprint for a reason.'

'Not for any good reason,' Alan said. 'The older couple are probably relations?'

'Probably,' Kim said. 'Parents maybe.'

'It's not a coincidence there were nine women in that room,' Alan said. 'This is a holding point for the port. It's part of a trafficking operation, which means, organised criminals. And if I'm right about that, Doctor Telford and his wife knew about it or turned a blind eye to people using their house for trafficking.'

'They turned a blind eye for a load of cash. Makes sense,' Kim said. 'Trafficking is a dangerous game to play.'

'Exactly. The penalties for screwing up are severe,' Alan said. 'Or if they decided they didn't want to play anymore. That's not an option open to most people and they may have found out the hard way.' He stood up straight, stiffening up. 'It still begs the question, who is Mary Adams and who pushed her through the window?'

'We can't ask them and the Syrian women didn't have any contact with any females after they left France,' Kim said. 'Do you want me to call the NCA and see if they're aware of the late doctor and his wife?'

'It can't hurt,' Alan said, nodding. 'The National Crime Agency will have them on a watch list if they've been linked to an operation somehow.' His mobile rang. 'DI Williams,' he answered.

'Alan. This is Anne Parry from Matrix.'

'Hello, Anne. What do I owe the pleasure?' Alan asked. 'It's been a while.'

'I am calling out of courtesy,' Anne said. 'My DI and I are on the way to a place called, Newry Beach.'

'Holyhead?' he said, smiling. 'Why would Matrix be going to the Newry?'

'It's a long story. Five years ago, a young couple went missing from our patch. The last place they were seen alive was at a fairground. They'd been to see a circus.'

'The Circus of Nightmares. It's caused quite a stir on the island already,' Alan said. 'They have pulled a few publicity stunts and frightened the life out of the locals in Llangefni. My sons are huge fans of it. I've got a feeling I'll be paying for all of us to go and see it live. What is taking you there?'

'To cut a long story short, we have recovered the remains of the missing couple stuffed in a metal drum. It was at the bottom of a pond, which was drained during a construction project.'

'Okay,' Alan said. 'It's a long way to go and it's an awfully long time ago. Who are you going to speak to?'

'Locally, this is a high-profile case,' Anne said. 'Leo Jobson is the son of a local villain. The guy is a bit of folk hero, so there's a lot of media interest. The jungle drums are beating and I want to get to the circus before it's all over the television. It was a dead end when we first picked up the case and it's still a dead end but we've got two families who want answers.'

'Tell me why Matrix is on this?'

'Initially, it was thought Leo Jobson might have been kidnapped for a ransom but when it became clear they weren't coming back rumours were he was killed as payback against his father, hence our involvement.'

'In case of any retaliation?'

91

'Exactly. Finding the bodies has fired up our critics and we need to be seen to be doing something. You know how it is. The last place they were seen was in the bar at the fairground and the drum they were put into was used to store the type of axle grease used on heavy machinery.'

'Like a fairground ride?'

'Exactly. It's unlikely to be a coincidence they were last seen at the fairground and then found in a barrel of grease that would be used there. I have the owner listed as Lottie Edwards. She's not returning my calls, which is why we're going tonight.'

'The element of surprise,' Alan said.

'It's all we've got at the moment. The circus has been in the same family for generations. I'm hoping she might be able to give me some names. People who worked around that time. People she may have had concerns about. You know the score.'

'I see,' Alan said. 'Fill your boots. If you need anything from me, you have my number. Are you staying over?'

'We're not allowed to,' Anne said. 'Budget restraints after covid-19 are biting every department. We can't buy a pencil without permission. A hotel in Trearddur Bay would be nice but beyond our reach.'

'I know the feeling.'

'What are you working on?' Anne asked.

'I'm in a lovely little seaside town called, Rhosneiger. We have a dead woman who was thrown off a balcony, a cellar full of dead doctors and nine Syrian women who were on their way to Ireland but only made it this far and were left in a cellar with a bucket and three bottles of water.'

'That sounds like a fucked-up situation,' Anne said, laughing. 'Trafficking is on the rise. People are worth more than heroin nowadays and if they get caught, the gangsters serve less time for moving humans than brown.' She paused. 'I might be able to help with a few names in the trafficking business.'

'You'll be top of my list when I have some details,' Alan said. 'I don't suppose you've heard of a couple called Telford. Both doctors working in Dubai?'

'No. That doesn't ring a bell but I can tell you working in Dubai is the new Cayman Islands. Having a business there is a great way to launder cash.'

'How does that work?' Alan asked.

'The Caymans were a tax haven but the government changed the rules and closed the loopholes but if you work in Dubai and you're out of the country most of the year, you don't pay tax in the UK,' Anne said. 'We've found a couple last year setting up dentist surgeries over there and writing off all their tax, laundering drug money for a local outfit by the millions and charging them forty-pence on the pound to clean it.'

'Forty percent,' Alan said, surprised.

'Everything is about the cash. It has to be clean or we'll take it off them. They are getting smart and smart costs more,' Anne said. 'Further investigation showed the surgeries were pieces of desert with planning permission on them and nothing more. The surgeries didn't exist.'

'I'll do some digging at the Dubai end,' Alan said. 'This place is full of wine. Hundreds and hundreds of bottles.'

'It's another sign of laundering, Alan. They're using wine, classic cars and coins as stock to hide bundles of cash they can't account for. Some of the vintage wine in our last raid was worth ten grand a bottle.'

'How big is a ten-grand bottle of wine?' Alan asked.

'Fucking massive if it's the dishwater you drink,' Anne joked. 'I remember the red vinegar you ordered after that course in London.'

'Dishwater?' Alan disagreed. 'That was the best rioja they had. It cost me fifteen quid.'

'Philistine,' Anne said. 'Look into it. You'll probably find your dead doctors are laundering money for some dangerous people.'

93

'That's food for thought,' Alan said. 'Good luck at the fair. I'll be in touch.'

Chapter 14

Len Jobson opened the window and let the fresh air in. It cleared the cigarette smoke from the Jeep. He coughed and flicked the stub into the night. It landed on the carriageway and bright red sparks flew into the air, burning bright for a second before being snuffed out by the rain. Just like a life. One minute we burn bright, the next we're gone, nothing but a memory, which fades in time and is eventually lost as our descendants grow old and die and the memory of us dies with them. Some people will remain only as a name carved into a headstone, others may be ashes blown into the wind, scattered by a grieving loved one. His son, Leo was neither of those things. He was a newspaper story long forgotten by most but not by his father. Not ever. Len had scoured the planet searching for Leo. He was convinced he'd been murdered and he'd been right. Someone killed his son and stuffed him into a barrel. They were close, closer than most fathers and sons get to be. Leo left a huge hole in his life.

Leo's disappearance changed Len. His blatant disregard for human life had been tempered by the loss of his son. The lives he had ended with the swing of a hammer, pull of a trigger or the flash of a blade had no meaning to him until Leo vanished. Losing his son put things into perspective. The sense of loss he felt was matched only by his sense of guilt. The guilt weighed heavily on his mind and twisted his dark soul into knots. He wanted to say sorry to those families who grieved because he had murdered their son, husband, grandfather, uncle, cousin or friend. But he couldn't. Not without being murdered himself or going to jail for what remained of his life and he wanted neither of those things. Karma brought the other option. The cancer spreading inside him was winning the race against the chemo and radiotherapy he had received. It had been sent into retreat for a while by the treatment he had received but it was back with a vengeance. He didn't have long, which meant finding Leo's killer was the most important thing he had left to do. If he did nothing else, that was all he had left to live for. Killing the culprit would be the last life he would take before he died.

He didn't fear God. God hadn't been there when he was slaughtering enemies as if they were diseased cattle who needed to be removed from the herd. Where was God when Leo was taken and stuffed into a barrel? Nowhere. When his time came, his light would be extinguished like the sparks of a cigarette in the darkness of the night and the darkness would become all-encompassing and infinite. And then there would be nothing. There would be no reckoning, no judgement and no atonement to make. He wouldn't be sent into the infernal pit of hell because it didn't exist. Hell was a place made up to control the masses, just like heaven. Be good and stick to rules and you will go to a good place. Become a killer for reward and burn in hell. Bullshit. He didn't fear what would come after death, his hell had been on earth. Life had punished him while he was alive. When he was gone, the universe would continue as it always had, with no care that he had existed. It all seemed so pointless.

He lit another cigarette and overtook the lorry in front of him. The Matrix detectives were three cars ahead on the A55, heading into North Wales. Whatever they had found in that metal barrel, was leading them to someone and he intended to find out who it was and what they knew about the murder of his only son.

****

Tiff was exhausted. The circus show had started and there was still no sign of Chelle. Wayne looked like he was losing the will to live but they walked around the fairground again and again, while announcements became more infrequent. The women in the lost children station were following their protocol but there were other announcements that needed to be made. Chelle's whereabouts were not their priority. Tiff was running out of options. She couldn't go home without her sister. Her mind and body were sapped of energy. She sat down on a bench and cried. Wayne watched her, unsure what to do.

'Do you think we should call the police?' Wayne asked. Tiff sobbed and shrugged. Calling the police felt like admitting something bad had happened to Chelle and she wasn't ready to do that. It was like giving up. 'It's half past eight,' he said. 'She's been missing for four hours.'

'I don't know what to do for the best,' Tiff said, sniffling.

'Do you think she might have met someone and gone to town?' Wayne asked. Tiff glared at him. 'I'm just trying to think of the possibilities the police will ask us, that's all.' He shrugged. 'They will ask us if she might have gone to town, drinking with someone.'

'I suppose it's possible but she wouldn't have left her bag and phone,' Tiff said. 'Even if she lost them and didn't know she didn't have them at first, she would have noticed and come back to look for them by now. A girl doesn't leave her bag and phone behind without going back to look for it. It doesn't happen.'

'What if she's gone home with a guy?' Wayne asked.

'She's not a slag,' Tiff said, shaking her head.

'She's not an angel either,' Wayne said. Tiff glared at him again. 'I'm not being horrible, Tiff. It's possible. Where else can she be?'

'Fuck off, Wayne,' Tiff said.

'Don't be like that.'

'You're insinuating my sister has come to the fair with me, met some random guy and gone home with him on a whim without telling me where she was going?' Tiff argued. 'Seriously?'

'What if she was so wasted, she didn't know what was going on and she's asleep on someone's settee?'

'She wasn't drunk,' Tiff said.

'You weren't drunk. You were spiked.'

'You're scaring me,' Tiff said, standing up. 'I've had enough of guessing games. I'm calling the police.'

Chapter 15

Jane Orange was exhausted. The doctors had sent her home to get some decent food and rest. The stress of Malcolm being so ill had taken a toll on her. He was sedated and recovering from surgery and there was nothing she could do to ease his situation. The surgeon said he wasn't out of the woods but she was happy with his progress. He would be heavily sedated for the next twenty-four hours and then they would access his situation. Remaining at the hospital was pointless. He was not aware of what was happening to him, so she may as well be at home, sleeping in her own bed. She had tried to eat a bowl of Heinz tomato soup and some crusty bread. It was her go to comfort food. Whenever she was poorly as a child, her mother made it for her. In tandem with watching Fingerbobs and a glass of Lucozade, it was the cure for all evils. The soup filled a gap but she had no appetite. She tried to listen to music. The best of Abba, ABC, Prince and Kings of Leon failed to settle her nerves so, she self-medicated with a half-bottle of Bells and some paracetamol. That slowed down her mind, which had been racing all day. What a nightmare day it had been. The worst for a long time.

Possibly the worst day ever, since she'd found out she was pregnant with their first child. As soon as she saw the results, she knew that her future would be with Malcolm Orange. She had cried for a week. As time went by, the hopes and aspirations she had nurtured since being a child, faded into the mists of time and she took on the role of wife and mother. In time, she actually began to love him in a sibling type of way. They were companions for life. Such a waste of what she could have been if she'd been more selfish. She couldn't terminate their child and so her choice had been made in a brief moment of passion when all sense and sensibility was lost. Malcolm was her husband and she was a good wife.

Malcolm had looked so poorly. She couldn't get his face out of her mind. Part of her was so angry at him. The bloody fool wouldn't listen sometimes. When he got a bee in his bonnet, nothing could stop him until he got stung. This time he had been stung good and proper. She could only hope they would have the opportunity to laugh about it one day in the future when the effing circus had effed off and they could recall the time he was punched in the head by a clown. What a story for the grandchildren that would be, when she finally got to see them again. They hadn't seen the grandchildren for over twelve months. Partly because of that dreadful virus and partly because their daughter-in-law couldn't stand Malcolm. He had a habit of telling her how to do things, then arguing with their son, Mark when he asked him to shut up. That would lead to another six-month cooling off period before they would visit again. Things were going to be different in the future. She was going to put her foot down when he got home. It was time to stop letting him run around like a bull in a china shop, pissing everyone off. It was always her that had to clean up after him, while he went on oblivious to who he had offended. Maybe the bang on the head would be the catalyst to make him think twice before jumping in with both feet. She could only hope so.

It wasn't late when she went to bed, probably before ten o'clock. She looked through the bedroom window at the fairground. The lights looked beautiful in the darkness but the noise carried on the cold night air. The beam from the lighthouse at the end of the breakwater pierced the night, turning relentlessly. The view seemed unfamiliar and surreal. She couldn't sleep so she went into the spare bedroom at the other side of the house and climbed into bed. It was quieter there. The sheets were clean and cool and sleep found her quickly. Whisky numbed her senses and allowed her to drift off.

Her dreams were plagued with thoughts of her long dead parents, their illnesses, deaths and funerals. She saw their grandchildren and shouted to them but they couldn't hear her. The images were all jumbled up in space and time with faces and people she didn't know. Somewhere in her dream she felt a draft on her face. It was gentle at first, tickling her skin. Gentle and warm. The draft touched her skin again, this time it carried the odour of food and peppermint mingled with cigars. Her subconscious mind told her it wasn't a breeze at all. It told her it was someone's breath. Then she felt someone lick her cheek.

Kelly was soaking in the bath. Her daughter was staying with her nan for the night. She had kept the details of the day to herself, simply saying they had witnessed a horrible accident at Rhosneiger beach. There was no need to frighten Elle. She was a sensitive girl, easily disturbed. Jack had been sullen and moody all the way back to Holyhead. He behaved like a sulky teenager, driving her further away. Her mind was made up and there was no going back. The news about his mother was devastating and she felt his pain but what they had witnessed was horrific. It wasn't the time to lose their dignity by being childish and sulking. The incident had shocked her and she wanted to go home and be alone. Self-preservation had kicked in. It had always been her self-defence mechanism. Kelly coped with whatever came along but she did it her way and alone. She didn't need a man in her life but that didn't mean she didn't want one. The fact was Jack wasn't the man she wanted to spend her life with. If she chose to share her life with someone, she would choose carefully for Elle's sake and her own. It was a tough ask but that was the way it was. She had seen her friends introducing one boyfriend after another to their kids without thinking it through. It always ended in tears. She had tried with Jack but it wasn't to be.

Jack had some dreadful times ahead of him but she couldn't be there because of pity for him. She needed to end the relationship despite his awful family news. His future didn't include Kelly and there was no point in dragging things out and pretending otherwise, only to hurt him further down the line. He didn't say goodbye when she got out of the van, which added to her contempt of how he had dealt with the situation. He had texted her a few times, asking to talk but she didn't want to talk to him or anyone else. Her walls had come up and they wouldn't come down for a while. That was just the way things were. She was a complex human being and she recognised she could be difficult to be around sometimes but that was the way she was made. For now, it was better for everyone if she had her own space.

The bath water was cooling and the skin on her fingers was beginning to ripple. She had topped up the hot water three times already. It was time to brave the cool air and get dried and dressed. There was a bottle of wine and a movie waiting for her downstairs. She climbed out, the water running from her skin. The cooler air touched her and goosebumps appeared on her arms. Wrapping herself in her favourite towel, she stepped out of the bath and patted her face dry. The mirror was steamed up and she couldn't see her reflection. Her dressing gown was in the bedroom. She dried herself off quickly and opened the bathroom door. Suddenly, she was plunged into total darkness.

Chapter 16

The crowd was hushed as Lottie introduced the next act. A troop of clowns pushed the set into position. A huge wooden wheel stood vertically on a platform; four shackles fixed at the centre. A second wheel was brought on. This one horizontal to the ground. The performers arrived and the clowns faded into the darkness behind them. The Great Arturo, a direct descendent of Greek royalty, who fought against the mighty Trojans, apparently. No one questioned the veracity of that claim. He appeared alongside his raven-haired beauty, Helen. Lottie said it was an act of incredible skill and coordination, timed to perfection and unrivalled by other performers of a similar ilk. The drums beat and trumpets blared, lasers cut the darkness. The music reached its crescendo and the clowns appeared again, fastening Helen to the wheel. Arturo grabbed the heavy wheel and released a lever. The wheel began to turn, Helen at its centre. Silence reigned.

Arturo took his position standing on the second wheel and the clowns pushed it until it was spinning quickly. Each time Arturo faced Helen, he threw a long dagger, which stuck into the wood between her limbs. The crowd whooped as each knife struck home. Six blades landed safely on the wheel, missing the smiling Helen. The crowd were impressed and Arturo took the applause. Enter Hugo, the giant clown. The crowd quietened. Hugo wagged a finger and looked unimpressed. He pulled the daggers from the wheel and handed them to Arturo along with a blindfold, miming that he should put it on. Arturo put the blindfold on, reluctantly. He looked nervous. Hugo pulled the lever on the big wheel.

Helen began to turn faster. Her expression turned to concern. She was shouting for it to be stopped. It was too fast. The timing would be wrong. It was too dangerous. Hugo ignored her and pushed Arturo's wheel faster, so he was spinning full circle every second. The crowd was silent as Arturo settled and adjusted to the increased speed. He released three daggers one at a time and they missed Helen but Arturo lost his balance on the fourth attempt. The next three blades tumbled wildly. The first wayward blade somersaulted through the air and severed Helen's left arm at the wrist. Her hand fell onto the floor; the fingers opening and closing. Then it crawled away into the shadows like a wounded animal. A scream pierced the tense silence and Lottie staggered into the light, the second wayward dagger in her guts. A sharp intake of breath filled the air as the crowd reacted. A split second later, the sixth blade tumbled through the air into the audience. The lights came on and a young man with shoulder length hair was slumped in his seat, the knife in his chest. People around him were sprayed with blood. Several of the audience screamed, others ran from their seats, to help, others ran away. The lights went out and the medical team responded in the darkness. An ambulance entered the arena. The audience could only see shadows and people rushing around in the strobing blue lights. Lottie and the injured male were put on stretchers and put into the back of the ambulance. The ambulance crew climbed in after them and closed the doors but the engine wouldn't start. A troop of clowns pushed it out of the big top and the murmur of voices filled the circus. No one was quite sure what to do. It was several long minutes before the lights came on and everything but the blood was gone.

The lights dimmed again and a spotlight illuminated Lottie at the other side of the arena, in perfectly good health. The crowd applauded, convinced it had all been part of the show. Lottie introduced the next act and the clowns changed the set.

****

Bob Dewhurst and April Byfelt were back at the fairground sooner than they expected to be. They met Tiffany at the entrance. Wayne had been to get coffees and burgers while they waited for the police to arrive. He was worried Tiff would appear drunk and wouldn't be taken seriously. Tiff manged a few bites of food and the coffee perked her up a bit. When she'd made the missing person call, she was directed to the correct station and told the report was classed as urgent and would be dealt with by the FDO. She had no idea what that meant but was told where to wait for officers to arrive. The Force Duty Officer was there to coordinate resources in the event of a serious event. A missing female in close proximity to the sea was classed as such. Within minutes, officers were deployed to the Newry Beach. Bob and April were the closest, being in the Holyhead station when the call came in. They were to set the ball rolling while senior officers were dispatched along with backup. A call was put into Alan as the closest detective inspector.

'Are you Tiffany Branning?' April asked as they approached. Tiff looked washed out. Her eyes were red from crying and her mascara had smudged. She looked like a frightened little girl dressed up as an adult.

'Yes,' Tiff said, nervously.

'Your sister is missing, right?'

'Yes.'

'Since what time?'

'About half-past-four.'

'Tell me what happened,' April asked, wondering why it had taken so long to report it. She heard the slur in Tiff's words.

'I don't know where to begin,' Tiff said.

'Take a deep breath,' April said. 'Her name is Michelle Branning but she's known as Chelle, correct?'

'Yes.'

'She's twenty-one?'

'Yes.'

'Do you have a picture of her on your phone?' April asked. 'If you have one taken today with what she was wearing visible, it would be perfect.'

'I have one here from earlier,' Tiff said. 'We took it in the Albert Vaults.'

'Great. That's perfect. I need your permission to upload this to our site on Facebook. We'll get her face out there immediately,' April said. 'If anyone has seen her, we'll know quickly.'

'I'm not sure about Facebook. My mum will see it,' Tiff said, shaking her head. 'I don't want to worry her. She worries about us all the time. If she thinks Chelle is missing, she'll have a heart attack.'

'Okay, Tiffany,' April said. 'Your sister is missing and your mother needs to know that. We can't disguise the situation to be anything but what it is. So, while I understand your concerns, we need to get this picture on Facebook.'

'Okay. If you think it's best,' Tiff said, reluctantly.

'Your mother will appreciate hearing this from you, before someone sees Chelle on Facebook and tells her,' April said. 'You must call her once we're done with the details, okay.' Tiff nodded that she understood. 'You have her bag and her phone, yes?'

'Yes.'

'They were found in the toilets by the cleaners?'

'Yes. Something must have happened to her. There's no way she would leave them,' Tiff said. 'She wasn't drunk, honest she wasn't.'

'But you had been drinking?'

'Yes. Chelle thought I had been spiked,' Tiff said. 'I was talking to three blokes in the pub and told them it was my birthday and they bought me shots.' Tiff choked back a sob. 'I was beyond drunk. There was something in those shots. I swear there was. Chelle said I'd been spiked so she went to get some coffee and food and never came back.'

'Did you know the men who bought you shots?'

'No but they were in a van with the circus on the side of it.'

'Have you seen them since?'

'No.'

'Has anyone messaged her phone since she went missing?' April asked.

'No.'

'I need you to check her Facebook page to make sure she hasn't posted from a different device,' April said.

'Why would she do that?' Tiff asked confused.

'She may be with a friend and used their device,' Tiff said. 'We need to know if she's been active on social media. Do that now, please.'

'Okay,' Tiff said, fumbling through the pages. 'Oh fudge, my fingers aren't working properly. Sorry.'

'Take your time.' April said. She was aware Wayne was nearby. 'Can you talk to this guy,' April asked Bob.

'Who are you?' Bob asked Wayne. He took him to one side.

'Wayne,' he answered. 'I'm just a friend. I've been helping Tiff to look for Chelle.'

'What's your surname?'

'Best.'

'I'll need a statement from you,' Bob said. He guided him away from Tiff. A constable approached them and Bob asked him to interview Wayne. The first patrol car arrived with two officers in it. Another four arrived on foot from the station.

'Gather around,' Bob said. 'We're looking for a twenty-one-year-old. Michelle Branning. She's been missing for about four hours. Her sister has scoured the fairground and she's not here and she's not at home. So, we need to begin the search beyond the perimeter of the fairground. If you can start a

105

search down near the Boathouse at the bottom of Porth-y-felin and work around the marina towards McKenzie pier, please.'

'Is it likely she's in a pub in town, sarge?'

'We're not ruling anything out, yet,' Bob said. 'I'll be sending a team through town next. I want the water's edge checked first.'

'What about the quarry park and the breakwater?'

'I want to concentrate on the immediate area first,' Bob said. 'It's dark and there's no light down there. There's too much ground to cover and not enough of us to venture down the quarry road.'

'Okay Sarge.'

'Let's get to it. Too much time has gone by for my liking.'

The officers trudged off the grassed areas towards the sea. The promenade was well lit and there were plenty of people about but it was darker near the shore. The tide was in and the stony beach was covered. The waves were lapping over the sea wall. Bob looked at the yachts anchored in the marina. The masts were still, which was a bonus. He walked back to where April was taking all the details from Tiffany. The misper report was four pages long but it covered most of the bases. Chelle had been missing too long. Most abductions go badly unless the victim is recovered in the first hour. The golden hour was long gone. They were against the clock and they knew it.

****

Anne Parry and Gill Robinson waited in Lottie's trailer, out of the rain. Her admin, Liz had checked with Lottie between acts and explained detectives from Liverpool were here to talk to her. Lottie was understandably flustered but told her to let them into her trailer, make them a coffee and stay with them. She was both irritated and baffled by their arrival. Uniformed police officers didn't call late in the evening unless there was something serious happening but these

106

were detectives. Senior detectives. A superintendent and an inspector, no less. The detectives were given coffee and told that Lottie would be there as soon as she could be. They watched the show on the screens in Lottie's trailer. Cameras covered different angles of the arena. It was being streamed by thousands. Neither of them had seen the Circus of Nightmares and they were fixed to it with increasing curiosity. There was no doubt, the performers and stage crew were expert at what they did. It was an impressive show but not for the fainthearted. Whether it was something they would pay to see again was debatable, neither were fans of horror and gore. They saw enough of that at work. Whatever their personal taste, it was undeniably professional. There was a pattern to each performance. A stunt or illusion was performed flawlessly but the big clown would appear and insist it be repeated with a few tweaks. Tweaks which led to accidents. The show was plagued by accidents, usually created by an interfering clown, who appeared to have the ability to be in two places at once. One second he was at one side of the arena, the next second he was across the opposite side causing havoc. Each time the big clown appeared, the crowd would shout, 'Oh no, not Hugo!'

The anticipation of something horrible happening combined with the audience participation created the exciting atmosphere. The accidents and unfortunate mishaps became more catastrophic as the show progressed. The effects were so convincing that the crowd questioned their reality each time. The expression of shock and horror was permanently fixed to some of the faces in the audience, unable to comprehend if what was happening was real or illusion. Several of the women in the audience were in tears. Some were clearly losing their grip on reality. When the finale began, clowns came on and began juggling chainsaws and power tools, tossing them high in the air. It was obvious the show was set to have a sticky ending. Arterial spray flowed like crimson aerosols, limbs were severed and the lovely Helen was put into a box and sawn in half with a chainsaw. Of course, the trick went horribly wrong and despite the best efforts of the clowns and several rolls of duct tape and some staples, they couldn't put her back together. The skill involved was only rivalled by the reality of the magic and special effects. Anne and Gill had to turn away at least a dozen times during the final show. Most of the cast were dead. Death, the greatest illusion. The lights came on for the final time at ten o'clock, with the entire cast in good health and one piece. Lottie came back to her trailer at twenty past the hour. She looked hot and her skin was glowing with perspiration.

'Good evening, detectives. I'm Lottie Edwards. I'm so sorry to have kept you waiting,' Lottie said, sitting down to unzip her boots. She didn't look to be in a hospitable frame of mind. There was an edge to her. 'This is the second time I've had a visit from the law this evening. I'm very tired and my patience is running low. So, what do you want?'

'I'm Detective Superintendent Anne Parry and this is Detective Inspector Gill Robinson,' Anne said. 'We're from the Matrix unit at Liverpool.'

'Liverpool?' Lottie asked, surprised. She thought Liz had made a mistake. 'You're a long way from home. This must be something of the upmost importance for you to come this far so late in the day.' Lottie took a packet of Golden Virginia and rolled a cigarette.

'Yes, it's urgent or we wouldn't be bothering you,' Anne said. 'We want to talk to you about a visit your circus made to the Speke area of the city some years back.'

'We haven't been on Merseyside for many years,' Lottie said. She lit her cigarette. 'I'm sure you can remind me when it was?'

'Five years ago,' Anne said. Lottie looked blank. 'I know it's late and it's a long time ago but you might be able to help us with a murder enquiry.'

'A murder enquiry from five years ago. Is this a joke?' Lottie asked, smiling. Her smile was infectious. 'Are you pissed off because I sent your uniformed officers packing?'

'What uniformed officers?'

'A couple of sergeants were here earlier,' Lottie said, leaving the details to their imagination.

'We haven't sent any uniformed officers here,' Anne said. 'As I said, we're from the Merseyside force.' Lottie took off her boots and rubbed her feet. She remained silent and pulled on the cigarette, inhaling the soothing smoke deeply. 'This afternoon we were called out to the discovery of two bodies. The bodies belong to a young couple who were last seen in the beer tent at your fair in Speke, five years ago.'

'Okay. I'm sorry to hear two young people lost their lives,' Lottie said. 'You have my attention, although I'm totally baffled why you are here bothering me at this time of night. How on Earth do you think I can help you after all this time?'

'We have a couple of questions, that's all,' Anne said.

'Ask away please,' Lottie said. 'It's getting late.'

'The couple were recovered from a metal barrel. The type of barrel which would have contained axle grease,' Anne said. She stood up and showed Lottie a picture of the product. Pamela Stone had identified it while they were driving to the island and sent her a link to the image. Anne leaned over and could smell Chanel Mademoiselle on her. 'The drum is a fifty-five-gallon barrel of Super Red Grease made by Miles lubricants. This is what it would have looked like when it was new.'

'So, the couple were killed and disposed of in that drum?' Lottie remained blank. She sighed and puffed on her cigarette, shaking her head. 'How awful. It must be dreadful for their parents knowing that is where their children ended up. How incredibly sad. I'm still not sure how I can help.'

'Do you recognise the drum?' Anne asked. 'Would that be a product you use on your mechanical equipment?'

'Ah, I see where you are coming from,' Lottie said, nodding as the penny dropped. 'You think the drum may have come from the fairground.' Anne nodded. 'Where was this drum recovered from?'

'A pond was drained as part of a building project on the outskirts of the city,' Anne said. 'It's not far from where you were camped. Do you use that product?'

109

'I don't recall that product or buying anything from Miles lubricants,' Lottie said, shaking her head. She went to her computer and logged in. 'Let me check. Miles lubricants,' she muttered to herself. 'Miles, Miles, Miles.'

'Do you have a maintenance team we could ask?' Gill asked. 'Maybe they will know what they use.'

'I know what they use. I do have a maintenance team but they just fix things. I don't need them to run the business side of things, like ordering,' Lottie said, without looking at Gill. Anne and Gill exchanged glances. Gill looked annoyed. Lottie caught her expression in the mirror. 'Don't be pissed off.' She smiled. 'I'm not being arsey with you but they don't buy anything. All spending is centralised. It makes it so much easier than chasing invoices and receipts and it limits the opportunity for theft. We run a cashless operation. All tickets are purchased online or with a card. No cash transactions, means no cash goes missing.' Lottie tapped on her keyboard. 'All purchases for equipment and machinery, chemicals and sundries are bought through my admin. Liz orders everything we use, from right here on this computer.' She scrolled through several spreadsheets and shook her head. 'We have only used Timken grease products since the late nineties, which is when we centralised all our purchasing and began storing it on computer. We have never purchased a Miles product. Sorry, I can't help with your barrel.'

'That answers the question for us. Thank you for looking,' Anne said, nodding her head. She couldn't help but be disappointed. It was the only lead of any real value. 'I know we're asking a lot from you here but if you cast your mind back five years ago, can you think of any employees you may have had concerns about?' Lottie moved away from the computer. She poured herself a glass of rioja and rolled another cigarette. She sat on the settee and lit it. 'Does anyone stand out in your memory.'

'Stand out how?' Lottie asked. She sipped her wine and blew smoke rings. 'I'm not sure what you're looking for. I don't recall anyone with a penchant for putting people in barrels. What exactly are you asking me?'

'Someone who may have had convictions for violence or sexual assault?'

'Wow,' Lottie said, smiling. She nodded as if she had suddenly understood. 'Do you think we would employ someone with a criminal record for either of those offences when we work directly with the public?'

'I'm just asking the question,' Anne said. 'Not every employer checks every reference and people tell lies. Could anyone have slipped through the net?'

'Most of our employees come into direct contact with children, adolescents and young mothers every time we open the gates,' Lottie said, sipping her wine. 'The days of fairground lads fuelled with testosterone trying to shag everything in a skirt are long gone. This is my business and my reputation is everything. The last thing I need is a paedo or a psycho sex offender working on the waltzers or the magic roundabout. We don't hire criminals.'

'I'm not suggesting you would willingly put people in danger,' Anne said. 'Predators are skilled at camouflaging themselves. They're good at fitting in.'

'This isn't just a circus and fairground. It's the way we live our lives,' Lottie said. 'We travel as a big family. This circus is our home and we travel as a community. There are close to two hundred people working with each other on a daily basis. Violent tendencies, aggressive personalities and sexual deviants are spotted quickly and dealt with accordingly. Sex offenders are no more welcome here in our community than they would be in yours.' Lottie gestured to her wine. 'Would you like a glass?' she asked, holding up the bottle. 'Faustino five. It's amazing.'

'No, thank you. We have to go back to Liverpool tonight. As much as I would love one,' Anne said. She steepled her fingers and looked Lottie in the eye. 'I haven't come to make accusations or offend you. Yet, I feel like I have probably done both of those things.' She ran her fingers through her hair, and sighed, deflated. 'It was a long shot but we had to ask.'

'I understand,' Lottie said. 'What you need to understand about the circus, is it's the heart of this operation. It always has been. Everything else comes after the circus.' Lottie finished her wine and refilled it. 'Everything else is an addition to enhance people's experience of coming to see the circus show. Not the other way around. I own the circus and most of the main attractions but there are dozens of satellites. There always are on any fairground. They feed off the circus and bigger rides.'

'Sorry. I don't understand,' Anne said. 'Satellites are what exactly?'

'Self employed traders who we allow to tag along. Most of the smaller food vendors and smaller stalls are owned by other families. Hook a duck, hoopla, darts, airguns, skittles, cans, basketball hoops and those type of attractions. They come and go as the business requires and they bring their own employees. Sometimes, they get a better offer at a Sunday market or a music festival or another travelling outfit may need some satellites to make their fairground look more attractive and we may part company with those families for a while, especially when we tour abroad. Not everyone can commit to a year away. Longer sometimes,' Lottie added. 'I try to only use satellites I know and trust but every now and again, bad eggs turn up.'

'I see,' Anne said. 'And when you came to Speke, did you know all the satellites that were with you?'

'I would need to think about that and go through my records,' Lottie said. 'I remember that was about the time there was a difference of opinion and we parted company with a large part of the operation. The community was split up. Some went to Ireland. Some went to Scotland and we went to France and Belgium. I would have to check who went where. That might take a few hours.'

'What was the difference of opinion?' Anne asked, curious as to why it had been mentioned. She could tell Lottie was holding back. 'If you can remember that far back.'

'I remember it.' Lottie stubbed out her cigarette and rolled another. 'Excuse me but I like to smoke when I finish for the day.' She lit it, inhaled and blew out the smoke. Blue strands made patterns in the air. 'The ghost train owner had tagged along with our operation for over a year. We had our own train but our machine had terminal mechanical issues and was very dated. It was a health and safety nightmare, so we scrapped ours and contracted the satellite to plug the gap for a while. Financially, it was a sound decision at the time.' Lottie paused to think. 'We became concerned the owner was mimicking the circus act and the illusions we performed. He was copying them inside the ghost train and he began streaming them online.'

'Why would he do that?' Anne asked, confused. She wanted to keep Lottie talking.

'Money, of course,' Lottie said. 'People love to watch other people being frightened. It's hilarious. Filming people inside a ghost train is a licence to print money on Youtube but he was copying our acts. We couldn't allow that. We wanted the ghost train to compliment the circus, not become a smaller version of it. There was talk of copyright infringement and they parted company with us and took half a dozen or so family-owned attractions with them. It was a tough time for my father especially. He'd known the owner all his life.'

'I see,' Anne said. 'Why do you mention this specifically?'

'Because the breakup sticks in my mind. It reminded me of what was going on back then. You asked me about people I had concerns with,' Lottie said, thinking. 'There were issues with some of the younger members of that family.'

'The family who owned the ghost train?'

'Yes.'

'What type of issues?'

'Issues with young women.'

'Issues like what?' Anne asked. She felt encouraged. 'Can you be specific?'

'The eldest son couldn't keep his dick in his pants,' Lottie said. 'He seemed to impregnate a girl in every town we visited. God only knows how many children he sired. There were always angry parents turning up looking for him with a baby in a pram. It was a weekly event. He spent more time hiding inside the ghost train than he did working outside of it. His younger sister was pregnant at twelve and there were rumours he was the father. He denied it and said his father was responsible, which really put the cat amongst the pigeons. His wife left and took the daughter with her.' Lottie shook her head at the memories. 'I'm being a gossip and I choose not to be a gossip. I remember nasty rumours about that family at the time and it's not my place to repeat it. The men in that family made me feel uncomfortable when they were around. I can tell you I was glad to see the back of them. We purchased our own ghost train and never looked back.'

'Do you have any idea where they might be now?'

'None at all,' Lottie said. 'I don't track other operations because what we do is so different. Sorry.'

'No problem. What was the family name?' Anne asked.

'Koresh was the family name. They were a big family,' Lottie said. 'The father was Tarek and his eldest son, Samiri. I can't remember the other brothers. They were only teenagers at the time but they were trouble. I can look through my records tomorrow for all their names if you think it would help. Now, if you don't mind, I'm tired and I want to go to sleep.'

'That has been extremely helpful. Here's my number. Please give me a call tomorrow, if you think of anything else. Thanks for seeing us,' Anne said. 'Amazing show by the way.'

Lottie opened the door and let the officers out. 'Good night, detectives. Have a safe journey home.'

Anne and Gill walked in the direction of the beach. They had parked their car near the marina. She could see uniformed officers down near the water. Lots of them. Whatever was going on, it wasn't good. The fairground was still running but the crowds were thinning. It would have to be silent by eleven o'clock. She saw three people walking towards her trailer from the fairground. Alan and Kim were approaching the trailer from a different direction. He didn't see Anne and Gill leaving. Lottie frowned as they neared. Liz was with them. She rolled her eyes skyward and swore beneath her breath.

'For fuck's sake, what now?' Lottie murmured to herself. She smiled at the people approaching. 'What is it now?' Lottie asked. 'There's no peace for the wicked.'

'I'm DI Alan Williams and this is DS Kim Davies.'

'More detectives. Just what I was hoping for. Good evening,' Lottie said. 'How can I help?'

'We've had a missing person report,' Alan said. 'A young woman has gone missing from the fairground. Her handbag and mobile phone were found in the toilets. We've been looking for a few hours and made an initial search of the surrounding area and the lifeboat is searching the marina.'

'Oh dear,' Lottie said, frowning. 'How awful. What can I do to help?'

'Her sister has told us she was spiked earlier today by three men she believes work here,' Alan said. 'We need to speak to them.'

'Does she know who they are?' Lottie asked, frowning.

'She thinks she might be able to recognise them but in the meantime her sister is still missing and we need to locate her. The drugging incident may be connected to her sister's disappearance,' Alan explained.

'Okay. What do you need from me?' Lottie asked.

'I'd like to be able to check every caravan and trailer without applying for a warrant. We could do with your help to gain access if you don't mind.'

'No one will have a problem with helping you find her. Liz will take you wherever you need to look,' Lottie said. 'I'll get changed and catch up with you. If any of my employees have spiked anyone, they'll wish they hadn't.' Lottie sighed, tired and frustrated. 'I'll be with you in five minutes.'

'Thanks for your help,' Alan said, 'It's much appreciated.'

'No problem.' She closed the door and locked it. A figure watched from beneath the tailer. It was cold now and he shivered. His sickness made him susceptible to the cold. His bones ached when it was damp. The Matrix detectives had traced Leo's disappearance to the circus where he was last seen. That wasn't beyond comprehension. He had listened to the conversation through an open window. The name Koresh had rung bells in his memory. It belonged to an Albanian outfit from the Green Lane area of London. They took over most of the capitol at one point in the nineties by being the most brutal gangsters the city had seen. They made the Krays look like Laurel and Hardy. He remembered them well and they had reason to remember the Quinn family. Ten years ago, Andi Koresh was sent north to establish a foothold in Liverpool and Manchester. He was a violent psychopath, unstable and unreasonable. His arrival was met with the vitriolic response it required. Things didn't go well for Andi and his crew. Len mulled over the memories. Could the Koresh family who ran a fairground business be connected to the criminals in London? A travelling fair would be a decent vehicle for transporting people and products from one place to another. He knew several men who had spent time travelling when they were on the run from the law and rivals. It was an ideal way to become invisible. Had his son Leo inadvertently walked into the wrong place and been recognised by a member of the Koresh family or had Katrin fallen fowl of a sexual predator and his son had become collateral damage? There was only one way to establish the truth.

Chapter 17

The lights went out and Kelly stood still, blinded by the sudden darkness. It took long seconds for her eyes to adjust. As her vision cleared, she could see the streetlights through the bedroom window. It wasn't a power cut. She was in credit with her electric provider so she hadn't been cut off. A fuse could have blown. Maybe. Or maybe someone turned it off. A million evil images flashed through her mind. Kelly tightened the towel around her and padded into the bedroom. She slid her feet into her slippers. Her dressing gown was hanging on the back of the door. She took it down and pulled it on. It was soft and warm on her skin but it didn't stop her from shivering. Her senses were on red alert, listening to every creak and sound from outside. She felt frightened, standing in the dark alone. She jumped when her phone vibrated and the screen lit up. She picked it up from the dressing table. It was a message on Facebook. She went into messenger and opened the unread message. There was no profile picture of the sender. It was a fake profile, probably from a pervert who hid behind his anonymity. Social media was crawling with pervs lately. She had to block or delete several profiles on a daily basis. It was becoming a joke. The last thing she needed right now was a pervert fishing for a sex chat. The muscles in her stomach were clenched in nervous anticipation of something bad about to happen. She opened the message.

Did you enjoy your bath? You have a nice house. Bet it's dark in there with no electricity?

Kelly shuddered as an image of her house appeared. In the picture, all the lights were out. Another image appeared, taken earlier. The bathroom, living room and dining room lights were on. Whoever took the photographs was outside right now. She ran to the curtains and peered through them. The alleyway across the road was shrouded in darkness. She imagined a hooded figure standing beyond the shadows watching her. A car drove down the street, taxi stickers on the doors. It didn't stop. She felt cold and vulnerable and ran to the underwear drawer. It took her less than a minute to put on knickers, a bra and pyjamas. She pulled her dressing gown over the top and fastened it tight. The clothing made her feel more secure. She thought about phoning the police but she had already lied to them once today. Her phone vibrated again. She thought about it. Don't open it. Not opening it didn't mean it hadn't been sent. They were sending her a message, whoever they were. She opened the message.

You have a nice daughter. Pretty little Elle. She looks like you. They are so vulnerable at that age, don't you think?

Another image appeared. It was Elle standing in the doorway of her nan's house. She was wearing her pyjamas. The set Kelly had sent her with earlier. Elle looked confused as if she was looking for something. Kelly ran downstairs into the kitchen her breath tight in her chest. She took the biggest knife from the block and ran back upstairs, looking through every window on the way. The streets and lanes around her house were empty but beyond the yellow glow of the streetlights was nothing but inky blackness. She imagined devils and serial killers lurking there, waiting and watching. All the crime thrillers and horror films she had ever seen flashed through her mind as her imagination ran riot. Another message arrived.

You are probably wondering what she is doing. She was looking to see who knocked on the door. Can't be too careful nowadays. Kids get snatched from the street all the time. She shouldn't be out there on her own.

Kelly wanted to puke. She knew who was sending the messages without asking. They must have followed them from Rhosneiger. Jack had his name and mobile number on his stupid van and he constantly posted pictures of them as a couple, despite her reluctance. She had told him not to tag her in them a million times but it was a possession thing with Jack. He had to make sure everyone knew they were together. Putting images of them together and tagging her in every post he made was like tethering her to him, branding her as his bitch for the other men in town to see. She's mine. Back off boys. He was such a dick sometimes. Every post left a route map for someone to follow to her profile. It took just seconds to follow the links. They knew her name and they had her number. She didn't know how they got her number but it wouldn't be hard.

Now they knew where she lived. It was obvious, they had followed her home. It didn't take a detective to find where her mother lived and take a picture of her Elle outside the door.

They were clearly criminals with intelligence. She had witnessed their handywork and didn't want any part of it. The man had seen her and she had seen him. She'd lied to the police to avoid being dragged to court as a witness. She had been there before and it had dire consequences. A young local man had gone missing from his home. The police appealed for witnesses and Kelly made a statement that she had seen a car being driven by a man she knew and her evidence placed him at the scene of the abduction. He was convicted of conspiracy to murder and jailed for fifteen years. Kelly thought that would be the end of it but it was far from over. His associates and family persecuted her for years. It had caused trouble for her and her family. Her dad was punched in a pub in town and six months later he was jumped on the way home from a darts match. Darts was his social life but he never went again. He no longer went for a pint at all. It had traumatised him. Her mum was spat at in the hairdressers, Morrison's and the bingo. Anglesey was a small island and avoiding people was not an easy thing to do. Elle had to go to school and they were in short supply. She didn't want to live her life looking over her shoulder, worrying about Elle and if she was safe. She needed these people off her back. She messaged back.

I haven't said anything to the police and I won't say anything.

She waited, holding the knife so tightly her knuckles were white. Her heart was pounding in her chest. She could feel the pulse in her forehead and the clock on the wall ticking. Tick tock, tick tock, tick tock.

The lights came back on and the profile vanished.

Chapter 18

Detective Sergeant Richard Lewis walked into the Albert Vaults. It was a small pub, longer than it was wide with the bar on the right-hand wall. A pool table filled the back room with the toilets beyond. Most of the tables were full of drinkers. It was the first pub on the way back into town from the Newry Beach. People were finishing off the night with a few drinks and maybe a kebab from Williams Street on the way home. There would be a rush at last orders. The taxi rank was just down the street and they would be busy with the circus in town. Taxis would be sparse.

Richard approached the landlord and spoke to him as a friend would. It was a decent pub, run well with decent staff and decent customers. It had to be as the police station was literally across the road. The landlord poured half a Directors and placed it on the bar. The dark ale settled, not quite as dark as Guinness but not far off. The froth was white. Richard sipped it and the froth stuck to his moustache. He licked his lips and smiled.

'It's a new barrel. What do you think?'

'Lovely drop of beer,' Richard said. He showed the landlord a picture of Michelle Branning. The landlord knew her and Tiffany. 'Chelle is missing,' Richard explained. 'She's been missing since half-past-four this afternoon. Obviously, we're retracing her steps.'

'I've seen the patrol cars coming and going. I wondered what all the fuss was about,' the landlord said. 'They were in here earlier on this afternoon. It's Tiff's birthday. They were in good spirits.'

'She had a few shots,' Richard said.

'It's her birthday. I think a few people bought them drinks. They're popular girls,' the landlord said.

'Tiffany thinks her drinks were spiked while they were here.'

'What, in here?' the landlord asked, offended.

'Possibly,' Richard said. 'I know you run a good pub and the locals wouldn't do such a thing but the possible suspects are from out of town. She thinks it was three men who might work on the fairground.'

'I know who you mean,' the landlord said. 'I knew they were from away. I had my eye on them. Let me check the CCTV. It's not the best system but you can see people's faces. They were here about an hour at least,' he said, flicking through the images. 'Here are Chelle and Tiff walking into the pub.' He scrolled on. 'Here. These are the men. They were playing pool until the girls walked in, then they moved to be near the girls. They sat nearby. You can see Tiff talking to them there, Chelle doesn't have anything to do with them. Here is a good shot of the men. I can take that as a single image. Do you want me to send all the footage from today to you?'

'Yes please. Send it to my phone,' Richard said. He downed his Directors and patted the landlord on the back. The image appeared on his phone. 'This is going to save us a lot of man hours and headaches. I owe you one.'

'I hope you find Chelle.'

'Cheers,' Richard said. He found Alan's number. It rang for a second or two.

'Hello Richard,' Alan said, sounding stressed. 'What have you got?'

'I've got images of the three men who were sitting next to Tiffany Branning in the Albert. The landlord pulled them from his CCTV. I'll send it over to you now.'

'Good man,' Alan said.

'Any joy finding her yet?'

'Nope. Not a sign of her.'

'Is the lifeboat still out in the marina?'

'Yes. No news is good news as far as they're concerned.' Alan went quiet for a second. 'I've got the image. Well done Richard. Check the other pubs in town just in case she's so drunk she doesn't know she's missing and I'll see you later.'

'Let's hope so. See you later.'

****

Lottie and Kim were looking at the CCTV footage from the circus cameras. They were drinking coffee with oat milk in an attempt to fight tiredness. The cameras covered most of the fairground but not the toilet blocks. It was deemed to be against the individual's right to privacy to be filmed going to the loo. The coverage was adequate to maintain a record of ninety percent of the fairground.

'We can't have a camera targeting the toilets. It's a crazy directive from Brussels,' Lottie said. 'Despite them being the place where all the shenanigans, goes on. Apparently, we can be fined for it anywhere in Europe, so we don't do it.'

'Does anyone check?' Kim asked.

'You would be amazed how often we're asked for the CCTV footage,' Lottie said. 'It's pretty much once per site, sometimes daily. I've set it up so I can capture a time slot and email it, otherwise I would be sat here for hours.'

One camera captured part of the area outside the ladies' toilet block but not the entrance or the approach. Another camera picked up the other side but there was a blind spot between them.

'We know Michelle left the beer tent at four-thirty and that her handbag and phone were found sometime before five,' Kim said.

122

'So, we have a nice tight window of time to search.' Lottie switched the camera feed to different angles, trying to find an image of Chelle near the toilet block but they had hit a blank.

'Wait. Look at that,' Kim said, pointing to the edge of the screen. 'Go back a few seconds there.' Lottie rewound the images. 'Look there. That's a pair of beige UGG boots and faded jeans. Michelle was wearing jeans and similar boots.' The image was of a female from the knee down.

'Her and a dozen others,' Lottie said. 'They're extremely popular boots in the winter. We can't say it's her for sure.'

'This isn't good. I can't track a woman when I can only see her feet.' Kim was getting frustrated. 'Let it run and see if she comes back this way towards the beer tent,' Kim said. Lottie turned it back on at fast forward. People whizzed across the screen. There was no sign of the UGG boots for a few minutes. Then Kim spotted a young woman wearing a pair similar. 'There. Can you zoom in on her?'

'I'll try,' Lottie said. She increased the image.

'The boots are the right colour but the jeans are wrong. That's not our girl,' Kim said, sighing. It had been a long day and she was weary. 'Which way would she go to get to the nearest burger van?'

'This way towards the beer tent,' Lottie said.

'Would she be able to see it from the entrance to the toilets?'

'Yes. It's a big trailer. She couldn't miss it.'

'So, she didn't go back towards the beer tent,' Kim said. 'What about the cameras on the exits?'

'The official fairground exits?' Lottie asked.

'Yes. There's only one, isn't there?' Kim asked.

'Technically, yes,' Lottie said. 'But if people want to get out, there are gaps between the caravans and motorhomes. There are dogs tied up as a

123

deterrent but people still come and go as they please. We can't seal the area with fences for fire reasons.' She pulled up the camera footage for the exit at four-thirty and then let it run on fast forward, stopping when a female of a similar appearance appeared. When the tape reached five fifteen, she stopped it. 'That is quarter-past-five and Michelle hasn't left the fairground through that exit. Do you want me to go further?'

'No. That's all we can do for now,' Kim said. 'Can I have all the footage from one o'clock this afternoon onwards, please?'

'Sure,' Lottie said. 'I'll email it to you if you like?'

'Yes please,' Kim said, handing Lottie her card. 'Use this email.'

A knock on the trailer door interrupted them. Lottie opened it and let Alan in. 'Any news?' she asked.

'No sign of Chelle but we have an image of the men from earlier this afternoon in the pub where Tiff thinks she might have been spiked,' Alan said. He showed Lottie the picture. 'I've got a clear image of the three men. Do you know them?'

'Yes,' Lottie said. 'They don't work for me directly. They're mechanics.' Lottie tapped at her computer. 'They took one of the circus vans into Holyhead this morning for an MOT and new tyres. It looks like they took a liquid lunch on the way back.'

'I need their names and where they are likely to be now,' Alan said. Lottie gestured to the screen.

'Carlos and Claus Vincentia are brothers and this one is their cousin David Prost.' Lottie stood up. 'I'll take you to their caravan but at this time of night, they'll be in the nearest pub. They don't need to be up at the crack of dawn like the rest of us.'

'Let's send uniform to the Vic on Porth-y-felin, the Boathouse at the bottom of the road and Langdon's in the marina,' Alan said to Kim. Kim walked out of the trailer in a hurry to arrange the sweep. 'You said they don't work for you. What do you know about them?'

'They've been mechanics for the circus for over a year. They work for a man called Ben Bronski,' Lottie said. 'He supplies us with fuel.'

'For the vehicles?' Alan asked.

'For everything. The cars, vans, motorhomes, trucks, lorries, and the generators that power the rides and lights,' Lottie explained. 'Ben Bronski has been bringing us fuel since my father ran the show. We can't travel as far as we do, paying forecourt prices. Bronski has a fleet of fuel tankers. He buys in bulk and resells to us and other travelling outfits. He also supplies us with mechanics and a mobile workshop. They keep us moving and road legal and I haven't had any issues with them until now. They keep themselves to themselves and seem polite. I haven't heard a bad word said about them.'

'Okay. Can you take me to their caravan please,' Alan said.

'No problem. It's up at the top of the field near Walthew Avenue,' Lottie said. They walked out of the trailer and through the fair towards the circus. It was still running but the number of people around was waning. The food outlets were closing down. The smell of onions reminded Alan he hadn't eaten since breakfast. His stomach was rumbling. Bob called him on his mobile.

'Hello Bob,' Alan said. 'Have you found her?'

'No. I've got a problem down here on the road leading up to Soldiers Point and the breakwater.'

'What's the problem?'

'I've got about forty volunteers down here, most of them locals, some of them Michelle Branning's family, insisting they are allowed to search the breakwater and the quarry park. Her mother is here mithering me about the ponds in the quarry.'

'She'd be better off at home,' Alan said.

'She's been on the vodka before she got here.' Bob lowered his voice. 'Emotions are running high. Tiffany has told her family she was spiked by men from the fairground and they're putting two and two together and coming up with five. You can imagine the speculation going on,' Bob said.

'We don't need an angry mob bouncing around the breakwater in the dark. Someone will end up in the sea,' Alan said. A dull blaring sound drifted from the mountain. 'There's mist rolling in from the sea. The foghorn up on North Stack is sounding.' Alan heard its deep mournful tone echoing from the mountain again. The sound was a warning to those at sea and those on land near the sea. Visibility was about to become a massive issue. 'It won't be long before that fog is on us.'

'I can't keep these people safe as it is. It's pitch-black over here and quite a few of them are pissed. If the fog settles, we haven't got a hope of knowing where they are. Most of them don't have torches. They're stumbling around in the dark shouting,' Bob said. 'More people are turning up all the time. Word is spreading across town and people want to help. The problem is most of the people turning up are pissed too. They've been at the fair all day.'

'Don't let any of them onto the breakwater road,' Alan said. 'It's time to wind the search down for the night. Tell them the fog has brought a halt to everything. We'll be back as soon as there's daylight to search safely. It's too dangerous now. Get your officers to cordon it off at the bottom of the Newry.'

'That's what I thought,' Bob said. 'Leave it with me. I'll sort it out.'

Alan acquired backup from four uniformed sergeants as they crossed the fairground. Lottie pointed out the caravan. It was an Elddis and looked to be nearly new. Alan didn't know a great deal about caravans but he knew they were expensive.

'That is their caravan and that is their pickup truck,' Lottie said. The Mitsibushi was this year's model. The mechanics seemed to be doing well servicing the circus. The lights were on at the front of the caravan. A silhouette moved past the front window. Someone was home. As they neared, they could hear the television. They were watching a war film, gunfire and the boom-boom of artillery shells drifted to them. Alan walked around the caravan and knocked on the door.

'Two of you cover the other side in case one of them makes a break for it through a window,' Alan said. 'Remember, we can't arrest anyone yet. Hold them for questioning and we can't search the truck or the caravan without their permission.' The officers moved into position. Alan knocked again. The television was muted.

'Who is it?' a voice asked.

'Police,' Alan said. 'We need to ask you a few questions.'

'What about?'

'Open the door before I come through it and take you away in handcuffs,' Alan said. Lottie looked surprised.

'Okay, okay. No need to be nasty,' the man moaned. The door opened. It was David Prost. He looked worried. The smell of cannabis drifted to Alan. 'What is all the knocking about?'

'Police,' Alan said, showing his warrant card. 'Are you alone in there?'

'Yes.' David shrugged. He scratched his testicles and looked around. 'This is a lot of policemen. What is the problem?'

'We're looking for this woman,' Alan said, showing him a picture of Michelle on his phone. There was a flicker of recognition in his eyes. His reactions appeared to be slow, dulled by the weed. 'Have you seen her since this afternoon?'

'I haven't ever seen this woman,' David said, shaking his head. 'I don't know her, so can I go back inside now.'

'That is your one and only chance to lie to me,' Alan said, showing him an image of the three men together. 'This is you and your cousins sitting near Michelle and her sister in the Albert Vaults this afternoon. If you lie to me again, you'll be in a cell so fast that your feet won't touch the ground. We can start with possession of cannabis and see what else we can come up with. Do you understand me?' David swallowed hard and nodded. Alan showed him an image of the sisters. 'Good. I'll ask you again. Have you seen this woman since this afternoon?'

'No. I haven't seen her since earlier today,' David said. 'That is the truth. We bought this lady some shots because it was her birthday but I didn't talk to this one.' He pointed to the images as he spoke. 'She wasn't so friendly. We offered them a lift to the fairground but this one told us to fuck off, so we did.' He held up his hands. 'I haven't seen either of them since then. I have been working on a truck until late and then I had a shower and I've been watching a film. I've smoked a bit of cannabis, okay but I haven't done anything wrong.'

'Do you mind if we have a look around the caravan?' Alan asked.

'Look around for what?'

'Her,' Alan said, pointing to Michelle.

'Let them look around, David,' Lottie said. 'It will take two minutes and you can get back to your film.'

'No problem, Lottie,' David said, stepping back. 'I don't want any trouble.'

'Where are your cousins?' Alan asked. 'Carlos and Claus Vincentia.'

'They have walked to the pub on the hill over there,' he said, pointing towards the mountain. 'The Victoria, I think it is called. They have been gone for hours. I bet they are pissed.'

Kim walked away and called the uniformed sergeant organising the search of the three pubs nearby. She told him the brothers were in the Vic. Alan and the uniformed officers went into the caravan. The air was thick with the smell of cannabis and sweaty men. Three pairs of oily boots were on a shoe rack next to the door. The fixtures were new but the caravan was untidy. Nothing matched. Carpets, curtains, blinds and soft furnishings were an assault on the senses. The kitchen section was cluttered with pots and pans. Dirty dishes filled the sink and a topless blond was the body of the month on a calendar sponsored by a brand of car paint. A cork notice board was covered in receipts and photographs. Alan looked at the photographs and waited while the sergeants checked the bedroom and bathroom. David sat on the settee looking nervous.

'There is nobody here but me,' David said. 'We're not criminals. We work hard. Lottie will tell you.'

'The woman you bought shots for this afternoon was unwell after drinking them,' Alan said. David blushed and looked away. 'Would you know anything about that?'

'Vodka makes people unwell,' David said, shrugging. 'She drank a few of them. We all did but her sister didn't. She seemed like a nice lady. Very sensible.' David folded his arms and sat back. 'She told us to fuck off, so we fucked off. What are we supposed to do?'

'The women think something was put into Tiffany's shots,' Alan said.

'I don't know anything about that,' David said. 'I bought a round of drinks, then Carlos bought one and then Claus bought the last one. Then the ladies left and we came back to the fair. They were fine when we left them. A little bit drunk but they were fine.'

'There's nothing here, sir,' one of the sergeants said. 'It's all clear.'

'We'll need to talk to you again tomorrow,' Alan said, stepping out of the van. 'Thanks for your cooperation.' He closed the door and from the corner of his eye, he caught David flicking his middle finger at him. He opened the door again. David blushed purple. 'How old are you?' Alan asked.

'Twenty-six.'

'Grow up and act like it,' Alan said, closing the door again.

Chapter 19

Carlos and Claus Vincentia were half-brothers. Carlos was the older by a year. Their mother was German. She'd been a bar maid in Dusseldorf most of her life. After a string of lousy relationships, she married the owner of an Irish bar in the Alt Strat area of the city. He was thirty years her senior. Her husband was father to neither of her sons and wanted nothing to do with them from day one. He wanted to fuck Elsa and unfortunately for him, her children were part of the deal. They came as a three-person package. The relationship was beyond stormy; it was violent. Elsa liked to drink and when she drank, she made poor decisions about the men she flirted with. Often, the flirting went much further, especially when her husband was so drunk, he had to go upstairs to their apartment to sleep. Elsa would entertain her male friends in the bar until stupid o'clock in the morning. Her husband would wake up, rough from drinking and interrogate her about the night before. He was insanely jealous. It was a cocktail of infidelity and deceit.

When Elsa unexpectedly had a stroke and died, the brothers were fifteen and sixteen, respectively. Their stepfather buried their mother and promptly threw them out onto the street the next day. The boys spent several weeks sleeping on the streets, making enough money to eat by begging and collecting empty bottles from the bins and cashing them in. They slept in doorways and in unoccupied boats on the river until a travelling fair arrived on the opposite side of the river. The fairground was huge with over a hundred stalls and attractions and luckily for them, they were short staffed. Manual labourers were needed desperately to continuously empty the litter bins. Litter in Germany is a huge no-no, and the fairground could only operate if it was self-functional and had no impact on the city's resources. Cleaning the litter bins and brushing the streets in the vicinity was down to the fairground operators. The boys worked hard and were likeable. They were given bunks with some of the travellers and became a permanent addition. Over the following five years, they learned how to set up and strip down the equipment and maintain the engines on the rides and on their vehicles. Nearly ten years ago, on a trip to the UK, they were spotted by Ben Bronski and they began working for him. Two years ago, he offered them a job with the Edward's operation. The job was simple. Keep the rides in good condition, the MOT'S in date and the circus vehicles moving. Bronski paid on time and he paid well and there were always opportunities to make bonuses. Their cousin David Prost had kept in touch on social media and joined them a year into their new venture. They got on okay but David was made to feel like an intruder. The brothers were a unit. Their upbringing had made them dependent on one another. The trip to Holyhead was exciting. Wales was a part of the world they hadn't explored and Ireland lay ahead. They had researched it and it was the land of green-eyed beauties and Guinness. Ben had insinuated there was a chance to earn a decent bonus too. It was all good.

In the meantime, they intended to enjoy the hospitality Holyhead had to offer. They were on their seventh pint in the Vic when the police walked in. The pub went quiet apart from Adele on the jukebox. She was still setting fire to the rain. Carlos was chatting up a pretty teenager called Cheryl and his brother was unsuccessfully trying to entertain her overweight friend, Candice. He had even offered to buy her some pork scratchings but apparently, she was on a diet. The brothers were oblivious when the police walked through the drinkers over to their table. The locals watched them with interest.

'Good evening ladies. Have these gentlemen bought you any drinks this evening?' Sergeant Gerrard asked.

'They might have. We're old enough to drink,' Cheryl said. The girls smirked but looked nervous. 'Do you want to see my ID?'

'I don't need to see any ID but if they have bought you those drinks, don't drink them.' Some of the regulars were listening to the conversation. A hush settled over the lounge. 'They might contain a little something you won't like,' he said, winking.

'Are they spiking women?' Cheryl asked.

'That's what we're here to check,' the sergeant said, nodding. 'At it again are we, gentlemen?'

'What are you talking about?' Carlos asked. He looked at the exits. One led to the toilets, the other went to the front door. There were too many regulars between them and the doors. 'We haven't done anything?'

'I think you know what I'm talking about.' The sergeant studied his response. His expression said he was nervous. Guilty of something. Sergeant Gerrard could spot a guilty man from a mile away. He didn't know what he was guilty of but he was guilty.

'I have no idea what you're talking about,' Carlos said. He sipped his pint. 'We're just having a drink after work and chatting to these young ladies. What's the problem?'

'We need a word with both of you,' sergeant Gerrard said. He lowered his voice. 'Probably better if we go outside then we won't disturb George and his customers,' he added, nodding to George Doutch behind the bar. George gave him the thumbs-up. He was a popular landlord known by everyone in town. Seeing a police officer in the Vic was rare unless they had a pint in their hand and their own clothes on. The brothers looked at each other. They spoke in German. Sergeant Gerrard didn't know what was said but the tone was aggressive. 'Don't cause a fuss in here. There's no need to do anything silly,' the sergeant said, sensing their nerves. 'We just want to ask you some questions.'

'What about?' Claus asked. He grabbed his coat and put it on. 'This is shit. It this because we are with the fair?'

'It won't take long. Come on outside.'

'We don't have to go anywhere with you if we don't want to.' Carlos said.

'You don't have to come with me but for your own sake, you should,' sergeant Gerrard said.

'Unless you tell us what this is about, we're not going anywhere,' Carlos said. 'It's up to you but we're not moving.'

'Okay. I didn't want to cause a stir in here but there's a young woman missing.' The pub became silent. 'She was last seen at the fairground and we need to ask you some questions about it. It's all routine. We can do it here but it would be much better for you and everyone in here if we do it outside.'

'Are they anything to do with Chelle Branning going missing?' one of the customers asked.

'They're as good as dead if they are,' another said. The locals were beginning to get agitated. 'Have they got something to do with it?'

'Are they fucking nonces?'

'Dirty pikeys,' someone shouted from the other bar. 'If they've touched Chelle Branning, hang them from a tree.'

'This is what I was worried about.' He gestured behind him to the glaring locals. Alcohol was fuelling the flames. 'I think we should go outside,' the sergeant said, lowering his voice. 'For your own sake. There are only three of us. We can't protect you if this turns nasty.'

'Okay,' Carlos said, emptying his glass. He put on is coat. 'Nice talking to you, Cheryl.' Cheryl scowled in disgust. 'Have you gone off me already?'

'Fuck off,' Cheryl said. 'I didn't know you were perverts.'

'We're not perverts,' Claus protested. Carlos took him by the arm and guided him away from the table. The locals glared at them. The atmosphere was almost flammable. The slightest spark could set it ablaze. The policemen flanked them until they reached the doorway. The door serviced both the barroom and the lounge, which were separated by the bar. The staff could serve both sides and see all the pub. They reached the doorway and one of the younger customers walked out of the gents. He threw his pint at the brothers. The stinking liquid hit Claus square in the face, stinging his eyes. It took only a second to realise he had pissed in the glass.

'Dirty pikeys,' the man said, laughing. A scuffle broke out. The brothers covered their heads and the policemen ushered them out of the pub onto the road, which was on a steep hill.

'That's disgusting! What is wrong with these people?' Claus shouted when they were outside. 'That man has pissed on me!'

'Calm down,' sergeant Gerrard said.

'What have we done for this to happen?'

'No one is accusing you of anything yet,' sergeant Gerrard said. Some of the locals followed them outside to listen to what was said. They lit cigarettes to justify being outside. 'Finish your cigs and go back inside.' The locals shrugged and ignored the order. The situation was volatile 'Let's start with your names.'

'I'm Carlos Vincentia.'

'I'm Claus Vincentia. We're brothers.'

'Have you seen these two women today?' sergeant Gerrard asked, showing them an image of the sisters. Look carefully. 'This is Tiffany and this is Michelle.'

'I don't recognise them,' Carlos said, shaking his head. He looked at Claus. 'I've never seen them.'

'Me too. I've never seen them,' Claus agreed. He looked at the floor. 'You should arrest that man who threw piss at me. That is assault.'

'You're both lying,' the sergeant said. He showed them the image of them in the Albert Vaults. 'This is you at lunchtime today.' The brothers looked shocked that he had the image. 'We'll try again. Have you seen these two women today?'

'I'm not saying anything else. We haven't done anything illegal,' Carlos said. 'Arrest me and get me a lawyer. Say nothing, Claus. They can't do anything to us. I know our rights.'

'Listen to me. A young woman is missing and we need to speak to everyone who has been in contact with her today and that includes you two. It's not difficult. Answer my questions and we can rap this up quickly.' Carlos folded his arms. 'Do we need to do this the hard way?' the sergeant said, shaking his head. 'Get a van down here,' he said to his colleague. 'We'll do this at the station. The locals are getting fisty. Take them in and lock them up until the DI has spoken to them. We can't mess about here. The locals will beat them to death if they think they're responsible for the Branning girl going missing.' He turned back to Carlos. 'Empty your pockets,' the sergeant said. Carlos shook his head. 'Empty them or we will do it for you.'

'Turn him upside down, sergeant,' one of the locals said. 'I'll do it if you want me to. Fucking pikey.'

'Do you want us to talk to them?' another asked. 'We'll get the truth out of them. Fucking perverts.'

Sergeant Gerrard stepped closer to Carlos and reached for his arms. Carlos butted the sergeant on the nose. Sergeant Gerrard grabbed him, stunned by the pain but Carlos shook him off. He ran down the hill before the other officers could react. He reached a stile and vaulted a drystone wall, which led into fields that ran all the way to the quarry and the mountain beyond. One of the sergeants grabbed Claus and cuffed him before he could run. The other gave chase but Carlos was younger and fitter and more motivated. He disappeared into the darkness, hidden by thick gorse bushes and rocky outcrops. In less than a minute, he was gone.

Chapter 20

Bob and his officers turned as many volunteers back from the breakwater as they could. Some were too incensed to be calmed down. He tried to talk sense to them but sometimes common sense is overruled by emotions. A few of the most stubborn men ignored their advice and ran off towards the Rocky Coast, which would take them to the base of the mountain and the quarry park. Without torches, it was a reckless trek at the best of times. The fog had descended and visibility was down to ten yards or so making it more treacherous. Bob and the other officers were powerless. If members of the public wanted to walk along the coast, they couldn't stop them, reckless or not. There were too many people milling about to control them all. They formed smaller groups of three or four and split off in different directions. Thankfully, most of the people had listened to what Bob had said and headed back towards the Newry where there was streetlighting. They could satisfy the urge to help by searching the water's edge in relative safety. Rumours were spreading like wildfire and tempers were running high. Michelle Branning was a popular young woman from a popular family on a big estate in a small town. Community spirit is a powerful tool in times of trouble and strife and the community was mobilised. The male members of the Branning family had convinced Tiffany and her mother to go home and wait for news. It was dark, foggy and freezing cold. Tiffany was suffering from exhaustion and the after-effects of alcohol and drugs. Drugs she hadn't ingested willingly. The police said they wanted to test her for Rohypnol to confirm her suspicions that she had been spiked. Samples of hair and urine were taken. The rest of the family joined the search. Finding Michelle was their number one priority. They joined the others searching the coastline.

Bob could hear the lifeboat trawling the marina, down near the McKenzie peer but he couldn't see it. Their job would be made harder by the thickening fog. As they walked past the ruins of the Soldier's Point Hotel, a shout went up from somewhere further down the road to his left. Another voice joined it. They were calling for help. It sounded as if it was coming from the jetty at Porth-y-felin House. Bob and several uniformed officers jogged in the direction of the voices. It was slow progress. The path was pitted with rocks and potholes and the grounds around the old mansion were littered with rubbish and junk. Fly tipping in the area was rife. They navigated several large pieces of furniture, a bath and a huge pile of building rubble. Their torches were the only lights available. The streetlights across the marina were merely a yellow glow in the mist. The voices called out again. This time they were closer. Bob found the path which led down to the jetty where the RAF used to anchor their rib. The Marine Core Unit had used Porth-y-felin house to accommodate their rescue crew where they could train on the sea, protected by the breakwater. He was concerned about the condition of the jetty. It had been many years since the unit operated there. Another call for help came from the fog; it was close. He shone his torch and picked out three figures down near the water. It was rocky there, covered in seaweed and cockles, which made it lethally slippery to walk on. The cockle shells and limpets were like broken glass on the skin. A fall there would be very nasty and if one of them fell, manoeuvring an injured male up the slope to safety would be difficult.

'Who is that?' one of the men shouted.

'Police. Sergeant Dewhurst,' Bob called. 'What have you found?'

'Over here,' one of the men shouted. 'We've found her.'

Bob made his way to the water. He slipped and fell forward. His feet went into the sea and the icy water numbed his skin. The water was up to his knees. He reached out to stop himself from falling. The shells cut his hands and ripped a fingernail. He tried to stand but slipped again and gashed his shin.

'Fucking hell,' he muttered. A colleague grabbed his elbow and steadied him, helping him find purchase on the rocks. 'Thank you,' Bob said. 'Bloody seaweed is lethal.'

'Are you alright?' one of the men asked.

'I'm fine. Where is she?' Bob asked, composing himself. The other officers pulled him to safety. Their expressions were grim. No one spoke. Bob could see a body in the water. It could have been a child. Michelle Branning was a tiny woman. She was floating face down in the water.

'We didn't want to touch her,' one of the men said. 'She's snagged on the rocks we think. The tide is going out but she's not moved an inch. We think she's snagged,' he repeated, nervously.

'Radio it in,' Bob said. One of the officers made the call. The atmosphere was solemn. Bob took a deep breath to settle his nerves. It was the outcome no one wanted. The condition of the victim indicated she hadn't entered the water voluntarily. 'Okay lads,' Bob said. 'Leave her to us now. We'll get her out of there,' he added. The men reluctantly moved back from the water. 'I'm going to ask you to keep this to yourself for a few hours. We'll need to make sure her mother and family know we've found her before it leaks out.' The men nodded. One of them was visibly upset. 'I don't want her to find out from Facebook,' Bob added. 'Let's show the family a bit of respect and keep it quiet for now.'

'Fucking bastards,' a volunteer muttered. 'It's those fairground men. They have done this.'

'We don't know anything yet,' Bob warned.

'Yes. We do. One of them spiked her sister.'

'We don't know what happened to her, so let's not jump to conclusions,' Bob said. The torchlight was enough to determine the body was undressed from the waist down. Her long blond hair floated around her head like a fan.

'She's got no pants on,' the man protested. 'It's obvious what they did to her. Bastards.'

'I know how you feel but we have to be absolutely certain of the facts before we start pointing the finger at anyone. Keep this to yourself.' The man nodded but looked angry. 'Get yourselves home safely,' Bob said. Sirens neared. He could see two patrol cars and an ambulance heading from the Newry, their headlights piercing the fog. The men who found her climbed over the rocks and made their way up the moss-covered steps. Bob could hear them talking angrily between themselves. There was no way they could keep it quiet. News that Michelle had been found would circulate rapidly. Bad news always did. They were near the gateposts when the emergency vehicles arrived and picked their way through the debris as close as they could to the jetty. The lifeboat appeared from the mist, its engine idling as it approached the body. The crew released the body from the rocks with boat hooks and pushed her towards the waiting policemen. Bob and his men pulled her in. A body bag was handed down and more officers helped to bring her up onto the jetty.

Alan and Kim had arrived by car and they knelt down to get a better view. They looked at the body in silence. There were signs of sexual assault, bruising and scratches on her thighs and wrists. Her eyes were open, staring and lifeless. Seaweed clung to her earrings. There were dark bruises around her throat and thumb marks beneath her chin.

'She's tiny,' Alan noted. 'She could have been strangled with one hand.'

'There's a crowd of locals coming up the lane,' an officer shouted. 'They're not happy.'

'Hold them back,' Alan said. He gestured to the ambulance crew. 'Let's get her out of here. I don't want them to see her like this.' Officers helped to move the body and seal her ready for the forensic team.

'How do you want to play this?' Kim asked.

'We've got three suspects. Carlos Vincentia is our prime suspect and according to sergeant Gerrard, he's running in the direction of the quarry.'

'Why run if you've done nothing wrong?' Bob asked. One of the ambulance crew was tending to the nasty wound on his leg.

'Who knows,' Alan said. 'He might have had a pocket full of Rohypnol and panicked.'

'There's no sign of her on the CCTV,' Kim said. 'I think she was taken from the cubicle, forced between the toilet pods and taken away from the fairground that way. If she was spiked, she would have been compliant and confused. She wouldn't have made a fuss.'

'Okay. So, the attacker followed her to the toilet and the drug took effect. So, it was an opportune moment and he decided to take her. That makes sense,' Alan said. 'She ended up in the water here, which means she went into the water on this side of the marina, probably near the boatyard?'

'Definitely,' Kim agreed.

'No doubt about it,' Bob said. 'If she was put in from the Newry, she would be by the McKenzie pier.'

'So, if she was drugged and taken from the fairground, where was she assaulted?' Alan asked. 'He must have taken her somewhere.'

'One of the apartments?' Kim asked.

'It will be easy enough to find out who lives there and rule them in or out but I'm ruling them out for now,' Alan said. 'What if she wasn't taken by a local?'

'There are a lot of people about,' Kim said. 'Undressing her needed some privacy.'

'What about a boat,' Alan said. 'The boatyard is packed with empty boats. There are thirty or forty yachts out of the water at any one time. It's easy to get into them.'

'The yachts are too high,' Bob said. 'Without ladders, he couldn't bundle a drowsy female onto a yacht and it would be too risky to make her climb. The cruisers are much lower and don't have a keel.'

'Okay, let's get the cruisers searched,' Alan said. Kim nodded and made the call, instructing the boatyard to be searched. There were angry shouts from the lane behind Porth-y-felin house. 'We need to get that crowd dispersed.'

'What do you want us to do?' Bob asked, pulling his trouser leg over the dressing. 'Good job. Thanks,' he said to the paramedic.

'Bring in the suspects. Carlos Vincentia will be cold and hungry and he'll be frightened,' Alan said. 'He has to stop running. At some point, he will make his way to one of the main roads, so put a unit in Llaingoch and another up at South Stack in case he makes it over the mountain. My money says he will realise there's nowhere to go unless he wants to swim to Ireland. We need to put a lid on this. I don't want a crowd of pissed-up vigilantes attacking the fairground looking for him. Claus Vincentia is in custody. Bring David Prost in too for his own safety. We'll interview all three of them as suspects. We'll need officers on the Newry to quell any retaliation.'

'Okay,' Bob said. 'I'll organise men at the fairground.'

'Let's get her body out of here,' Alan said. Michelle was loaded into the ambulance and police officers escorted the vehicle through the angry crowd. Questions were shouted and accusations made but no confirmation was given. The crowd were quietened and some of them drifted away. Whatever the outcome, the search was over. All hope of finding Chelle alive was gone. Alan and Kim went back to the patrol car. 'Go home and get some rest,' he said to Kim.

'Bad day, eh,' Kim said.

'Today will go down in the annals of history as possibly the shitiest Sunday on record.'

'Aren't we going to speak to Claus Vincentia?'

'He's drunk,' Alan said. 'I don't want anything he says being thrown out of evidence because we didn't give him chance to sleep it off. Let him sweat overnight. Go home and get some sleep and we'll go at him fresh tomorrow.'

'What about you?' Kim said.

'I need a large whisky, a shower and a few hours sleep,' he said. 'I don't see tomorrow being any better than today has been to be honest. In fact, it will probably be worse.'

Chapter 21

Len Jobson stopped for coffee at McDonalds at Abergele. He grabbed a cheeseburger and small fries and ate them in a few bites. He was hungrier than he thought. His mind was racing. There were things to do and not much time to do them. The clock was ticking and he was running out of time on this planet. He still had his strength although it wasn't anything like what it used to be. His muscle wastage had been distressing. He could see it in the expressions of everyone he met. Shock, horror, surprise, sadness and pity. The pity was the worst. He had been a strong man with a powerful physique. For those that had known him, it was visibly shocking to see him so thin. It was one thing knowing someone was ill but another to see them wasting away before their eyes. It was more obvious for those he didn't see regularly. His decline was more acute to those who remembered him in his heyday. In his prime, he would eat two steaks in one sitting and bench press his own bodyweight for eight sets. His strength had been God given. God gave it to him and God had taken it away. Fuck him. He'd given him a son and taken him too. There was nothing Len could do about that but the reality was that someone had snatched Leo away. Another human being or human beings had murdered Leo and his girlfriend and stuffed them into a barrel and dumped them in a pond, where they should have remained for the duration of time. Whoever was responsible for their murders would soon be acutely aware that their bodies had been discovered. They might panic. They might not. They might believe enough time had gone by for them to remain anonymous, hidden in the shadows of the past. There would be a ripple of fear running through them, no matter how cool, calm and collected they were. Hopefully, the ripple would turn to a tsunami of anxiety, wondering if they had left clues to their identity behind. Leo's killers would not get the opportunity to live with the peace of mind that their victims would never be found. They had been found and now Len was going to find them and his retribution was going to be biblical. Len vowed he would bring vengeance for his son. He would sort that one before he bowed out for good. He had to act before the cancer sapped all his energy completely. He felt enthusiastic for the first time in a long time. It had taken five long years to get a sniff of what had happened to Leo. There had simply been nothing to go after but now he had a direction to go in. Better that that, he had a name. A name he knew well. Koresh.

A tap on the window made him jump. He nearly spilled his coffee. His right hand went to the switchblade he carried on his belt. It was an instinctive reaction for a man in his profession. Detective Inspector Gill Robinson gestured for him to open the window. He shook his head and half-smiled, his finger on the button. The glass retreated into the door and the cold night air rushed in.

'It's cold out there,' he said. 'Hello Gill.'

'Hello Len,' Gill said. She was holding a large latte. 'Fancy meeting you here. What a coincidence.'

'It's a small world. To be honest, this is the only place open at this time of night,' Len said. 'It's not such a big coincidence really.'

'Granted, there's not much open. What brings you to this part of the world?' Gill asked.

'I often drive around at night,' Len said. 'I have trouble sleeping but then you know that.'

'That was a long time ago, Len,' Gill said. She smiled sadly. 'A different lifetime.'

'It wasn't so different,' Len said. 'We were a bit younger but we're the same people. You've got a few more stripes on your sleeve but you haven't changed much. You still make the blood pump faster when I look at you.'

'It's dark out here and you can't see the wrinkles around my eyes but thank you. You always were a charmer,' Gill said. 'It's late. Go home and get some sleep.'

'I hardly sleep nowadays,' Len said. 'I think it's knowing I'm going to die soon.' He shrugged. 'I don't want to waste the time I have left, in bed sleeping.'

Gill nodded. She had nothing sarcastic to say to that. 'There's so much I want to do and so little time to do it in.'

'I'm sorry,' Gill said. Len grimaced and shrugged. 'No. Seriously I am sorry. I can't imagine what you're going through.'

'I don't need your pity. Most people would say it is just payback. Karma is a bitch and all that type of nonsense.' He smiled. 'Payback for all the shitty things I've done in my time, inspector,' Len said. He finished his coffee and started the engine. The headlights came on and illuminated raindrops. 'It's started to rain,' Len said. 'You have a safe journey home, Gill. You're okay for a Dibble.'

'You too,' Gill said. She put her hand on the window frame before he could close it. 'I don't know if it's a coincidence you're here but I have a suspicion it isn't.' His face didn't give anything away. 'Did you follow us?' she asked, studying his expression.

'Follow you where?' Len asked. 'Maccies?' Gill smiled thinly. 'Don't flatter yourself. I wanted to see the moon on the sea and I enjoy the drive over the top of the big hill, looking over the Wirral and the lights of Liverpool.' The clouds parted and the moon shone brightly. 'It's very therapeutic.'

'Don't get involved in this investigation, Len. Let us do our jobs.'

'What investigation?' Len asked. 'You haven't lifted a finger to find Leo for years.' His eyes gleamed with intelligence but they gave nothing away. 'Are you telling me you have a new lead to investigate?'

'I didn't say anything like that,' Gill said. 'If we have anything to tell you, we'll be in touch.' She turned to walk away. 'Don't interfere, Len,' she added.

'I wouldn't dream of it,' Len said, closing the window. He watched Gill climb into her vehicle. She closed the door and he put the car into gear and drove towards the A5 slip road. Len knew she had no clue that he had followed them. He could tell. She was confused as to why he was there and she didn't believe his explanation but that was all. He put his foot down and drove into the night.

Anne and Gill watched his taillights fade into the darkness. They drank their coffee. 'What the hell is Len Jobson doing in Abergele?'

'He said he likes to drive around at night to clear his head,' Gill said.

'Bollocks,' Anne said. 'He's up to something.'

****

The Victoria emptied out and the locals filed onto the road. Some of them struggled to cope with the gradient. One leg higher than the other after a skinful of lager was not compatible with standing upright. They gathered in groups, chatting about the night's events. Another group of locals were walking up the hill from the Newry. Their conversation was agitated and emotive. Some of the men and women were angry and aggressive. Others were clearly upset. The drinkers overheard them talking.

'Excuse me. Did you say they've found Chelle Branning?'

'Yes,' one of the women answered. She was crying, her hands curled into fists. 'They found her floating in the marina near the old MCU jetty. Raped and murdered by the looks of it.'

'How do you know that?'

'She's got no clothes on,' someone answered.

'The police were here earlier wanting to talk to two of the pikeys from the fair. They mentioned Michelle Branning was missing,' a man said. 'One of the men butted sergeant Gerrard and fucked off over the fields towards the quarry.' He shrugged. 'I'm no detective but why would he run off if he had nothing to do with it?'

'You don't headbutt a copper for the fun of it,' another man said. 'He is guilty. Why else would he butt a sergeant and run away?'

'When was that?'

'About twenty-minutes ago. Right here where we're standing.'

'Baz threw a pint of piss at one of them,' a man laughed. He wobbled on unsteady legs. 'It hit him right in the face. Funny as fuck it was.'

'I say we go and find him,' Baz said.

'We know the quarry and the paths like the back of our hands.'

'The police are at the bottom of the Newry stopping anyone going down the quarry road.'

'We'll go over the fields and follow him that way. The police won't see us. Has anyone got a torch in their car?'

'I have.'

'Me too. I'll get mine. I have a baseball bat in the boot too.'

'Nice one. Let's get this pervert and smash his head in. Murdering, rapist isn't getting away with it in our town.'

Chapter 22

Lottie was sitting in her trailer, tired and concerned. It had been a dreadful day at the circus of nightmares. How ironic. The thought made her put things into perspective. Things could always be worse. Liz was sitting opposite her and the twins were on the settee. They were all drinking honey flavoured Jack Daniels. The twins were out of costume, showered and looking handsome. They were both dark haired with olive skin and brown eyes. The similarity between them was striking. Not identical but not far from it. Hugo was an inch taller.

'Why didn't you tell me earlier?' Lottie asked Liz. 'What if something terrible has happened to her?'

'Because the police have been around all evening,' Liz said, shaking her head. 'I've been trying to tell you. I thought she was just late and had gone to the port or something. With everything that's been going on, I didn't even know she wasn't back in her trailer until an hour ago.'

'You don't know where she went to meet him?' Hugo asked.

'No. she didn't say.' Liz shook her head. 'You know what she's like about him. She pretends there's nothing going on. She always has.' She paused. 'Sometimes, she stays out with him but she always answers her phone. She's not answering. Neither is he. That is unusual.'

'I'll ring him,' Lottie said. She scrolled through her contacts. The phone rang and switched straight to voicemail. She left a brief message. 'He's not answering to me either.'

'She didn't say what he wanted?' Hugo asked.

'No.'

'Well, we need to speak to him pronto,' Boris said. 'If his mechanics have been spiking local women, we're going to struggle to replace them before the crossing on Friday. We need to refuel everything before we get on the ferry.'

'It's not the end of the world. We'll cope,' Lottie said. 'If his men have been stalking women, I don't want them anywhere near us. I won't have perverts anywhere near my circus.'

'I say we wait and see what comes out in the wash,' Hugo said. 'The police always blame the travellers first and investigate later. Those women were drunk. Anyone could have spiked them. The missing woman is probably asleep somewhere she shouldn't be.'

'I understand that,' Lottie said, nodding. 'But the fact is, a young woman is missing. Missing women are not good news for anyone, us or the town. The press will be down here tomorrow. We need to make sure no one makes a comment to the newspapers. They'll twist anything we say. I have a bad feeling about this.'

'Lighten up, Lottie. You have a bad feeling about everything,' Boris said. 'Let's not worry about it until we know the truth. The woman is probably in town pissed in a pub or gone home with someone she's met at the fair. How many times have we seen this?'

'You're right,' Lottie said. 'I'm tired. We need to keep on our toes tonight. That missing woman is worrying me. If the locals think it is one of our employees who is responsible for her disappearing, there will be a backlash. The police have been all over us as it is.'

'Are you still worried about councillor Orange?' Boris asked. He shook his head and grinned. 'Stupid little man might think twice before he goes shooting his mouth off.'

'You need to take it seriously,' Lottie warned. 'If the councillor doesn't recover, they'll be back to speak to you two. His wife said he was punched by a big clown.' The twins laughed. 'That's you and it's not funny.'

'He'll be fine,' Hugo said. 'Stop worrying.'

'I'm worried. It's easy to say don't worry but I do. The police said Malcolm Orange told his wife he was punched by a big clown,' Lottie protested. 'How can I not worry about it?'

'No one hit the silly old fool. He had a turn, fell and banged his head. We all saw that happen,' Boris said. Hugo nodded in agreement. 'Anyway, it's he said, she said. There were no witnesses to back him up.'

'Did you punch him?' Lottie asked. She frowned.

'Don't be ridiculous,' Boris said, shaking his head.

'Ridiculous?' Lottie frowned. 'It wouldn't be the first time you two have been overprotective.'

'We look after our little sister,' Hugo said. 'You should be grateful.'

'I am but if he pushes the assault allegation, you two could be in trouble.' Lottie emptied her glass. 'I don't want you two locked up in a cell. We're on that ferry on Friday with or without you.'

'That's a Bono song,' Hugo said. 'He's Irish.' Lottie looked at him unimpressed. 'They only have his wife's statement to go on,' Hugo said. 'And that's second-hand information from a man with a brain injury under the influence of drugs.'

'Nothing will come of it,' Boris said. The twins exchanged glances. Lottie caught it but didn't challenge them. 'Don't worry about it.'

'I hope you're right,' Lottie said. She topped up her glass, sipped her drink and rolled another cigarette. 'With everything that's been happening, I haven't been over to see dad today. Is he alright?'

'He's the same as he always is,' Hugo said. 'He thinks mum is coming home this week. I found him looking for a paintbrush this morning. He said he was going to paint the caravan blue before she came home. Apparently, blue is her favourite colour. It took me twenty minutes to convince him she liked it as it was.' Hugo finished his drink. 'Ten minutes later he was looking for the paint. He's away with the fairies half the time and sleeping the rest. We're going to

149

have to put him in a home at some point. The sooner the better. He's becoming a liability.'

'He's not going into a home,' Lottie said. 'We've discussed this before. It's not happening.'

'We can't watch him twenty-four hours a day. I found him in the prop tent last week, messing with a flamethrower,' Hugo said.

'That's his memory returning. He would spend all day in the prop tent if we let him. That was his thing,' Lottie said. 'It happens sometimes but it doesn't last long.'

'We can't afford to look back through rose-tinted spectacles,' Hugo said. 'At some point he will hurt himself or someone else. Again.'

****

Carlos stopped running when his lungs were fit to burst. His eyes had adjusted to the dark but he'd run straight into a fog bank. He couldn't see more than a few yards in front of him. The grass was becoming longer and the ground boggy. His trainers were soaking wet and caked in mud. He'd nearly lost them on a couple of occasions as the bog tried to suck them from his feet. The further he went, the deeper his feet sank into the mire. He had to turn back before he got stuck completely. Carlos pushed his hands into his pockets and felt the bottle of flunitrazepam tablets. It pained him to lose them but he had no choice. He took them out and dropped them into the bog. The bottle remained just below the grass. He stood on it and pushed it deep into the mud. That was the end of that problem. The police had nothing. Assaulting the policeman wouldn't be taken lightly but he was under the influence of alcohol and they'd been assaulted by the locals. Everyone saw the youth throwing piss at them. He could plead that his actions were provoked by fear of being attacked. It was an impulse reaction. Not his usual behaviour by any stretch of the imagination. His record was clean. He'd made sure of that. The police had never discovered who slit their stepfather's throat while he was drunk and sleeping next to his new barmaid, who was also too drunk to know what was happening. She'd woken up covered in blood and immediately called the police. The police had suspected her but there was no murder weapon and the back door had been broken into. His blood was found on the wall and gate outside in the backyard, which was enough to cast doubt that she'd killed him. Of course, the brothers were travelling with the fair and no one knew where they were. If the police ever traced them, they had an alibi. Each other.

Carlos backed out of the marsh and headed down the slope. He had no idea where it would lead him. The incline would hopefully be easier to navigate than the marshland. After what felt like an age, he reached a hedge and followed it until he found a gate. He stopped and listened for the sound of an engine, imagining police cars searching for him but it was quiet. The fog gave him some confidence, offering him a grey shroud to hide in. He heard voices on the wind and tried to understand what they were saying but the words were blown away. They were further away than he imagined. He climbed over the gate and jumped down onto the gravel path on the other side. It wasn't a proper road. A shadow appeared on the other side of the gate. His heart stopped. Something loomed in the mist. He relaxed a little when his brain identified the silhouette of a horse. Its breath formed a cloud of condensation in the air. A second animal joined it and they stood in the mist staring at him. They made him feel uneasy. He patted them on the nose and looked to his left and right. Picking which direction to go in was impossible. He had a fifty-fifty chance of getting it wrong. The voices he'd heard were to his left. He decided to go in the opposite direction.

****

Baz and three other men from the pub had crossed the muddy fields and found the quarry road beyond the police cordon. They were all in their early twenties and unpredictable. Two carried baseball bats and the other, a tyre iron. It was cold and their feet were wet. The bottom of Baz's jeans was rubbing his leg painfully. Hunting down the pikey didn't seem like such a good idea anymore. The novelty of being part of a vigilante mob had worn off, especially as only three of them had actually joined the mob. Three others made it down the hill as far as the stile, which led into the fields before turning back. They flagged down a passing taxi and flicked the middle finger as they drove away laughing. It wasn't as much fun as they thought it would be and it was hard going. Baz was panting like a dog and he could hear the other two puffing and blowing. The alcohol and testosterone fuelled aggression had worn off. Baz wanted to go home and crawl into bed but he couldn't lose face now.

They walked towards the quarry in silence, none of them wanted to be the first to say they wanted to go home. The road was narrow and thin with high banks on either side. It was once the railway track which carried thousands of tons of rock from the quarry to build the breakwater. Over a mile long, it was straight as a die. About halfway to the quarry, there was a stone bridge over the road. It was used to allow cattle to cross the railway line, moving the grazing from one stretch of fields to another. Baz jogged up the slipway onto the bridge to get a better view and called to the others, in hushed tones.

'Up here,' he said. They joined him on the bridge. They crouched against the wall, resting. All three were completely miserable. 'I say we wait here for ten minutes and if he doesn't turn up, we go home. I'm freezing.'

'Me too. I've had enough.'

'Do we have to wait that long?'

'Yes.'

'But I'm knackered.'

'This was your shit idea in the first place,' Baz said. He heard footsteps and put his forefinger to his lips. A shadow immerged from the direction of the quarry. He could see the shape of a man appearing from the gloom. His shoulders were hunched, hands stuffed deep into his pockets. 'Shush. Look there,' he whispered. 'That's the rapist.'

'Is that him?'

'Who else would be down here this late at night?' Baz said. 'Duck behind the wall until he goes underneath.' The three men hid while the solitary figure reached the bridge and walked underneath. Baz felt his shoulder pressed against the big stone blocks the bridge was built from. They were three times the size of a house brick. One of them felt loose. 'Psst,' he whispered. He pointed to the block. 'Let's drop this on the fucker.'

The three men wrestled with the block and lifted it free of the wall. They carried it to the opposite side and rested it on the guard wall. The lone male appeared from underneath the bridge and they pushed the block. It landed on the target with a dull thud. The man crumpled to the road his skull broken and his neck at an awkward angle.

'Bullseye,' Baz said, excited.

'One hundred and eighty,' his companion laughed.

The men jogged down the slipway. Baz shone his torch at the crumpled body. He stepped closer but there was blood all over the face. The man was unrecognisable.

'Is he dead?'

'Yes, he's dead,' Baz said. 'We need to get out of here before anyone else comes along.' He checked around to see if they'd been seen. 'Let's go. Quickly.'

****

Richard Lewis arrived at the boatyard. The Newry was quiet now. He could see Fred Garret, the marina manager pacing up and down, arguing with someone on his phone. Several detectives were chatting to a group of uniformed officers near the gates. The marina consisted of a H shaped block of apartments with retail units beneath them. There was Langdon's bar, a sailing shop and a newsagent with a café in it. They were all in darkness. Lights burned in a couple of the apartments, reflecting from the dark sea. The waves appeared black like oil. The buildings were built on the water's edge. Behind them was the boatyard where vessels were stored out of the water. The heart of the boatyard was a cavernous stone-built workshop, tall enough to fit even the biggest yachts inside. It was a skeleton now, a shadow of its former self, having burnt down a few years before. Only the walls and metal roof beams remained. The insurance company were delaying payment for whatever reasons they could come up with to delay paying for the rebuild. A lot of the tools lost in the fire could never be replaced. They were handmade by the craftsmen who had worked there a hundred years ago, building boats from timber that had been prepared and cured for months. Those skills had been lost to fibreglass and moulded plastic production. Richard remembered going there with his friends after school to watch the boat-builders work. It felt like a long time ago. He climbed out of the car and headed towards Fred Garret.

'Good evening, Fred,' Richard said, sensing it wasn't a good evening at all. Fred was having a shit evening.

'Good evening?' Fred muttered. 'It's the middle of the night. Why couldn't this wait until the morning?'

'Forensic evidence degrades quickly,' Richard said. 'This is now a murder investigation and as such, it takes precedence over the time of day, I'm afraid. We have reason to believe Michelle Branning was brought to this side of the marina and sexually assaulted before she was murdered. We're in the process of eliminating the residents in the apartments and we need to search the boats that are out of the water to rule them out or in as the case may be.'

'You want to search the boats?'

'Yes.'

'They're not my boats,' Fred argued. 'They are not my property. They belong to private owners.'

'I appreciate that and the problems it might cause, but we need to look at them anyway.'

'Have you got any idea what you're asking?' Fred paced up and down again. 'The insurance company are being arseholes about the workshop fire and the boats lost in the storm. I can't just let you lot break into our yachts without the owners' permission, looking for whatever it is you're looking for. They won't pay out as it is.'

'Calm yourself down,' Richard said. 'The way I see it is our killer walked down here with Michelle and found somewhere by chance. It was an opportune moment, which means, he found a boat that was already open or he broke into one, in either case, we don't want to break into anything, it will already be open,' Richard said, shrugging. He smiled. 'What we're looking for could be in one of those boats but we don't have to break anything to find it. We will not do any damage at all. Do you understand?'

'Oh, I see what you mean,' Fred said. 'That's okay. What do you need from me?'

'We think the yachts are too high to access from the ground, so I need you to show us all the cruisers and fishing boats that can be climbed onto easily,' Richard said. 'Have any of them been worked on recently and may have access ladders fixed in place?'

'Follow me. This way. They're all over here.' Fred walked towards the boat storage area. A vast patch of the shore that had been concreted. It was like a graveyard for vessels of all shapes and sizes. They loomed above them in the darkness. Some were broken, some were old and needed repairing. Others belonged to individuals who had bought them as a toy. A floating gadget to impress their families and friends. *"We have a yacht on Anglesey. We have a yacht but we have no fucking idea what's involved in its upkeep or how to sail it and the last time we went on it; it rained all day and was so windy we could hardly stand up. The kids hated it and never want to go again.'* Like any toy, their owners tire of them eventually and keeping them in the water is expensive so, they have them stored with best intentions to re-float them one day. Others belonged to dead people.

'I used to play down here as a kid,' Richard said. 'Some of those boats were still there back then. They've never moved.'

'You're right.'

'I've been in the sea more than some of them,' Richard joked.

'Some of the vessels closest to the sea wall have been there for donkey's years, their owners passed away,' Fred explained. 'We try to contact relatives but as soon as an outstanding bill is mentioned, they don't want to know. We keep the cruisers over there,' he said pointing. Richard counted seven vessels. Next to them were bigger fishing boats.

'Over there, ladies and gentlemen,' Richard said. The officers moved towards the vessels with torches. It didn't take long for a boat to be identified as a possible crime scene.

'This one is open.' A uniformed officer was standing on the deck of a white day cruiser. It was being painted. A set of wide wooden ladders was fixed to the bow.

'This could be what we're after,' Richard said. 'Come down from there. Don't contaminate it.' He took his torch and pointed it through a porthole. There was a small galley kitchen and dining table and a seating area with padded bench seats, which converted into a bed. There was a pile of clothing on the table, jeans, UGG boots, a belt and socks. He could see a pair of black knickers on the floor. 'Bingo,' Richard said. 'Get me a forensic team down here,' he ordered. 'This is where Michelle Branning was assaulted.' He called Alan to give him the news.

Chapter 23

Monday Morning

Lottie woke up, made a coffee, added oat milk and rolled a cigarette. She slumped on the settee and put her feet up. Her muscles were stiff and aching. She needed a hot shower to loosen her up. It was still dark but she could hear the camp stirring into life. An engine started and a dog was barking, then one of the Mathew's kids started crying. The family were three trailers away but she could hear him like he was outside the door. That kid was always crying. His mother said he was teething but he was five. Lottie hadn't had any children but she knew five-year-olds didn't teeth. She put on the news and turned up the volume. The lead story was the discovery of a couple at their holiday home in Rhosneiger. It was being described as a robbery homicide, possibly connected to serious organised crime. There were several victims as yet unidentified and they were appealing for anyone who knew a woman called Mary Adams from the Cork area of Ireland. They posted her passport photograph. Lottie nearly spilled her coffee.

'No, no, no,' she muttered. She reached for her mobile and dialled Liz. After a dozen rings, Liz answered in tears.

'Have you seen the news?'

'Yes,' Liz sobbed. 'She wasn't in her trailer this morning and I knew something bad had happened to her. I was hoping she would be in her bed when I woke up but she's dead. Oh, poor, poor, Mary.'

'Have you told anyone?' Lottie asked.

'No.' Liz sniffled. 'I've only just seen it on the news.'

'Come to my trailer now,' Lottie said. 'We need to contact the police before they trace her back here. If we contact them first, it won't seem suspicious.'

'I hate that man and everything to do with him,' Liz said. 'I told you he was bad news. He struts around like he's Jesus Christ, pretending to be helping the poor but he's nothing but a crook.' She choked a sob. 'I warned her to stay away from him.'

'It's too late now,' Lottie said. 'Come over here. We need to get our stories straight.'

****

Alan was woken by the phone. Not his mobile, the landline, which confused him as it never rang. His mobile was on silent ensuring he would get at least a few hours unbroken sleep. He hadn't left the landline off the hook, which was a schoolboy error. His initial reaction was to tell whoever was calling to fuck off, turn over and go back to sleep but he realised it was probably important. It was always important. It was rarely good news, that was a fact. He answered the call. The duty sergeant had been left with two pieces of bad news by the nightshift and so, he felt it important enough to call him. Alan needed a pee. Once upon a time, he would have been able to wait until he'd spoken to him but not anymore. His bladder was a bully.

'Morning sir,' the sergeant said. 'Terrible news about the Branning girl.'

'It's not the outcome we wanted,' Alan agreed.

'Shocking it is. I've known the family since before she was born.' He paused. 'I was at her christening.'

'Have you spoken to the family?' Alan asked.

'They're devastated,' he said. 'They're a close family. Families can be broken by things like this. We've seen it more times that I wish to mention, haven't we?'

'We have.'

'Anyway, back to business. I have a couple of pieces of news left by the nightshift officers. They said to ring you at eight o'clock if you weren't here already.'

'Eight o'clock?' Alan said. 'Oh shit. I set my alarm for six.' He checked his phone. 'I've turned it off,' Alan said. 'You're going to have to wait a minute. This phone is attached to the wall and the wire doesn't stretch to the bathroom.'

'Right you are,' the sergeant said. 'We don't want you making a mess. I'll hang on here.'

Alan went to the bathroom. The window was open and it was freezing. He grabbed his dressing gown from the back of the door and struggled into it. His knee was sore today and he rubbed it as if rubbing it would make it better. It didn't. Empty toilet rolls were stacked along the window ledge in an ever-decreasing triangle four rows high, built by one of the boys to remind him to buy some. The boys had been home for a few days, miraculously timed so they all descended at the same time. Jack was back from travelling in Vietnam, Kris had had a row with his missus and Dan was decorating his own house and didn't like sleeping with the smell of paint. The fumes gave him a headache. They exhausted his limited stocks of toiletries in the space of twenty-four hours and the kitchen had been ravaged as if a plague of locusts had descended and devoured his food. Still, it had been nice to see them all together. The memories of the bungalow as a family home, the boys still children, the log-burning fire roaring and Kath in the kitchen cooking something hideous, were bittersweet. The past was such a happy place yet thinking of it made him sad because it was gone. He peed, flushed the loo and went back to his phone call, wrapping the gown tighter. His memories were swept into a dark recess in the corner of his mind for now. He picked up the phone.

'Okay. I'm back. Sorry about that.'

'No problem at all. I've been asked to relay that David Prost was not in his caravan when officers went to bring him to the station last night.'

'Oh, that's not good.'

'Apparently, his pickup truck was gone, so they assumed he might have gone somewhere to work, picking up parts or to tow a vehicle but when they called back this morning, he still wasn't in and there's no sign of his vehicle.'

Alan had the sinking feeling he was in the wind. What would make him run was anyone's guess. Michelle Branning had been raped and murdered and only a guilty man would run following a routine visit from the police. But what was he guilty of?

'I've put an alert out on his plates.' He paused. 'I don't want to jump the gun but is he a suspect in the Branning case?'

'He's a person of interest,' Alan said. Not sure if he was a suspect or not. He was still debating it. 'His cousins certainly are.'

'I'm asking because I would be in Ireland by now,' the sergeant said. 'If it was me on the run, that is.'

'Good point. The circus is booked to sail over on Friday. Extend the alert to the port,' Alan said. 'Ask them to check if that truck travelled overnight.'

'Will do.'

'What is the second nugget of bad news?' Alan asked.

'Unfortunately, we have another incident which took place in the early hours of this morning,' the sergeant said.

'What happened?'

'Trevor Branning, Michelle's uncle,' the sergeant said. 'We found him this morning on the quarry road under the farmer's bridge. Someone dropped a block on his head. Crushed his skull and fractured his neck. His ID, wallet and phone are on him, so he wasn't robbed. He's in the ICU at Bangor. The doctors are saying it's touch and go.'

'What do we know?'

'We know he was out looking for Michelle. Bob Dewhurst says he saw him last night heading down the rocky coast towards the quarry. He was with a

160

couple of others but it was foggy. Apparently, they got split up. The others are safe at home but Trevor must have reached the quarry and then headed back towards town along the quarry road.'

'Have the family been told?' Alan asked.

'Yes, but not until after his wife reported him missing. She was flapping because the rest of the family were home and Trevor wasn't. They knew Michelle had been found, so she feared the worst.'

'When did she report him missing?'

'About half an hour ago.'

'Get someone to go and see her at the hospital,' Alan said.

'Will do.'

'Has he said anything?'

'Nothing. He hasn't regained consciousness.'

'Who would be on the quarry road at that time of night to drop a block on his head?'

'I've got no idea,' the sergeant said. 'My money is on the Vincentia man. Sergeant Gerrard said he was last seen heading in that direction.'

'Of course, he did,' Alan said, thinking. It didn't add up. 'Who is at the scene?'

'Chod Hall. He was asking if you wanted to have a nosey before they clean up?'

'Tell him I'll be there shortly,' Alan said. 'I want to have a look at it.'

'Will do,' the sergeant said. 'Shall I let them know you're up and about and on the way in?'

'Let who know?'

'Kim Davies and Richard Lewis are waiting to interview the Vincentia brother.' He paused. 'They have some interesting footage from the landlord at the Albert Vaults. I don't know the details but it's good news I believe.'

'Okay. Tell them to carry on,' Alan said. 'I want to go to the quarry first. I'll be there in half an hour.' Alan thought for a second. 'Has Pamela Stone finished at the boatyard?'

'She took the entire vessel to their warehouse facility at Caernarvon,' the sergeant said. 'Fred Garret is doing the war dance apparently.'

'I bet he is,' Alan chuckled. 'Why does she want the entire vessel?'

'She said it's something to do with the decking being porous?'

'Of course,' Alan said. 'Porous decking. What other type is there?'

Chapter 24

Kim and Richard went into the interview room. Claus Vincentia was sitting at the table, flanked by a very professional looking brief. Kim had no idea who he was. His suit was the price of a two-week holiday at least. They sat down and went through the legal requirements. Claus looked washed out and tired. Dark circles underlined frightened eyes. His night in a cell hadn't refreshed him one bit, nor had it washed away the stink of stale ale. He looked like he needed a good hot shower and a toothbrush. The introductions were made for the camera and the tape.

'Henry Graff,' the brief said, speaking for the camera. His accent was indiscernible. Probably public school educated, Kim thought. Expensive. Everything about him was expensive. Too expensive for a travelling mechanic to afford and definitely arranged by someone they were yet to encounter. Claus had been snoring all night and his brother had his own problems, so neither of them had arranged representation. Whoever arranged for Henry Graff to be there, had money and influence. 'I'll be representing Claus and his brother Carlos and their cousin David Prost until we can assign them a solicitor each from our practice. If any charges come to fruition this morning, I'll advice my clients and their representatives accordingly. I have a few colleagues who fit the bill.' He scribbled on a note pad while scrolling on his iPad. Graff had fired the first warning shot across her bows, letting them know his firm was formidable. 'So, it's just me for now.'

'Just you is fine, Mr Graff. Carlos assaulted a police officer, so that will be a section eighteen but he's on the run and we can't find David, so there's no rush to wheel out the big guns just yet,' Kim said. 'Keep your powder dry for now.' She smiled. 'However, I must say that was very impressive. I can imagine an inexperienced detective quaking in their boots listening to that.' She smiled again but Graff ignored her jibe. 'Before we begin, I need you to know that we've recovered CCTV footage from the Albert Vaults. The coverage includes the time your client and his relatives entered the pub, until they left.' The brief nodded. Kim turned to Claus. 'Do you understand what I've just said?'

'Yes,' Claus said. 'You said you have CCTV from the pub. I'm not worried. We didn't do anything wrong.'

Kim placed photographs of the Branning sisters on the table. 'This is Michelle Branning and this is her sister Tiffany,' she said. 'Do you recognise them?'

'Yes. I recognise them. I met them briefly yesterday,' Claus said. He pointed to Tiffany. 'We bought her some shots because it was her birthday. Is that a crime?'

'Buying someone a drink is not a crime but adding Flunitrazepam to it is,' Kim said. She waited for a response but Claus folded his arms and remained silent. 'Flunitrazepam is a drug commonly used in date rape cases.'

'I don't know what that is,' Claus said, staring at Kim, his expression defiant. 'I've never heard of it.'

'Really,' Kim asked, frowning. 'You've never heard of Rohypnol?' she said. 'Roofies, ruffles, Mexican Valium, the forget-me-pill. Do any of them ring a bell?'

'No. I don't to need to drug women,' Claus said, irritated.

'Tiffany Branning was tested last night and she has residual traces of Flunitrazepam in her blood,' Kim said. 'The results of tests on her hair will confirm it.' Claus blushed. 'We think you added the drug to her drink.'

'I didn't do anything like that,' Claus said. 'Maybe somebody else put it in her drink. It's a busy pub. They had been in other pubs before they met us. Anyone could have done it. You've picked on us because we're travellers.'

'I'm showing your client a sequence filmed by the CCTV system at the Albert Vaults, which covers the inside of the public house, specifically the seating area where Claus and his brother were sitting,' Kim said. Claus looked shocked. The colour drained from his face. She pressed play on a digital monitor

164

which was fixed to the wall. The footage showed Tiffany Branning turning away from the three men to her left to talk to her sister. The sisters were giggling about something. Carlos could be seen leaning over to sprinkle a white powder into her drink. Claus stirred it with a cocktail stick. Kim stopped the recording. 'That is your brother Carlos adding a white powder into Tiffany's drink and that is you making sure it was dissolved.' She paused. 'What do you have to say about that, Claus?'

'In light of this evidence, I need a word with my client,' Henry Graff said, removing his spectacles. 'Don't say another word, Claus.'

'You can have a break,' Kim said. 'Before you do, watch this.' She started the recording again. 'The footage showed the sisters standing up, taking cigarettes from Tiffany's handbag and walking out of shot as they went outside to smoke. Claus leaned over and added white powder to Michelle's drink. 'That's you adding Flunitrazepam to Michelle Branning's drink.' Claus blushed darker this time. He slumped down in his chair. 'To bring you up to date, Michelle Branning was raped and murdered yesterday afternoon. Her body was recovered from the marina last night.' She watched the brief turn white. He shifted uncomfortably in his chair. Claus closed his eyes and shook his head.

'I didn't rape and kill anyone,' Claus protested. 'This is crazy.'

'Please don't say anything at all, Claus,' Henry said. 'A break is required, detective. If you don't mind.'

'We'll leave you to it for five minutes,' Kim said. She smiled and shrugged. 'I'm going to have a coffee. Would either of you like one?' she asked. Claus and his brief shook their heads but neither of them answered.

****

Alan parked his BMW in a passing point on the quarry road. It was a hundred yards from the farmer's bridge. Uniformed officers were manning a cordon and crime scene tape fluttered wildly in the wind. It wouldn't last long. The wind was becoming stronger. Chod Hall waved to him from the farmer's bridge. The injured man had been removed but the block was where it fell. A kidney-shaped patch of congealed blood stained the grit and gravel. Alan walked up the slipway and greeted Chod with a handshake. Chod was a DS with talent. His analytical skills and powers of observation had earned him a secondment with Greater Manchester Police. He worked in their murder squad for two years before deciding he wanted to move back to the island.

'This has me baffled,' Chod said, pushing his dark hair from his face. 'You can see where the block came from, there's a gap in the wall over there and you can see where it ended up but there's no way one man moved that block. Arnold Schwarzenegger couldn't pick that up and carry it from there to there. It doesn't make any sense at all.'

'I agree,' Alan said. 'There was more than one person up here.' He looked at the banks on either side of the road. Some of the grass to the right was flattened. 'There look,' he said, pointing. 'Let's have a little wander.'

The detectives walked along the bank to the flattened grass. A path had been trudged from the road, up the bank and into the fields beyond. From their elevated position they could see tracks leading across the field, skirting the marshland and heading into the next field. The gorse and grass had been flattened and there were footprints in the muddy patches.

'Two or three sets of footprints?' Chod said. 'I'm saying three.'

'I agree,' Alan said, nodding. 'They knew where they were going,' Alan said. 'It was pitch black and foggy last night. Even with a torch it would be difficult to navigate across that field yet they did it and avoided the marsh. They have local knowledge.' Alan pointed to the drystone wall. 'They knew if they followed the boundary wall to the next field, they would stay dry. The next field leads over to Porth-y-felin.'

'They were definitely locals,' Chod said. 'I was told there was bother at the Victoria Inn last night, wasn't there?'

'Yes. Sergeant Gerrard went to interview brothers from the fairground about the Branning women. He was butted and the culprit ran across the fields. Those fields over there. He would have come in this direction.'

'So, he could have been followed by locals from the pub?'

'Followed or chased more like it,' Alan said. 'If there was a vigilante mob hunting Carlos Vincentia in the dark, they'll be bragging about it somewhere. Wait for the pub to open and find out who was in there late last night. There may be some names that will jump out at you.'

'I will do,' Chod said. 'I'm going to walk across the fields to Porth-y-felin following their tracks. They will have been in a rush.' He pointed to the muddy patches. 'It would have been hard going in the dark. They may have left something behind.'

'I'll get uniform to pick you up outside the Vic,' Alan said.

Carlos Vincentia had spent an uncomfortable night in a garden shed. He slept under some potato sacks and a plastic tarpaulin. His head was banging and he was thirsty. There was nothing in the shed of any use to him. It was daylight and the fog had lifted. There was no cloaking device to be had. He would be clearly visible wherever he went. His phone was dead. The battery was shit and he'd used what little charge he had trying to get David to pick him up. The problem was David didn't know where he was and he couldn't tell him because he didn't know either. David sounded squirrely. He was a first-class pussy. The police had been to the caravan and it had sent him off at a tangent. The police were working blind. They had nothing, stumbling around in the dark trying to find a needle in a stack of needles. The sisters had been on a pub crawl through town. Anyone could have spiked them. No jury on the planet could convict them of drugging them. The police were looking for a patsy to crumple under the pressure and admit to it. That wasn't going to happen while he had breath in his body.

Carlos opened the shed door and tried to get his bearings. He was on the edge of a housing estate at the bottom of the mountain. Behind him, about a mile away was the sea. He had come from that direction in the safety of the dark. It wasn't an option to go back that way in the daylight. He needed somewhere to rest up, eat and drink, charge his phone and make contact with Claus. The situation wasn't ideal. It was a mess but it wasn't irretrievable. They would be on the move on Friday and it would all be behind them. If he could avoid the police until then, everything would be fine. His boss would be furious that they had attracted the attention of the police. Bronski didn't like the police and they didn't like him. There was always something dodgy going on around Bronski. He sold fuel and Carlos was sure he sold a lot of other stuff too. There was always a bag of skunk spare when he arrived. He would tell them to enjoy it as a thank you for all their hard work. One time it was a bag of flake, well over a gram. It was the best coke he had ever snorted. He asked Bronski if he could buy some more of it and Bronski flipped, ranting about not being a drug dealer. It was a gift and nothing more. Bullshit. Carlos was aware of some of his dealings but he knew it was just the tip of the iceberg. They would have to keep their indiscretion and the resulting police involvement to themselves. There was no way Bronski would find out unless someone told him and they weren't about to do that. Keep your mouth shut and say nothing about nothing. That's what Bronski always said when he was paying them a bonus. Bronski was touchy about the police. He said it was because he was of Russian origin and that the British police hated Russians. Carlos wasn't sure if they did or if they didn't but he didn't want to piss him off. Bronski wasn't the kind of guy you wanted to piss off.

Carlos ventured a few yards from the shed and looked over the garden fence. The houses were all detached with fields behind them. There was washing hanging on the line next door and some of the bedroom windows were open. A dog was barking nearby. He tiptoed along the fence to the kitchen window and peered inside. It was empty. The worktops were clean and tidy and the table and floor tiles were spotless. In the corner was a walking frame. The owner was probably old. He ducked low and moved to the lounge window. The curtains were open and he could see through the room to the driveway at the front of the house. He couldn't see a car. There was no sign of life. He crept back to the kitchen and checked the back door, trying the handle. It turned but the door wouldn't budge. There was a mortice lock below the handle, so there was probably a key on the other side. Most people leave the key in the lock. He checked around and kept low as he ran back to the shed. There was a spade hanging on the wall. That would do the trick. He took it and went back to the kitchen. Leaning the spade against the wall, he knocked on the door and waited.

****

Jane Orange was cold and wet but too scared to move. The thing that had visited her in the night told her if she opened her eyes, he would cut them out. She knew he had gone but the fear had not left with him. The urge to urinate had been so intense, she couldn't stop it from happening. The mattress and her nightdress were soaking wet and cold on her skin. She wanted to open her eyes and go to the bathroom, shower and put on, fresh clothes but she was too frightened. The bedding would need to be changed and the mattress turned. If Malcolm knew what she'd done, he'd be disgusted. She was disgusted with herself.

The thing that had woken her was inches from her face. She could smell its breath, feel his warmth on her skin. When she'd stirred from her sleep, he had spoken to her. He said such disgusting things to her. So vile that they could never be repeated. Just thinking about what it had said made the tears stream down her cheeks once more. What he said he would do to her if she ever spoke to the police was inhumane. Beyond evil. He knew her son's name and the names of her grandchildren and he swore he would hurt them too. All the time he spoke, she had kept her eyes screwed tightly closed. Her chest was so tight with fear she couldn't release her breath. Her muscles began to cramp but she didn't move. Not even an inch. Not even when its hands travelled beneath the quilt touching her, squeezing her in places no woman should be touched involuntarily. His voice would stay in her head for the remainder of her life. She would take it to the grave. The sensation of his face so close to hers and the incessant whispering had made her feel as if she would die right there; her heart would burst from fright. The evil things it wanted to do to her made her sick. They were feelings that would never fade. Could never fade. They would scar her deeper than any knife could have. They had cut into her soul. She had suffered the most traumatic few hours of her life and for what exactly? Malcolm and his effing ego.

She opened her eyes but didn't move. Her beathing was shallow and fast. She could feel her heart beating in her chest, like the bass drum in a marching band. Was it still there, waiting for her to move? Jane looked left and right as far as she could without moving her head. Nothing bad happened. She turned her head and looked around the bedroom. It was empty. There was no sign of the malevolent being that had been there last night, yet she could feel it. The memory of his touch on her skin made her want to vomit. She threw off the covers and ran to the bathroom. A stream of puke hit the porcelain and splattered across the seat. Her chest heaved again and her stomach was emptied of the nervous bile. The taste in her mouth was acrid and stung the back of her throat. She felt as if her heart was about to explode.

Eventually, she couldn't remember how long, the panic subsided and she removed her nightgown. There were tiny scratches on her breasts. His fingernails were sharp like nails. The tips rough and uneven. She looked in the mirror and saw more scratches on her thigh. The sensation of him touching her, whispering, taunting, threatening, the disgusting words he used, the overwhelming evil that radiated from him swamped her senses. She felt her knees buckling and she folded onto the tiles next to the bath. It was five minutes before she felt strong enough to stand and turn on the shower. She waited for the water to reach temperature and climbed into the cubicle. The water touched her skin like warm silk washing away the filth on her. She rubbed shower gel onto her skin until the bottle was empty but still didn't feel clean. The hot water soothed her nerves and calmed her a little. She used a bottle of shampoo to wash her entire body again. And then she washed it again.

Half an hour later, she felt recovered enough to get out and dress herself. She wrapped her hair in a towel and went back into the bedroom. Her nerves were on edge, her senses ultra-aware. Fear still gripped her soul. Could it have all been in her imagination? The scratches said no. It had happened. It had been there. She saw her mobile on the bedside table and picked it up. She wanted to call the police and tell them she'd been threatened and her family had been threatened and she'd been touched. Assaulted. Touching without permission was assault, wasn't it? She wanted to ring them and tell them. She wanted to ring Malcolm and tell him what a stupid stubborn arsehole he was and that this was all his fault. Councillor effing Orange and his effing crusades. One effing ridiculous crusade after another. This was his fault but she knew she could never phone the police and she could never tell Malcolm what had happened. He said he would come back and she believed him. She went into her phone with shaking fingers. A photograph was still open, taken on her camera. She stared at the image, mouth open, tears flowing down her cheeks. It was a selfie. The flash had made her skin look deathly pale. Her eyes were screwed tightly closed and the expression of sheer terror was etched into every line on her face. The face next to hers belonged to a clown. A very evil looking clown with crooked teeth and dull emotionless eyes. It was smiling. Jane dropped the phone and ran from the room. This time she didn't make it to the toilet before she vomited.

****

Kelly Williams had hardly slept. She made a pot of tea and turned on the news. That was a mistake. The local station was full of the gruesome find at a house on Rhosneiger beach. The images of the house were taken from the exact spot they had been standing when she'd first seen the woman at the window. The camera zoomed in on the balcony. The window had been boarded up with shuttering, which looked ugly against the rest of the building. She shook her head as the details were revealed. Four dead in the basement, two as yet unidentified. It was suspected to be linked with serious organised crime. What is that? Serious organised crime. As opposed to what exactly? Not very organised crime. Unorganised crime. Not so seriously organised crime. What was the difference? Whoever was responsible for the murders, organised or not organised was a fucking nutter. She had seen his face and looked into his eyes and she could confirm he was a nutter. And she could confirm he hadn't been alone. So, there was actually a bunch of fucking nutters working together. Whether they were organised or not was irrelevant, she was frightened.

The news changed to the rape and murder of Michelle Branning. Kelly shook her head and closed her eyes. She knew Michelle and Tiffany. They were ten years younger than her but she had met them socially a few times. They were typical Holyhead girls. Bubbly and confident. Loud and proud, fun until the fun stops and then beware. Mess with one at your peril. The thought two young women could go out to celebrate a birthday and end up with such a tragic ending was incomprehensible. Kelly felt for her family and friends, especially her mam. She would be destroyed. The news of her murder made her twice as anxious as she was already. She felt more vulnerable than she had ever felt. Everything felt like it was fragile and could shatter into a thousand pieces at any moment.

The online encounter with a murderer had unsettled her. Her mind had been in turmoil ever since. She had to do something but there weren't many options open to her. She could stay put and do nothing and hope it all goes away but that was like burying her head in the sand. It was unlikely that this would be the end of the matter. Women falling to their death from a balcony in a small Welsh village tended to attract attention. This one certainly had. The news bulletin was nearly half an hour long and they were promising an hour long special to be broadcast after the evening news. This was a huge news story and the culprits would be sitting watching it, planning how to avoid being captured. Removing any witnesses would be high on their list.

Kelly couldn't see how the men would get away with what they had done. They had threatened her into silence but there would be other witnesses out there. People must have seen them coming and going from the house. She still wasn't sure how they had got her mobile number but she had a good idea it was something to do with Jack. The electricity being turned off was concerning.

It could only be done from close quarters. She went to the front door and unlocked it. Her heart was beating faster than it should. She opened it and checked the street for anything out of the ordinary. What that was, she had no idea. It looked the same as it always had but now it was frightening. Every nook and cranny, doorway and alleyway had become a hiding place for a murderer. A murderer who had taken a picture of her daughter outside her mothers' home. She couldn't think clearly. Doing nothing and waiting wouldn't solve the problem. It wasn't an option.

Kelly stepped outside into the covered porch. There was a gas cupboard there, which housed the meter and the electric cupboard was next to it. They were always locked and could only be opened with the triangular key thingy which her dad had given to her. It was open. She pushed the door and saw that the main fuse for her house had been tampered with. It was held in place by a fuse wire that was sealed by the utility company who supplied her. The concept was the fire brigade could turn off the gas and electric from the outside in the event of a fire. The fuse wire had been cut, which meant they had removed the fuse, messaged her and then replaced it. They had been at her front door the entire time. How brazen was that?

Kelly scrolled through her phone and found Jack's number. She rang him and he answered within a few rings. His voice was excited, like a teenager with his first girlfriend.

'Hello babe,' he said. 'I was just thinking about you. In fact, that's a lie. I've been thinking about you all night. Not in a pervy type of way. You know what I mean,' he stammered.

'Don't get yourself all hot and bothered,' Kelly said. 'I'm not calling to make up. Everything I said yesterday still stands but I need to talk to you.'

'Oh, okay. What's up then?' Jack asked, sulkily.

'I need you to take all the pictures you've tagged me in, off Facebook,' Kelly said. 'All of them, Jack and I mean they need to be taken down this morning.'

'Why can't I have pictures of you on Facebook?' he moaned. 'Is this about what happened yesterday?'

'Yes.'

'I thought so,' Jack said. 'You're overreacting. I thought so yesterday if I'm honest.'

'I'm not overreacting,' Kelly said, calmly. Although she didn't feel in the slightest bit calm. 'I want those photographs removed please.'

'I'm at work,' Jack said. 'I'll do it later. What did the detective say last night?'

'What do you mean?'

'He called and asked for your mobile number,' Jack said. Kelly stayed quiet, simmering beneath the surface. 'He said they'd written it down wrong and needed to clarify something with you. What was it about?'

'You are such a stupid idiot,' Kelly said, shaking her head. 'It wasn't the police. It was them.'

'Who?'

'The murderers, stupid,' Kelly said. 'They got your name and number from your van. Now, they know where I live and thanks to you, they have my mobile number. You gave it to them.' She was fuming. The urge to shout and scream at him was powerful but she resisted. 'They cut off my power and threatened me last night, you bloody fool.'

'They cut off the power to your house?' Jack asked, shocked.

'Yes.'

'Oh my god,' Jack said. 'Have you told the police?'

'No, of course not and you had better not say anything to them either,' Kelly said. 'You've done enough damage, thank you very much. I can't believe you gave them my number. I wondered how they got it. I should have known.'

'I'm so sorry,' Jack said. 'He sounded so genuine. Why would I think he was lying?' Jack sighed. 'I am really sorry, you know.'

'I know you are,' Kelly said, sighing. 'I know you mean well but I think it's probably best if we don't see each other.' Jack remained quiet. 'I want to leave the relationship, Jack. It's not good for me and Ellie right now.'

'I understand,' Jack said. She felt relieved.

'Good. It's for the best, especially now this has happened.'

'You need a break. Take as long as you want, Kelly,' Jack said. 'A few weeks or so and you'll think differently. This has been a massive shock for both of us. Take a bit of time off and I'll be here waiting for you.'

'Take a bit of time off?' Kelly said, sighing. 'I'm not calling in sick at work, Jack. I don't want to take a bit of time off. I'm trying to tell you that we're finished. I don't want to be in a relationship with you anymore.'

'You feel like that now but give it a few weeks and you'll feel better.'

'I haven't got fucking measles,' Kelly said. She could feel her heart sinking. She didn't want to hurt him anymore than necessary but he wasn't getting the message. 'I don't want to fall out with you. Please remove all those pictures of me.'

'I will,' Jack said. 'I'll do it right now. Whatever you need to get over this.'

'Get over what?' Kelly asked. She was confused and felt her anger rising again. 'Look. Take the photos down. I'm going to block you because I don't want them to be able to find me through your profile and then I'm going to deactivate my account. Don't take it personally.'

'I'm not sure how else to take it,' Jack said. 'I don't see why you need to block me. That's way over the top. Everyone will think we're finished.'

'Oh my god,' Kelly mumbled. 'You're not listening to me.' She took a deep breath. 'I might have to go away for a while.'

'Where to?'

'It's best you don't know,' Kelly said. 'Bye, Jack. You take care of yourself.' Kelly hung up and cried as she blocked his number. He was sweet but just not the one. She shed a tear as she deleted the number that had messaged her the night before. Then she deactivated her Facebook, Twitter and Instagram accounts. To anyone searching for her online, she was invisible. That was a good start. She had to be proactive. Elle would need to do the same with her social media and that would cause eruptions and tantrums but they needed to vanish for a while. The newshounds wouldn't leave the Rhosneiger murders alone until they'd squeezed every last drop from it and that meant it would be in the spotlight for weeks. Killers in the spotlight are ten times more dangerous. A hundred times, probably a thousand times. The more focus there was, the more the public's expectations would grow for a result from the police investigation. The closer the police got to the truth, the more edgy the criminals would get. They would have to tie up all loose ends and Kelly was a loose end. She was an eyewitness and witnesses get criminals sent down. They wouldn't let her live. They couldn't let her live. Not if they wanted to remain at liberty. Threatening her into silence was one thing but could they be sure she wouldn't recant and tell the police what she'd seen? No. They could never be sure she wouldn't talk which meant they could never rest easy. Killing her would be simple and disposing of her a simple task. She didn't want to be thrown into the sea, weighted and bound, alive or dead. It was a horrible thought but her mind was racing at a million miles an hour. Her daughter, mother and father were her weak points. She would have to explain to them as a family what she'd seen and get them all somewhere safe. It was the only way to be sure. They could hide and wait it out until the police caught them and locked them up without her evidence, then things could go back to normal. That was the plan and it was the best she could hope for.

Chapter 25

Lottie and Liz waited in an interview room. They were numbed by the death of their friend, Mary. It had come as a massive shock. Mary had been like a sister to Lottie and the twins since the day they met. The twins had saved them from a life of sexual slavery. For Lottie and Mary, the traumatic nature of their meeting had bonded them to each other. Their whispered conversations through bamboo and rattan walls kept them going when desperation saturated their souls. Lottie couldn't imagine a time when Mary wouldn't be there.

Hearing the news of her demise on the breakfast news had been a devastating shock. The circumstances of her death were baffling. She could only imagine what had happened and the more she thought about it, the more distressing the situation became. Her relationship with Benaim had been taboo and nobody spoke about it. His presence had haunted the circus for years. It was only her loyalty to her father that stopped her finding another supplier. That and the prices he charged. If the truth be told, she knew he couldn't sell them diesel at those prices if it was sourced legitimately. The twins were certain he was buying red diesel tax free and filtering the colour dye from it chemically. Either that or he was stealing it by the tanker load. She knew he was trading on the wrong side of the tracks but ignored it, especially after she realised Mary had fallen in love with him. She couldn't do anything to hurt Mary.

After speaking to Liz about it, Lottie had called the police helpline and asked to speak to Alan Williams about the appeal for information. The telephone operator had put her on hold for a few minutes and then asked her to make her way to the station at Holyhead as soon as possible. It was simpler for her to talk directly to him, face to face. Lottie had told the twins where she was going and they reluctantly agreed it was for the best. Hugo was adamant he wanted to break into the Vincentia trailer and search it to see what they were doing but Lottie persuaded him to leave well alone as the men were being investigated by the police. If he broke into it, he would compromise any evidence they recovered. Whatever the Vincentia brothers were up to was nothing to do with the circus. She wanted them gone whether the police charged them or not. For Lottie, there was no smoke without fire and the police had one of them in custody. Enough said.

Alan walked into the room with three cups of coffee and a handful of sugar sachets, which he dropped on the table. He smiled and handed the drinks to them, keeping his, he put two sugars in it. The women didn't appear to be nervous, which was odd. Everyone is nervous when they first go into a police station. Even innocent people. Perhaps it was working in the performance industry, he thought. They spent their lives not looking nervous, no matter how big the crowd. He'd seen Lottie's performance as the ringmaster when the boys had watched the circus online. She was impressive. Stunningly attractive and impressive. She directed the show he'd watched with an intensity that was magnetising to the viewer but then that was all part of the show. While all eyes were focused on her when she spoke, something was happening out of sight behind the scenes. She was part of the illusions and they were jaw-dropping. The woman sitting opposite him now, appeared to be very ordinary in comparison to the domineering presence she portrayed in the circus.

'So, how did your first day in Holyhead go?' he asked. Stupid question, he thought as soon as he'd said it. He sipped his coffee and burnt his top lip, dribbling it back into the cup. 'Excuse me,' he said. 'That's way too hot.' The women laughed and Alan blushed. 'I'm clumsy, sorry.'

'We didn't get off the best start to be honest,' Lottie said. 'All that fuss with the local councillor was blown out of all proportion but obviously, you have to investigate these things if someone is in hospital,' Lottie added. 'How is councillor Orange?'

'He's out of the woods, I believe,' Alan said, cautiously. He didn't want to be distracted from the topic he was there to talk about. One incident couldn't become a smoke screen for another. 'I'm not aware of all the details about what happened. It will be a case of he said, she said but it does appear some of your entourage have been misbehaving elsewhere,' he added.

'They're nothing to do with me or the circus. The fact they travel alongside us is embarrassing. I'm so ashamed,' Lottie said. 'I'm so sorry to hear about that young woman. It's dreadful news. I am aware of the link to the fairground and obviously, I don't want the entire operation tarred with the same brush.' She paused for thought. 'To think anyone linked to our community could do anything like this is beyond belief. You're sure the Vincentia men were involved in drugging those poor women?'

'Positive,' Alan said, nodding.

'Obviously, we want to help you with your enquiries as much as we possibly can. If there's anything we can do, just ask.'

'Okay, thank you,' Alan said. 'First things first. Do you have any idea where David Prost has gone?'

'No,' Lottie said. 'He doesn't work for me directly. He wouldn't feel the need to let me know if he was leaving for a few days. As long as there is a mechanic available, they pretty much do as they please.' She shrugged.

'He hasn't gone on business for your vehicles?'

'No. Like I said, they don't report to us,' Lottie said. 'If they need a part or take a vehicle into a local town, they do it. They are nothing to do with our business.' Lottie felt she'd probably laboured the point. 'Have you found Carlos Vincentia?'

'No,' Alan said. 'Have you heard from him?'

'No,' Lottie said. She looked at Liz. 'I would be surprised if he even has my number. He's in charge of the workshop but I don't deal with him directly. The vehicle owners deal with them on an individual basis. They're an independent business.'

'Okay. I understand,' Alan said, blowing his coffee. 'Let's talk about what you came here for. Tell me how you know Mary Adams.'

'I met her abroad. She's worked for the circus since she was a teenager,' Lottie said. 'She's only a few years older than me. We met when we were backpacking in Sri Lanka twelve-years ago.' Lottie put sugar into her coffee. It was black as there was no oat milk available at the station. 'It's a long story but we were thrown together by chance. Do you need to know the story? Is that relevant?'

'I don't know yet but I'm listening,' Alan said. 'Tell me all about it. I need to know who she was to understand what happened to her.'

'Okay. I'll give you the short version. I was in Sri Lanka for two months, travelling around the coast alone and I rented a room at a beach bar in the south near Yala. It's very isolated, about as remote as it could be, which was part of the attraction,' Lottie explained. 'I was there for a week before I realised, I was in trouble. My passport went missing and then my wallet, cards and cash were stolen. I was stranded. It turned out the owner was a bad man called Nok. As well as running his bar, renting rooms and a small restaurant, he had another business. He was identifying vulnerable tourists who could go missing without any fuss. Lots of backpackers travel alone and some disappear without a trace. Of course, you will understand that some of those people wanted to disappear. They don't want to go back to their lives, so no one knows if they've fallen foul of men like Nok,' Lottie explained.

'I get that,' Alan said.

'Nok identified people who had been travelling a while and were not expected to be anywhere else anytime soon. People with no schedule or flights booked. If they went missing, no one would know. People trafficking in the south is rife, especially women,' she said, shaking her head. 'I was an experienced traveller but I didn't see that coming. He was so polite and friendly. Anyway, he locked me in my room and threatened to have me taken away by the traffickers unless I paid him the equivalent of twenty-thousand pounds. He was so blasé about it as if it was nothing. I didn't have twenty-thousand pounds and I had no idea what to do. As it turned out, Mary was in the next room being held against her will. He was planning to sell us both. We began talking through the wall and devised a plan. He let me contact my father on the internet, which took a while because they were travelling. I convinced him my father was wealthy but was a circus owner and only dealt in cash. The circus was near Amsterdam at the time. I promised Nok that the money for both of us would be brought to Sri Lanka by my family and transferred into an account of his choice at the end of the week, as long as we were unharmed.' She shook her head and sighed at the memory. 'Can I smoke?'

'No. I'm afraid not,' Alan said.

'Just thinking about it frightens the life out of me. We didn't believe he would let us go even if he got the money and we both knew the local police drank there for free. They weren't to be trusted. To cut a long story short, I made the call on the Tuesday and my brothers were there on the Thursday and we were released Thursday evening. Mary came back to the UK with us and she stayed. She's worked for us ever since. We've been like sisters since that ordeal.'

'I can imagine,' Alan said.

'Losing her like this is devastating.'

'That's a scary story,' Alan said. 'It's hard to imagine it goes on in this country too, isn't it?'

'It goes on everywhere,' Lottie said. 'At least six of our performers are waifs and strays we picked up along the way.'

'Picked up how?' Alan asked frowning.

'Girls in trouble,' Lottie said. 'Greta and Judy for instance. The two girls who work at the lost children's station were on the run from gangsters in Prague. They'd been tricked into prostitution by traffickers. They came to the fairground begging for a job and somewhere to hide. Mary used to do all the interviews for casual workers, wherever we arrived at. We took them in and hid them. They've been with us for two years now,' Lottie said. She sipped her coffee. 'Helga, our trapeze artist was given to a cattle trader in Bulgaria to settle a debt. She was six. My parents took her in and kept her safe.'

'Six years old?' Alan asked, shaking his head.

'Hard to believe someone could give their child away to pay for a cow but life is cheap there,' Lottie said. 'Mary was instrumental in picking up waifs and strays and our experience in Sri Lanka made it impossible not to help and take them in. I've lost count of the number of people the circus has saved. It's a good feeling to be able to help them.'

'I should imagine it is,' Alan said, impressed. A traveling community would be virtually invisible to normal society. Forever just passing through town after town unseen by most people. 'You say Mary has been with the circus for years.'

'Yes. Ever since we returned from Sri Lanka.'

'We have her passport at an address near Cork?' Alan said. 'She had it on her.'

'That was her mother's house. She died a few years back. Mary rented it out and kept her Irish passport.' Lottie explained. 'She flew to Malaga last week for a break. That's why she had it.'

'Did she go alone?'

'I don't think so but I can't be sure.'

'Best we stick to what we know is a fact,' Alan said. 'We can come back to that later. Do you know what she was doing in Rhosneiger yesterday?'

'We have a rough idea,' Lottie said. She looked at Liz and Liz squeezed her hand. 'Mary has been in a toxic on off relationship with a man called Benaim Bronski for years. None of us are exactly sure how long it has been going on as she kept it secret from us until recently.'

'Benaim Bronski,' Alan said, writing it down. 'You've mentioned his name to me before.'

'Yes,' Lottie said. 'He supplies us with fuel and employs the Vincentia brothers and David Prost. The mobile workshop belongs to him.'

'That's interesting,' Alan said, writing. 'So, Mary went to meet Benaim Bronski yesterday?'

'Yes, but we didn't know where she was meeting him or why,' Lottie said. 'She didn't come back to her trailer last night and we saw the news this morning.' Her eyes filled with tears. 'That's the first we knew of it.'

'What do you know about Benaim Bronski?' Alan asked. The women looked sheepish. 'Come on. He sells fuel to you but neither of you like him, that's obvious.'

'Is it that obvious?' Lottie asked.

'Yes. Don't ever play poker. So, what does he do that you don't like?' Alan asked.

'There are always rumours about what he does outside of the fuel business,' Lottie said.

'What are the rumours?'

'We think he might be involved in smuggling, using his tankers,' Liz said, interrupting. Lottie looked taken aback. Alan caught her expression. Liz had crossed a line she didn't want to cross. It was too late now; the door had been opened.

'Smuggling?' Alan asked, looking at them both.

'Yes. We think so.' Liz paused.

'You think so?' Alan asked, smiling.

'We're quite sure,' Liz said. She looked at Lottie and frowned. 'In fact, we know he's involved in smuggling with his tankers.' Lottie shook her head, wide-eyed. 'Don't be angry with me. I'm sick to the back teeth of lying.'

'Under the circumstances, it would be prudent to put your cards on the table and tell me the truth,' Alan said. 'Your friend is dead and you might be able to point me in the direction of the killer.' Lottie nodded to Liz to carry on. 'How can you be sure he's smuggling?'

'Mary told me, Bronski persuaded her to smuggle five Africans across the channel from France when we crossed in September,' she said. Lottie looked shocked.

'I didn't know that at the time,' Lottie said. She threw Liz a withering glance.

'When did you become aware of it?' Alan asked, slightly amused by Liz's frankness.

'This morning,' Lottie said. 'Liz and Mary thought it best to keep it from me.' She smirked at Liz. 'Didn't you, sneaky buggers, you are.'

'I told her when we heard the news about Mary,' Liz said. 'Benaim is a bully. I think she would have done it thinking she was helping the people he was smuggling and keeping him happy at the same time. I'm certain he persuaded Mary to put people in her caravan. That means the Vincentia brothers smuggled people too.'

'Did she agree to do it?' Alan asked.

'Yes. She felt sorry for them. She told me, all they wanted was the chance of a life better than the one they left and Mary thought she was helping.' Liz started crying. 'The women she hid had been in one of the camps near Calais for months. They had absolutely nothing. The women were prostituting themselves for food and blankets. Bronski played on her heart strings. He knew she couldn't say no.'

'Under the circumstances, it would be difficult for her to say no,' Alan said. 'Because of your experience in Sri Lanka.'

'The thing is, Bronski was getting paid, thousands I heard. He would contact families to collect payment. They fell out about it. Mary was furious,' Liz said, angrily. 'Mary wouldn't have taken a penny. I know she wouldn't.'

'Can I just add that we didn't know anything about this until after the event,' Lottie said, looking at Liz as if she wanted to slap her. She smiled and shook her head. 'If I had known, I would have been very annoyed. Mary is her own person and what she does in her own trailer is up to her. She's a grown

184

woman. Even if I don't approve of her choice in men. I couldn't have stopped her. Each owner is responsible for their own vehicles and trailers and what's in them when we cross borders. I don't have eyes in the back of my head.'

'I get that,' Alan said. 'How did she smuggle five Africans in her trailer?' he asked, frowning.

'What do you mean?'

'Each vehicle is checked at the port,' Alan said. 'They weren't sitting in the living room watching the television.'

'Oh, I see. The Vincentia brothers adapted her trailer,' Liz said. Lottie rolled her eyes skyward.

'How do you know that?' Lottie asked.

'She told me not to tell you,' Liz said. 'She knew you would be mad with her.' She shrugged and held Lottie's hand. 'They did something to her bedroom so that people could be under the bed but the heat sensors can't detect them. She told me they altered it somehow. I didn't see it because I didn't want to know all the details but that's what they did.' Liz shrugged. Lottie smiled. 'There. I feel better now. I've been telling her for years to leave him alone. He's bad news, always has been. I wouldn't leave him to look after my parrot. He'd sell it or eat it. Bastard.' Alan remained quiet. 'How did she die?'

'She fell from a balcony,' Alan said.

'Fell or was pushed?' Lottie asked.

'There was an altercation,' Alan said. 'We think she was trying to get away from someone when she fell.'

'Oh god. She hated heights,' Liz said.

'I don't think she had much time to think about it,' Alan said.

'That's a good thing, I suppose,' Liz sniffled.

'She died instantly when her head hit the concrete,' Alan said, sipping his coffee. Another stupid thing to say, he thought. Liz sobbed harder. He'd

185

thought telling her would help deal with the situation. Clearly too much detail. 'Do you have a picture of him?'

Lottie searched her phone and found an image of him. Benaim Bronski had been burned. He was scarred on his neck and one side of his face. His hair was missing in places.

'He had an accident when he was delivering fuel many years ago,' Lottie said. Alan noticed a tick in her eyes when she lied. Why she would lie about Bronski's scars was a mystery. That question could wait until another time.

'Where will we find Benaim Bronski?' Alan asked Lottie.

'I've got his mobile number but he hasn't been answering it,' Lottie said.

'But it is on and it's ringing?'

'Yes.'

'That's all we need to track him.' Alan stood up. 'This information hasn't been released yet but there were nine Syrian women in the house where Mary Adams died. They were waiting for passage to Ireland.' Alan looked out of the window, thinking about what he'd learned. 'Now I have spoken to you, I think Mr Bronski may have been trying to persuade Mary to smuggle some of them over to Ireland with the circus. Obviously, she said no this time,' he said. 'It would explain the altercation. We'll need a full statement but there's no rush. I'll have a detective call at your trailer later on today.'

'As long as it's before six-thirty,' Lottie said. 'The show tonight is sold out.'

'The show must go on, eh?' Alan said.

'Absolutely.'

'I'll say goodbye for now,' Alan said, standing up. The women stood and picked up their bags, keys and coats. They headed for the door. 'Thanks for coming in.'

'No problem,' Lottie said.

'What was the name of the bar in Sri Lank?' Alan asked. Lottie looked stunned. 'Where you were held captive,' he added.

'Forgotten Beach,' Lottie said. He could see the wheels turning in her mind. 'Why?'

'I'll drop a line to Interpol. If there are traffickers still working in the area, they should know about it,' Alan said. 'It might stop it happening to other lone travellers. It certainly doesn't hurt to flag these things up.'

'It was a long time ago,' Lottie said.

'Some people never learn, especially criminals,' Alan said. 'This man Nok could be back out on the streets by now, doing the same thing again. It can't hurt to have the place checked out by the locals.'

'No. Of course not,' Lottie said. She smiled and walked out of the room. What had happened to their captor, Nok was something they never spoke about but his end was swift and brutal. The twins arrived at the bar and broke him and several of his henchmen. Their bodies were dismembered in his own kitchen and scattered into the sea from his own boat.

Chapter 26

Alan and Kim were holding an update briefing for the team. There were sixty detectives working across the cases, drafted in from Caernarfon and St Asaph. The initial confusion about the Rhosneiger incident was becoming clearer. Carlton Barrymore from the National Crime Agency had joined them to offer advice. The NCA were keen to be involved in anything to do with trafficking. It was their current hot potato. Over the last eighteen months, their interest in Benaim Bronski had become more intense, only trumped by their interest in Dr Gerard Telford and his wife Elisha. DCI Barrymore and his colleagues were not surprised the Telfords had wound up dead. They were swimming out of their depth. The fact they were intrinsically linked to Bronski had made the trip to North Wales worthwhile. Detective Chief Inspector Carlton Barrymore was a black officer from the West End of London. His mind was as sharp as his suits and his positive attitude was refreshing. He had high cheekbones, wide shoulders and pockmarked skin. His cockney accent was a dead giveaway as to where he grew up. Alan liked him immediately. Once the final few detectives had shuffled into the room, Alan called the gathering to order.

'We need to rattle through a lot this morning, so let's get on with it,' Alan said. 'It's important you take away what is relevant to your piece of the investigation but don't lose sight of the bigger picture. This is a complex operation as it stands and I would gauge it's going to take a few more twists and turns before we know exactly what we're looking at and who we're looking for.' He turned towards the Anglesey detectives. 'Locally, the investigation into the murder of Michelle Branning is the focus for teams A and B. Any interaction with the press goes through me and me only,' he said. The detectives nodded they understood. 'One wrong word to the local press and the town could react against the travellers. We need to play down their involvement in public. The involvement of David Prost and the Vincentia brothers means it's running parallel to the Rhosneiger investigation, linked because they work for our prime suspect, Benaim Bronski.' The detectives in the room were focused on images of the suspects on digital screens. 'Carlos Vincentia, Claus Vincentia and David Prost are German nationals with clean records. Europol are digging for us. There may be charges pending in Germany relevant to our investigation. They operate a vehicle mechanic service to the fairground and its community, which means they travel with it. It appears they've been involved in smuggling migrants in their trailer across the channel at the bequest of Bronski and they may have been about to transport the Syrian women found in Rhosneiger.' Alan pointed to their images. 'These three men are our favourites for taking Michelle Branning simply because we know they drugged Tiffany and Michelle.' He shrugged. 'That is a fact and we have it happening on CCTV. Tiffany felt the effects almost immediately, because she'd consumed more alcohol. Michelle didn't drink any shots and so the drug took longer to take effect on her.' Alan emphasised the point. 'We have them on CCTV putting white powder in the Branning sister's drinks. Fact. Is this the first time they have used Flunitrazepam to drug women for sex?' Alan scanned the faces in the room. The shaking heads and murmurs indicated everyone was of the same opinion. 'This is not their first foray to trap females. I'll put money on it.' Alan turned to Richard Lewis and his team. 'Richard, I want you to track where the circus has been for the last eighteen months. See if there are any similar cases reported. We're looking for women who think they may have been drugged and assaulted. There will be more of them out there, guaranteed.'

'We'll get on it,' Richard said. Their dates and venues will be on the internet.'

'We have Claus but we need to find these two,' Alan said, showing the images of Prost and Carlos. Kim took over.

'We interviewed Claus this morning and charged him with administering drugs for sex after he was advised to make a no comment interview by his awfully expensive brief,' Kim said. 'Henry Graff works for Graff, Gladstone and Brookes based in Chester. Some of you will have dealt with them before. They are the big guns for organised crime families in Liverpool and Manchester, Chester and Wirral. The Vincentia brothers couldn't afford to hire that company but their employer, Benaim Bronski can. If he's prepared to fork out that kind of money to defend them, then there's a good reason why. He wants them out of the cells ASAP. Whatever Bronski is up to, these three men are involved and he needs to guarantee their silence.' The images of their pitch at the fairground appeared. 'They have a trailer, which they share and a mobile workshop and are continually on the move. It's the perfect cover for moving people and contraband.'

An image of Benaim Bronski appeared on the screens. He was handsome in a rugged way, even with the burns. His left cheek and ear were scarred, the hair missing. His physique had been built by manual work and pumping iron for many years. The image of Mary Adams appeared. It was obviously a passport photograph.

'Benaim Bronski has been in a relationship with this woman, Mary Adams who died at this house in Rhosneiger. She has worked for the circus for over twelve years. We know Bronski persuaded Mary Adams to have her trailer adapted to accommodate five African nationals on the crossing from Calais to Dover.' Alan pointed back to the Vincentia brothers. 'Carlos and Claus made the alterations to her trailer. The going rate for transport across the channel in a vehicle is twenty-grand. Obviously, it's cheaper to cross by dingy but the odds of surviving are less. We're quite sure the Vincentia vehicles smuggled more too.' Alan waited for the images to change. 'So, we know Bronski moves people and we know he's been in a relationship with Mary Adams, who died in this house in Rhosneiger. The house belongs to a limited company owned by Doctor Gerard Telford and his wife Elisha. They were found dead along with Elisha's parents, George and Mildred Troutman in the cellar.' He looked towards Carlton Barrymore. 'Chief Inspector Barrymore from the NCA is going to brief us on the Telfords.'

'Doctor Telford appeared on our radar about five years ago when he began buying up properties around the West End. Mostly old pubs and big retail units that had gone out of business and been empty for over two years. If a property is empty for a certain length of time, there's no need to apply for planning permission for change of use. The period varies from borough to borough but Telford appeared to be doing his research cleverly,' Carlton began. 'At face value, it sounds like a wealthy man trying to make his money work for him but he bought fifteen properties over eighteen months, which in the West

End is some going. They were converted into flats, high end quality properties with top of the range appliances, fixtures and fittings and they were all flipped within six months, bought by one of three companies registered in Dubai. We all know doctors working in the private sector can earn a lot of money but this type of development costs millions for each site.' Images of the flats appeared. They were impressive buildings. 'He couldn't cashflow this type of development, so we wanted to know where the money was coming from. The money went into businesses in Dubai, Ukraine and Moscow and never came back, which means the Inland Revenue never got their sticky mitts on any of it.' A ripple of amusement ran through the room. 'Something fishy was going on so, we began surveillance of all their activities. The good doctors bought a number of rundown retail units in Dubai and renovated them. The units were rented out to legitimate businesses selling prestige cars on the ground floor and they built surgeries above them. They had four surgeries up and running and another two under construction. The entire Dubai business was simply the machine to wash millions of pounds of serious organised crime money for a Russian cartel run by Hector Karpov.' Carlton let the information sink in. The image of the house on the Rhosneiger beachfront appeared. 'What were they doing on Anglesey, I hear you ask. Gerard Telford was a clever man. He knew that once the machine was in motion and the money was being laundered, they would become superfluous to requirements. He didn't want to be a long-term asset for the Karpovs. Elisha Telford was never comfortable with their association with them. They developed an exit strategy and bought this house, another in Bari, Italy and a villa in Naples, Florida. He bought them to hide his own money from the Inland Revenue and to make them difficult to find when they retired. They had this bolthole renovated for when they broke away from the operation.' He pointed to the house. 'A lovely spot and beautifully renovated. It was also fitted with a secure room where contraband could be stored while passage from Holyhead to Dublin could be secured. It was a perfect plan except the Karpovs wouldn't accept his retirement notice. No one walks away knowing what the Telfords knew. Doctor Telford began squirreling money away, ready to leave but he'd massively underestimated the Russian machine. They realised what was going on and threatened Elisha's parents. The Telfords panicked and ran here to try and hide them from harm but there's no hiding from this type of operation.' He changed the image. Benaim Bronski appeared. 'Bronski is a Russian national. He's been feeding on the scraps of the Karpov empire for decades, moving product and people for them. He's a bottom feeder but a wealthy one. In turn for what he does for them, they supply him with fuel at a massive discount. The businesses fit hand in glove until Brexit happened. Brexit changed everything at Holyhead. Everyone was so focused on there not being a hard border on Ireland that they failed to realise that the border would be the Irish Sea itself and Holyhead would become the checkpoint Charlie between the UK and the EU. Everything is being searched, checked, probed and measured. Bronski had a shipment of people to move to Ireland who had paid half their fare upfront to the Karpovs. The other half would only be paid when they reached their destination and that was Bronski's share and he wanted his money. He had to come up with a plan-B but the Telfords turned up with their relatives before the women were shipped from Calais. Whatever happened, there must have been a dispute, which ended in the Telfords and their relations being restrained in the cellar.'

'We know Mildred Troutman had a heart attack during all this, hence she wasn't tied up,' Alan added. 'The others were put into the cellar.'

He switched the image to an arrest record and custody suite photograph of Bronski.

'This is where the Telford's charmed life ran out.' Carlton pointed to the screen. 'We arrested Bronski two weeks ago on conspiracy charges and held him on remand. He was granted bail three days ago when one of the key witnesses was found dead in the Thames.' A murmur ran around the room. 'Bronski was in jail and there was no one to give the Telfords food or water. Which explains why they were emaciated when you found them in their cellar.' Carlton looked around the gathering. 'Bronski was in jail and left them there to starve to death. He was trying to tidy up at the house when Mary Adams fell through the window. That wasn't part of the plan and it scuppered his. If things had gone to plan, the Syrian women would have been in the fairground trailers on Friday sailing to Ireland and he would have disposed of the Telford family's bodies and no one would be any the wiser. The Telfords were transient and had no children to worry about them. No one would have noticed they were dead for a very long time,' Carlton looked around the room. 'Are there any questions?'

'Why take the women to Rhosneiger?' a detective asked. 'Why not just take them on the ferry as foot passengers?'

'That would involve letting them go and they owed ten-grand each,' Carlton said. 'This wasn't Thomas Cook arranging their journey, they're people traffickers. They would never have let them go. Not even when they paid what they owed. Those women were destined for a life in slavery in some shape or another. There was no happy ending waiting for them in Ireland. There never is a happy ending with these people.' Carlton nodded to Alan that he was finished.

'Thank you, Chief Inspector,' Alan said. 'Benaim Bronski is our number one focus. He is the linchpin in all this,' Alan said. 'We have a warrant for the Vincentia trailer and the workshop and we can crosscheck what Pamela Stone has recovered from the boat. She has fibres, DNA and footprints. Whoever took Michelle Branning to that boat and raped her was in a hurry because they left a lot of clues behind. They never went back to tidy up.'

'Do you think they were disturbed?' someone asked.

'Yes. Probably, although the boatyard is closed on a Sunday,' Alan said. 'Michelle Branning had water in her lungs. She drowned.' The expressions on the faces of the detectives in the room said exactly was he was thinking. 'She was still breathing when he put her in the water.' He paused. 'In the meantime, I want to eliminate everyone else. What was the name of the man who helped Tiffany look for Michelle?'

'Wayne Best,' Kim said. 'We know he dated Michelle for a few months about a year ago but she finished with him when she caught him cheating. He could be deemed as a suspect. Best to make sure one way or the other.'

'We have a statement from him but I want him interviewed, swabbed and removed from the picture,' Alan said. 'We know what we need to do. Let's get to it. Find David Prost, Benaim Bronski and Carlos Vincentia.'

Chapter 27

Len Jobson swallowed three pain killers and brushed his teeth. He felt better than he had for a long time. It was all about focus. Instead of focusing on what had happened to Leo and Katrin, he could focus on "who" had happened to them. After a phone call to a cop on the Quinn's books, he found out Tarek Koresh had a criminal record. Assault, rape, sexual assault, grievous bodily harm with intent, robbery, going equipped to burgle and conspiracy to supply. He was a busy man when he wasn't moving his ghost train around from fairground to fairground. The ghost train was used predominantly as a cover for ferrying class A's for an outfit linked to Manchester, Blackburn and Leeds. It hadn't taken long to get his details from another cop on the Quinn's payroll. He had his home and business address, mobile number, vehicle registration plate and tax details. The police were watching him for the purpose of gathering information on his employers. Len had everything he needed except permission. He needed permission to act against anyone in the business as they may be associates of the Quinns; he also needed permission to act alone.

Dale Quinn called the shots and he said Len could do whatever needed to be done with impunity. The Quinn organisation would lend him as much help as he needed to find the man who killed his son. Len had been honest that the Koresh family could be implicated and Dale had told him they were a spent force, running from the shadows of their past. Their violent reign in London was over and had generated many dangerous enemies and they were too few, too poor and too weak to fight them. Most of the London based family had gone back to Albania to avoid being chopped up and fed to the pigs. Only a few kept the family name and they were all in the relative safety of the north. London was off limits. Most had changed their names for fear of reprisals for their ruthless past but Tarek and his son, Samiri had kept it. They liked the sway it gave them with wannabies in the north. The reputation of the Green Lane gang still lived in the annals of gangster history. The true players knew the family was done but they didn't deal with true players. They dealt with minnows and those on the periphery of the drugs industry and the weak, where they could toss a name in to create fear. Fear was good for business. Len was going to show them they didn't know what fear was. It was something they were about to learn the hard way.

Len was waiting for a call from Reggie Quinn, a man he'd known as long as he could remember. They had worked with each other for decades with complete trust and total respect for each other. Len Jobson proved he was lethal, discreet and could be trusted. When the Quinns had a problem that needed to be resolved, Len sorted it with the minimum of fuss. Some problems needed to vanish, some needed to be left in a very public place as a message to others. Whatever was required, Len was the final solution. The Quinns had clean hands yet were responsible for dozens of killings. Len loved Reggie like a brother and the feeling was mutual. Reggie was the oracle of the family. If they needed to know where someone was, Reggie could find out. His contacts reached far and wide and deep into police forces all over the country. He had intelligence providers in most of their rival operations. If Reggie wanted to find someone, it didn't take long. Len felt his mobile vibrate. The number was withheld. He answered it.

'Len, Reggie speaking. How's it going?'

'As well as can be expected,' Len said. 'I'm taking each day as a bonus.'

'Good man. Did you get the case of scotch I sent to you?'

'I did,' Len said. 'Very nice it is too. I was going to save it for a rainy day but they're all rainy days from here on in so I'm halfway through the case.'

'Good for you,' Reggie said. His tone changed. 'About that bit of business, we were talking about. A little birdie has told me what you're looking for is in Chester tonight, down by the racecourse on the other side of the bridge.'

'Down by the castle?'

'That's the place. There's a coach park there near the river, which is used for events.'

'I know it,' Len said.

'You should do. It's next to the Crown Court,' Reggie chuckled. 'We've been in there few times over the years, haven't we?'

'Too many times,' Len laughed. 'Do you remember that paedo we lifted from the racecourse?'

'How could I forget him. He thought he'd got away with it because they found him not guilty,' Reggie said, laughing. 'Horrible bastard. I'll never forget his face when he saw the wood shredder and realised what was going to happen. Pissed his pants on the spot. Horrible bastard.' He stopped to think. 'We've had some good times, Len,' he added. 'You go and do what you need to do to make amends for your boy and make sure you fucking hurt him, Len.'

'Oh, I will, Reggie,' Len said, smiling at the thought. 'Does Tarek work the ride anymore?'

'No. His boy Samiri works it,' Reggie said. 'He's a wrong one too. If you get the chance to gut the pair of them, take it. You'll be doing the world a favour.' Reggie went quiet for a second. 'Listen to me, Len. Are you going after Koresh because you know the name and have history with the family or because you know he's responsible?'

'I'm following the police and they don't know their arse from their elbows. It's a hunch,' Len said. 'My boy and his girlfriend were found in a grease drum. The type of grease that would be used on wagons and fairground rides. The woman who runs the circus told the police they didn't use that brand of lubricant.'

'Meaning what?' Reggie asked. 'You've lost me.'

'Koresh was an independent trader and would have purchased his own grease. He owned the ghost train independently of the circus, so it fits.'

'I see where you're coming from but it's a stretch, Len.'

'Koresh and his sons are sex pests,' Len said. 'Tarek has got form for it. My boy and his missus were last seen at that fair and she was found with no clothes on. Leo was tied up and had a broken arm but wasn't badly hurt, which worries me.'

'Why?'

'I was convinced he'd been taken because he was my son but now, I'm not so sure. If they wanted to hurt me, they would have tortured him and dumped him somewhere where he would have been found, so that I would know exactly why he was killed,' Len explained. 'They hid his body. If it wasn't for the supermarket project, he would never have been found. I don't think it was another outfit squaring things up. This is something different. I can feel it in my bones.'

'I get you,' Reggie said. 'I can see where you're coming from.'

'Finding their bodies, the way they did tells me it's more likely whoever killed them was after Katrina and Leo was in the way. I think the attack was sexually motivated.'

'The way I see it, you have two choices,' Reggie said. 'It was business related or it was perverts.'

'Exactly. Either way, Tarek and his offspring fit the bill.'

'I see what you mean.'

'I'm going to ask them the question. I'll know when I look in their eyes if they had anything to do with it. If they do know anything, they'll tell me.'

'Of that, I'm completely sure they will,' Reggie said. 'Good luck my old friend. Happy hunting. Let me know if you need anything else.'

'I will do. You take care of yourself, Reggie,' Len said. 'Make sure you give your grandkids a massive hug every time you see them. Don't take any of them for granted.'

'Oh, I won't. You go and do what you need to do, Len. All the very best.' He hung up and smiled. He felt good about his mission. If it was to be his last, so be it.

It was after eight o'clock when Malcolm Orange arrived home. Jane was on tenterhooks listening to him. He spent an hour in the window ranting about the effing circus. She couldn't tell him about her visitor. He would implode if he knew what had happened and he would make things worse. The bump on the head had done nothing to quell his notion of self-importance and superiority. She wished there was an off switch somewhere. They ate a meal in awkward silence. Malcolm was angry that she'd demanded he drop his accusation of assault. He point-blank refused. Jane cleared the plates and washed the dishes and poured herself a large brandy. When she went into the living room to ask Malcolm if he would like one, he was gone. His coat wasn't on the hook where it always was. Jane was terrified that the bloody fool had gone to the fairground to cause trouble. She knew her husband well. That's where he had gone. She paced the room and gulped her brandy for what felt like an hour. Fifteen minutes later, he walked back through the front door.

'I've told her exactly what I think of her,' Malcolm said.

'Please don't tell me you've been to the fair making a bloody fool of yourself again,' Jane said. 'After everything I've said to you.'

'I'm not going to sit here and do nothing, and I'm disappointed you are prepared to let these pikeys get away with it,' he said, taking off his coat. 'I went straight to the boss, Lottie Edwards and I told her she's in charge of a bunch of thugs. That's what they are, thugs.'

'And what did she say?'

'She told me to fuck off,' Malcolm said, offended. 'I can't bear women who swear like that. It's not big or clever and it's certainly not attractive.'

'Oh, shut up, Malcolm.'

'I beg your pardon?'

'I said shut up!' Jane said. 'I'm sick of listening to you drone on about what you think about this and what you think about that. I couldn't give a shit what you think anymore. You're a boring, irritating big bag of piss and wind and everybody thinks the same,' Jane said. 'That woman is trying to run a business and I bet she has to put up with wankers like you everywhere they go.'

'Jane Orange,' Malcolm said, astounded. 'I don't think I've ever heard anything so vile come out of your mouth. What on earth is wrong with you?'

'You!' Jane snapped. 'You are what's wrong with me.' She stormed upstairs. 'And don't even think about coming into this bedroom tonight or any night until you can stop being a wanker and be effing normal for once.' The bedroom door slammed.

'Typical woman,' Malcolm muttered. 'They have to overreact to everything. Boring, irritating bag of piss and wind?' he said, to himself, shaking his head. 'The poor woman has lost her marbles.'

Malcolm made a hot milk and added a little scotch. It would help him to sleep. He turned out the light and headed for the hallway. A knock on the window made him turn around.

Tap, tap, tap.

Malcolm opened the blind and looked into the back garden. He couldn't see anything but his reflection.

Tap, tap, tap.

On the back door. Malcolm put down his mug and stormed over to the door. He picked up a steel ladle and opened the door. The cold night air and sound of the fairground rushed in. He looked outside but couldn't see anyone there. A balloon was attached to a piece of string on the lawn. It was weighted down by something. He walked over to it, angry but baffled.

'Bloody pikey kids messing about, playing knock and run,' he muttered. 'They can't control their dogs or their kids, no wonder they can't control their employees.' He bent down to inspect the balloon. It was weighted by something. He patted his pocket for his glasses case but it wasn't there. Reaching down to the grass, he picked up the balloon and what was attached to it and carried it into the kitchen where he could see it in the light. 'How the hell did that get there?'

His glasses case was tied to the string. He opened it. His spectacles were twisted and flat, the lenses shattered. He was confused. How did they get his glasses? He thought.

Tap, tap, tap.

On the window. He looked up into the face of a clown. It grinned and waved. Malcolm slammed the back door closed and shut the blind. He stood waiting for something to happen but nothing did. Malcolm put the whisky bottle in his pocket, went upstairs and picked up the landline. The phone was dead. He wondered if it was a coincidence. How did they get his glasses? He peered between the curtains and looked out of the window. There was no sign of the clown. Had there been one there at all? His head ached; the pain reminded him of what he had endured in the pursuit of a trading licence. Jane was probably right. Maybe he should stop being such a wanker. There was a feeling of dread in his guts. He added more scotch into his milk and went to bed.

Chapter 28

Carlos waited and listened. He could hear shuffling inside the kitchen, then the clicking sound of the walking frame against tile. A shadow appeared at the back door. And he could see the hunched figure of an elderly female. The lock rattled as a key was turned and the handle twisted. It seemed like an age before the door opened. A confused looking lady with white hair and a jaundiced complexion blinked against the daylight. She smiled, her teeth slipping from her gums slightly.

'Hello lovely,' she said, looking at the spade. 'Have you come to do the garden?'

'I have but I could murder a cup of tea and I'm desperate for the loo,' Carlos said. 'Do you mind if I use your bathroom?'

'Of course, you can,' she said, stepping back to let him in. 'Harold said you would be here this week if the weather was alright. I wasn't sure when you would turn up. The frost has killed most of the bedding plants and the roses all need cutting back.'

'Don't you worry,' Carlos said. 'I'll get all that done and I've noticed the borders need a tidy up.'

'Oh yes. Ted used to do the garden but he died of covid-19 last year and it's too much for me.'

'I'm sorry to hear about that,' Carlos said. He walked into the kitchen and looked around. A single egg cup, mug and plate were soaking in the sink. She'd had breakfast alone. 'Where is the bathroom?'

'Up the stairs to the right,' she said. 'I'm Martha,' she added as Carlos went into the hallway. 'What's your name?'

'Gus,' he lied. He glanced in at the living room. Very tidy and very empty. The television was on but there was no volume.

'Do you take sugar in your tea?' she called after him.

'Two please, Martha,' he said, climbing the stairs. The bedroom doors were open and he checked each one quickly. There was no sign of anyone else living there. He used the bathroom and sighed with relief. There were two toothbrushes in a glass, one blue, one pink. She kept his toothbrush, he thought. Sentimental value. Grief and letting go can be powerful emotions. The poor old dear. He washed his face and patted it dry with a clean towel. That cleared the cobwebs from his mind. He felt a bit more human. A drink and something to eat would bring him back to full power.

'Have you had any breakfast?' Martha asked. 'I can do you a bacon buttie if you like?'

'That would be great, Martha,' Carlos said, coming down the stairs. 'It's truly kind of you. My mother's name was Martha, you know,' he said smiling.

'Was it really?' Martha asked. 'Where is your mother?'

'Germany,' Carlos said. 'She was a doctor. Retired now.'

'I thought you weren't from around here,' Martha said, putting some bacon into a small frying pan. 'I could tell by your accent. I thought to myself, he's not from around here. What brings you to Anglesey?'

'My wife is from here. I met the love of my life at University,' Carlos said. 'Alison Jones. She's a vet.'

'Is she a local girl?' Martha asked, sliding bread into the toaster.

'Oh, yes. Holyhead born and bred. All her family are from here going back generations. They used to run the Vic pub many years ago.'

'Oh lovely,' Martha said. She passed him a mug of tea. The smell of bacon and toasted bread filled the air. 'Here you are. That will warm you up. How do you know Harold?'

'He's a friend of a friend,' Carlos said, slurping his tea. It soothed his parched throat. He looked at all the plug sockets above the worktops. 'Do you use a mobile phone?'

202

'Pardon?' Martha looked confused. 'Harold said you worked with him.'

'Yes. But we were introduced by a friend,' Carlos said. 'Do you use a mobile phone?'

'Yes. But I can't get used to it,' Martha said, buttering the toast. She took the bacon from the frying pan and placed it on the toast. 'Do you want brown sauce?'

'Do you have any red?'

'Red sauce on a bacon sandwich?' Martha frowned. 'Maybe that's what you have in Germany. I only have brown.'

'Brown is fine,' Carlos said. 'What type of phone do you have?'

'Sampson,' Martha said.

'Samsung,' Carlos said, chuckling. 'Can I borrow your charger please?'

'Yes.' Martha put the sandwich on a plate and put it on the kitchen table. 'It's in the living room plugged in next to my chair,' she said. Carlos walked out of the kitchen and into the living room. It was decorated in the eighties and had remained there, trapped in a time warp. The carpet was a floral nightmare which boggled the senses. The television was on. Martha must have been watching it when he knocked on the back door. She'd muted the volume. Carlos looked at the headlines on the screen. A reporter was standing on the Newry Beach, the fairground in the background. The circus tent and Ferris wheel dominated the picture. He read the headline and his guts twisted. 'Take a seat in there and I'll bring this into you and fill up your tea.'

'Thanks,' Carlos said. He plugged his phone in and the charger icon appeared. 'Do you mind if I turn the volume up?'

'Not at all,' Martha said from behind him. She handed him the plate. 'This is terrible news,' she said. Carlos turned the volume up. The reporter was talking about the rape and murder of Michelle Branning. He felt sick but bit into the bacon buttie anyway. The taste was amazing. His senses reeled as he swallowed the first mouthful of food, he'd eaten for over twenty-four hours.

Raped and murdered. Raped and murdered. Murdered, echoed through his mind. 'She was a lovely looking girl, so petite. Like a little angel she was. I heard a woman earlier saying they used to call her Tinkershell like the fairy because she was so tiny. What a crying shame.' Carlos finished the sandwich in minutes. He swigged the fresh cup of tea and reassessed his situation. The girl was dead. That was not the best news by a long chalk. His head was spinning with the news. Michelle Branning had been murdered. This had turned into a nightmare. The police would assume he was responsible and they would be hunting high and low for him and they would be pointing the finger of guilt at him. 'They say they're looking for a man who is associated with the fair but isn't employed by them,' Martha said, parroting the news reel. 'What does that mean?'

'I don't know, Martha,' Carlos muttered, glued to the screen.

'Either he works on the fair or he doesn't. They're always bad news these travelling types. Trouble always follows them and the crime rate goes up wherever they are and comes back down when they've gone. That can't be a coincidence, can it?' Martha said, nodding wisely.

Martha stopped talking and stared at the television. Carlos inhaled deeply as a photograph of his face appeared on the screen. Wanted, Carlos Vincentia. Martha covered her mouth with her hand, shocked. She sat in her armchair and looked at Carlos. Carlos shook his head and frowned.

'That's you, isn't it?' she asked.

'Yes,' he said. 'I'm afraid it is.'

Chapter 29

Benaim Bronski was sitting in his truck wondering how so many things could go so wrong, so quickly. A long conversation with a representative from high up in the Karpov business had told him to clean house or be cleaned. The police would have connected him to Mary Adams by now. There was no doubt about that. The stupid bitch had completely flipped out when she realised what he was up to. The women he wanted her to hide in her trailer, were downstairs in the cellar. It clicked that they were being held captive, trafficked not rescued. It was like flicking a switch. One minute she was cautiously compliant, the next she was threatening to call the police. That was the one thing he couldn't allow to happen, so he'd grabbed her to calm her down and she banged her head on the wall. That was that. She became hysterical, banging on the patio doors and the people on the beach saw her. Stupid bitch. He'd pulled her back but she punched him in the balls, so he pushed her but underestimated his own strength. She smashed through the glass as if it wasn't there and tumbled over the balcony. That was the beginning of the end. Everything was starting to unravel.

He had to irradicate anything that connected him to her death in that house. The Telfords were gone, silenced forever. The greedy bastards. They wanted it all their own way and tried to take their ball home before the game was over. That's not how the game was played. He hadn't meant for them to die like that but he couldn't change it now. He didn't know he was about to be arrested and remanded in custody. That was unfortunate for them. Not that he would lose any sleep over them. They had a good run for a while and all good things come to an end at some point. There was no hard evidence against him apart from the Holyhead woman. She was an eyewitness, who could place him leaving the scene of the crime. Kelly Williams and her boyfriend Jack Henderson would have to be silenced permanently. He wasn't sure if the boyfriend had seen him but he had to assume he had or that she would have described him. His burns were too distinctive to ignore. They were unique. She was sent a message and hadn't said anything to the police yet and he needed to keep it that way. It was only a matter of time. Everything else would hinge on what they found on the Vincentia brothers and what they coughed up in interview. The fucking idiots. He couldn't believe he could be brought down because they were drugging women for a shag. If he went down, the Karpovs would have to take him out or risk him squealing for a lighter sentence. Everyone was out for themselves if the truth be told. Honour amongst thieves was bollocks. There was no honour to be had from this, only survival. Survival of the fittest or the dirtiest as the case may be. It was time to be as dirty as possible to survive.

He saw a vehicle across the motorway. A pickup pulled onto the site and flashed its headlights three times. He flashed his in reply. David Prost got out of his pickup and walked towards the bridge from his side of the expressway. Benaim climbed out of his truck and walked to the bridge from his side. They met in the middle. Four lanes of traffic roared beneath them. David looked nervous and frightened. Benaim reckoned he was lost without the brothers to guide him. He was always one step behind them, lurking in their shadows.

'You look like you're going to cry,' Ben said, shaking his head. 'You're not going to cry, are you?'

'No,' David said.

'Why the sad face?'

'I feel guilty for running away but I didn't know what else to do. The police were going to find Carlos and Claus and I panicked.' David shrugged. 'I called you because I thought you would know what to do for the best.'

'What the fuck happened, David?' Ben asked. He looked pissed off. His eyes were dark and brooding at the best of times but today his face was like thunder.

'I don't know, Ben,' David said, shrugging. 'The police came to the trailer looking for the brothers. There were detectives and uniformed police all around the van. Lots of them.'

'What were they looking for, exactly?'

'They said two women had been spiked and one was missing. And they said they knew we had seen them in a pub in the town. They searched the trailer for them and I told them the brothers were in the pub. They went to find them and said they would be back to talk to me later on. They told me not to go anywhere,' he shrugged and lit a cigarette. 'I shit myself and got in the truck. I didn't want anything to do with missing women. That is bad news.'

'She's not missing anymore,' Ben said.

'What do you mean?' David asked. 'That's good, surely. They found her?'

'Haven't you been listening to the news?'

'No.'

'They found her dead in the sea, idiot. She was stripped from the waist down, raped and murdered,' Ben said angrily. David was speechless. 'What the fuck was going through your heads drugging women in town?'

'It is Carlos and Claus. They think it is like a game. I didn't know this would happen,' David said. 'Sometimes they bring women back to the trailer but I never thought anything like this could happen.'

'Women they have drugged?' Ben asked, frowning.

'Yes. They're like zombies on that stuff they give them,' David said. 'Then they put them into a taxi and send them home like nothing happened. I told them they were playing with fire. I have nothing to do with this.'

'Shut up,' Ben snapped. David was going to protest but thought better of it. 'Don't pretend you didn't know what they were up to. You three were together twenty-four-seven. You knew what they were up to. Are you telling me you didn't know what they were up to?'

'I didn't know anything about the woman being killed, honestly I didn't,' David said. He held his face in his hands. 'I told you. It's a game to them. They have gone too far this time. They will arrest them for murder for sure.'

'Welcome to the party, idiot,' Ben said. 'The police will take that trailer and workshop to bits looking for DNA.'

'If they search the trailer, they will find the compartment where we hid the migrants from Calais,' David said. 'They won't be able to prove we smuggled them into the country, will they?'

'They will find a lot more than that,' Ben said, shaking his head.

'Like what?'

'Stuff that shouldn't be there,' Ben said. He studied David's face to see if he knew what he was talking about. Carlos assured him David didn't know everything and that they kept him in the dark. They called him the mushroom, kept in the dark and fed horseshit. 'Stuff which is unbelievably valuable and doesn't belong to me.'

'What stuff?'

'Grow up, David. What do you think I'm talking about?'

'I don't know and I don't want to know.'

'Tough because you're in this up to your neck. They will find drugs,' Ben said. David shook his head. 'There are a lot of drugs in the lining of that trailer. They belong to extremely dangerous people. If they don't get their drugs delivered to Ireland on Friday, they will want their money. If they don't get their money, they will kill me and you and the Vincentia brothers and anyone related to us.' David looked suitably frightened. 'Do you have family in Dusseldorf?'

'Yes. Father, mother and sister.'

'They know where you're from. They will kill them all,' Ben said. 'You need to get the drugs out of the trailer.'

'What?' David asked. 'You said the police will be searching it.'

'They will be looking for forensic evidence inside the trailer, not drugs in the shell. That will be the last place they look. As long as the shell remains intact, we can retrieve them.'

'I don't understand,' David said.

'It's simple. We need the drugs out of the trailer or we're all dead.'

'What do you want me to do?'

'I need you to listen very carefully. They will move the trailer to a secure compound. There are only two in North Wales. I'll find out where it is being stored and you need to get some tools. You need to get to the trailer at night when the forensic teams have finished for the day, ring me,' Ben said. 'I'll tell you where the drugs are stashed. You can cut into the skin with a power saw. I reckon it will take you twenty-minutes at the most to recover them. There are twenty packages in total. They weigh a kilo each, so you'll need a rucksack to carry them.' David looked as white as a sheet.

'Are you listening to me?'

'Yes. But I don't think I can do this.'

'If we can get them back, we have a good chance of getting out of this alive.'

'What if I get caught?'

'You will go to jail and the Karpovs will have your throat cut on the inside,' Ben said. 'You don't want to think about what they will do to your mother and sister.'

'No.'

'What did you say to me?'

'I said no,' David said, shaking his head. 'I'm not getting involved in smuggling drugs. I won't say anything to the police but I'm not getting involved by moving them.'

Ben grabbed David by the legs and lifted him over the railings. David was dangling upside down, held by the ankles. The traffic screamed beneath him. His mind began to spin. He could hear Ben shouting at him but he couldn't understand what he was saying. The blood was pooling in his brain, pressure building to bursting point. He could hear the blaring of horns and claxons from horrified drivers passing below. Ben dragged him back onto the bridge and squeezed his cheek hard.

'Are you listening to me?' Ben snarled. He slapped him hard across the face. 'David!'

'Yes. I'm listening,' David muttered. 'I think I've shit in my pants.'

'You need to get in your truck and stay out of sight until I call you,' Ben said. 'Get a rucksack and wait for me to call you.' David nodded. 'Do you have tools on the truck?' David nodded again. 'Good. Do as you're told and you'll survive this and come out of the other side with some money in your pocket, understand?'

'Yes,' David mumbled. Ben turned and walked away and didn't look back.

Chapter 30

Pamela Stone and her team were working their way through the Vincentia trailer. It was a DNA festival. She concentrated on the individual bedrooms, capturing samples unique to their occupant. Toothbrushes, and men's underwear and a couple of used condoms, which were guaranteed to yield evidence linked to one person. Rarely were multiple samples taken from a toothbrush or condom. The evidence was bagged and tagged and rushed to the lab to be processed urgently. The police wanted the findings crosschecked with what was found on the boat when the results were produced. They were still waiting for them. Processing the small samples of blood, semen, saliva and fibres was a painstakingly slow process as they couldn't afford to waste any of the precious trace elements. There was enough for a couple of tests to be run and not much more. If the tests were faulty, they may not get a second opportunity. They had to be right first time. With the interior processed and its contents removed for further analysis, they began to investigate the structure of the vehicle itself.

Beneath the beds and seating areas were pods big enough to accommodate two people in each. The spaces had been lined with thermic board and insulation, which would mask the heat given off by a human body. If heat sensors were used on the trailer, which was highly unlikely, the chances were, they wouldn't see anything untoward. There were no guarantees but there never were. The odds were stacked in their favour. They had been designed to take six beneath each divan and another four in the seating areas. Twenty-two berths in total. The manufacturing was precise and skilled. Pamela called Alan to tell him the news.

'Hello Pamela,' Alan said. 'Have you found anything interesting?'

'The trailer was occupied by three single males,' Pamela said. 'It's awash with DNA. There's plenty to compare to whatever comes back from the boat.'

'How long are we looking at?'

211

'Forty-eight hours minimum, even with a rush on them,' Pamela said. 'The traces from the boat are so minute, we have to be right with the first test. As soon as we have anything back, I'll call you. Have you caught your suspects yet?'

'Nope,' Alan said. 'We know they're not in Ireland, which is good but they're still at large. Their faces are all over the news. They can't hide forever.'

'We found pods in the trailer, welded beneath the beds and seating areas,' Pamela said. 'They've been insulated to avoid heat detection cameras. The fact they haven't been stopped and arrested is testament to the fact they worked.'

'I think you'll find the same in Mary Adam's trailer,' Alan said.

'We have. She had pods to accommodate six people,' Pamela explained. 'The Vincentia trailer is adapted to carry twenty-two.'

'That's a very lucrative side-line,' Alan said.

'The workmanship is top quality,' Pamela said. 'Welders with that level of skill could adapt anything they wanted to.' She paused. 'It makes me wonder what else they've made.'

'Do you think the trailer may be adapted to carry more than just people?'

'What do you think?'

'I can feel a big bill heading my way,' Alan said, smiling. 'Are you going to take the trailers away and strip them down?'

'The question is, do you want me to take them away and strip them down?'

'Is it going to be awfully expensive?'

'Very.'

'Okay. Let's do it,' Alan said. 'In for a penny, in for a pound.'

****

Kelly left her house with the curtains closed upstairs and the bedside table lamp switched on. She had four sets of clothing on, one layer over the other. She packed as many of Elle's clothes as she could into four shopping bags and put them into the boot of her car. It looked like she was washing rather than leaving. Her nerves were tingling as she started the engine and drove towards her mother's house. Elle was at school until three-thirty. The street was quiet as she drove away, wondering when she would be able to return. She still had to convince her parents to come with her. Elle would not be happy but she would come around. Making shit decisions to protect your children was all part of being a parent.

It was a short drive to their house but she took the long route. Kelly drove around Land's End and up the high street in an attempt to confuse anyone following her. There wasn't much traffic and she was certain there was no one behind her. When she arrived at her mother's house, she parked at the back next to the garages and waited a while. There was no sign of anyone following. She climbed out and went through the garden gate to the back door. It was open, as usual. The kitchen was full of steam when she walked in, the windows misted with condensation. The aroma of lamb stew filled the air. It reminded her of her childhood.

'What are you doing here?' her mother, Sheree said.

'Look at what the cat's dragged in,' her dad, Steve said, walking into the kitchen. He kissed her on the cheek. 'Is everything okay?' he asked, noticing her eyes were swollen from crying. 'What on earth is wrong?'

'I don't know where to start,' Kelly said. She went into the living room and removed three layers of clothing, folding each item on the arm of the chair. Her parents watched, completely bamboozled by her behaviour. 'Let me get these clothes off. I can hardly move.'

'Have you finally cracked?' Steve asked.

'Nope. I've never thought with more clarity that I am right now.'

'Why are you wearing extra clothes?' Sheree asked, frowning. 'Have you been shoplifting?'

'I need to take a few outfits but didn't want to put them in a bag. They might be watching me.'

'Oh, they might be watching her.' He nodded to Sheree. 'I see. That's all perfectly clear now,' Steve said. 'What drugs have you been sniffing?'

'Sit down and listen to what I'm going to tell you.'

'This sounds serious,' Sheree said, her face stern. 'You're not pregnant already with that Jack bloke?'

'Are you pregnant?' Steve asked, blushing. 'I'll bloody kill him if he's dumped you.'

'I'm not pregnant and Jack hasn't dumped me,' Kelly said. 'It's much worse than that.' Her parents looked at each other, worried. 'Have you been watching the news about people murdered in Rhosneiger?' she asked.

'Of course, we have,' Sheree said, winking. 'Why? You didn't do it, did you?'

'No, mam,' Kelly said, smiling at her sarcasm. 'I didn't do it but I saw who did.'

'Oh, for fuck's sake, not again,' Steve said, shaking his head. 'Don't tell me you're going to be a witness again. Last time I got my arse kicked in the Blossoms. I don't think I can cope with that again.'

'Shut up, Steve,' Sheree said. 'Let the girl speak.'

'Okay, I'm just saying,' Steve said. 'Can you please explain to me in simple terms, what the bloody hell you're talking about?'

'I'm talking about the Rhosneiger murders on the news,' Kelly said. Her parents still looked confused. 'Look. I was on the beach with Jack and we saw a woman called Mary Adams banging on the glass, screaming for help. The next thing we knew, we saw her crash through the window and fall from the balcony,' Kelly said. 'She's the woman on the news. The police are saying she was pushed through the glass. It's murder and I saw it happen.'

'You never said anything about seeing her fall,' Sheree said. 'Why didn't you tell us?'

'I didn't want you to worry,' Kelly said. 'Not after everything that happened last time. I thought being a witness was the right thing to do back then but I couldn't have been more wrong. Just look at all the trouble it caused the family.'

'You can tell us anything. We're here to support you.'

'We're your parents.'

'Exactly,' Kelly said. 'That's why I was protecting you. I don't want any harm to come to any of us.'

'Well, you've started telling us what happened now, so let's hear what you saw,' Steve said. He scratched his bald head.

'When Mary Adams fell from the balcony, Jack phoned the police and I went to see if she was alive. She was dead. Her eyes were open and there was blood coming from her ears. She was gone.'

'That must have been awful,' Sheree said.

'It was. I knew she was dead as soon as I saw her. I heard a door slam at the front of the house so, I ran down a path between the houses and I saw two men running away from the house. They were getting into a van. One of them was a big guy with scars on his head and tufts of hair on his scalp, like he'd been burnt or scalded. I'll never forget him. He turned around and looked right at me. We looked at each other in the eyes.' Kelly put her hands to her face. 'I was frozen to the spot. He just stared at me and then he put his finger to his lips telling me not to say anything. It was the weirdest feeling. I was so frightened.'

'Did you know him?' Sheree asked.

'No.' Kelly shook her head. 'I've never seen him before.'

'That's a relief,' Steve said. 'So, he knows what you look like?' he asked.

'Yes. They know what I look like.'

'That's not so bad if he doesn't know you, I suppose.'

'It's not that simple. He knows who I am,' Kelly said. Her mum and dad exchanged worried glances again. 'He knows where I live, my mobile phone number, my Facebook and worst of all, he knows where you live and they know I have a daughter.' They looked shocked and confused. 'They sent me a photograph of Elle in her pyjamas outside your front door.'

'How did they find all that out?' Steve asked.

'Jack's van,' Kelly said. Her dad frowned. The wrinkles on his forehead creased, making deep lines which reached onto his scalp. 'He has his name and mobile number on the side of the van. They searched the internet for jack Henderson, found his Facebook page and found pictures of me that he had tagged me in, so it was simple to jump to my Facebook and get my name. They must have followed us from Rhosneiger, so they knew where I lived and they followed Elle here.' She paused. 'They called Jack and pretended to be the police asking for my mobile number. They told him they'd written it down wrong and he gave them my number.'

'Bloody idiot,' Steve said.

'Oh my god,' Sheree said, biting her nails. 'What have the police said?'

'I haven't told the police.'

'What?' Steve said, standing up. He became agitated. 'Are you mad?'

'We need to phone them right now,' Sheree said.

'Sit down and listen to me!' Kelly snapped. Her parents looked shocked. 'Sit down, please.' They sat down. 'I haven't told the police because of what happened to us last time, remember?' Her dad was going to complain. Kelly

216

held her hand up. 'These people are different to the last time I was a witness. They're not local lads thinking they're gangsters. These men are the real thing. The news reports are linking this to serious organised crime. People trafficking and drug smuggling. These are dangerous men, dad.'

'I've heard them say that they were traffickers,' Steve said, biting his bottom lip. 'What did they message you?'

'They threatened me,' Kelly said. 'They cut off my power from outside my front door and sent me messages on my mobile and a picture of Elle.'

'They've been to your house?' Sheree said.

'Yes, and they've been to your house too,' Kelly said. Steve stood up and went to the window. It was an instinctive reaction. 'They knocked on your front door and Elle went out to see who it was.'

'I remember her doing that,' Steve said. 'I thought it was those bloody kids from number eighty pissing about playing knock and run again.'

'That's when they photographed her and sent me the picture.' Her parents were open mouthed with shock. 'Five people died in that house in Rhosneiger.' She paused to let it sink in. 'Five people were murdered and I saw the men responsible leaving.'

'They're worried you're going to talk to the police,' Steve said.

'Of course, they're worried about me talking to the police. I can put them at the scene of a crime. They want to make sure I keep quiet.'

'Of course, they do,' Steve said.

'What are you going to do?' Sheree asked. 'I can see you already have a plan. It's written all over your face.'

'Am I so easy to read?'

'I'm your mum.'

'I've turned everything off, phone Facebook, Twitter, computer, tablet, the lot. I need to disappear for a while with Elle but for that to work, you have to come with us,' Kelly said. Her parents looked gobsmacked. 'If we run and hide and you stay here, they'll come for you to keep me quiet.' Her parents nodded in agreement. 'We all need to go. We go now and we take Elle out of school and take off. Right now.'

'Where will we go?' Steve asked. 'Not that it matters. A long as we're all together. We'll be fine.'

'I'll pack a few bits and pieces,' Sheree said. 'Let's go to Barmouth. We haven't been there since you were a child. Elle would love it there.'

'Okay Mum,' Kelly said. 'Barmouth it is.'

Chapter 31

Len bit into his hotdog and watched the ghost train in operation. He recognised young Koresh immediately. There was a strong family resemblance. The Koresh males had strong facial features, prominent noses and protruding foreheads and thick eyebrows that seemed to join in the middle. He looked like a younger version of Andi Koresh. Len could remember Andi Koresh well. Andi was one in a million. Psychopath, sociopath, narcissistic and paranoid. Living inside his head must have been like living in a box of snakes, where everything you touch is repellent and a threat to your life. Andi was sent from London to muscle into the action in the big northern towns and cities with the aim of gaining a foothold to launch a takeover. Taming the local outfits was the first priority. A task the Albanians massively underrated. The timing of his foray north couldn't have been worse. Manchester and Liverpool were in a state of fragile peace for the first time in decades. It was a peace which had been brokered following years of mutual assassinations and political infighting between the powerful outfits. Gangland funerals became a rare event. Everyone was happy and everybody was making money, until Andi Koresh appeared on the scene with half a dozen apes and twenty kilos of good quality brown from Afghanistan. The stuff every smackhead dreamed of putting into their syringe. They set up shop in a lockup beneath the arches of the Manchester railway near Piccadilly and began trading immediately. A fortnight later, they bought a kebab house on Smithdown Road in Liverpool and were the talk of the town within days. Everyone wanted the Afghan scag.

There were four shootings in the first fortnight of them arriving. Three of them fatal. They began by identifying street dealers and robbing them of their money and product, hurting them so badly, they would never venture onto the streets ever again. With the street corners conquered, they worked up the food chain. Andi and his goons worked to a pattern. They identified key members of the local gangs and tracked them to their homes. Then they would storm their houses in the middle of the night while their families were sleeping, terrorising their wives and children. They made each visit as dramatic as they could, bringing shotguns, power tools and machetes. Threats were made which could not be ignored. Children were hung upside down by their feet from bannisters and threatened with drills and circular saws. Mothers were traumatised so deeply their bags were packed the following day. Marriages were destroyed in an instant. No one could protect their children twenty-four-seven and no one was in any doubt Andi Koresh wouldn't follow through on his threats. It was enough for most to step away from the life with immediate effect. Those who retaliated by attacking the Koresh dealers, were kidnapped and given the special treatment. Andi enjoyed subjecting them to torture and horrific experiences that would break the strongest men. Not a single man who was taken by the Koresh family ever returned to the business. Not one. Considering who these people were, that's quite a remarkable statistic and testament to what an evil bastard Andi Koresh was.

When two senior members of the Quinn family were subjected to a visit in the small hours of the morning, their families completely traumatised, Len was called in. Nobody wanted a war with the entire Albanian outfit. Tit for tat killings put a strain on the business and destabilised the cities fragile balance. This was a mission which needed to be swift and deadly. There was no chest beating or flag waving. With the aid of three handpicked specialists, Len cut the head off the snake. Literally. Andi Koresh was mailed back to the Albanian headquarters in London in six parcels. His head was sent by special delivery in a cakebox with his genitals shoved into his mouth, to the home of the Koresh patriarch in London. Three of Andi's lieutenants were pulled from the Mersey missing their eyes, teeth, fingers and toes, their genitals found in the contents of their stomachs. A day later, the Koresh foray north was brought to a close when the remainder of their crew were found in the ashes of their newly acquired properties. They had been tied together and soaked in accelerant before the buildings were torched. It meant they had plenty of time to sit and contemplate what they had done and what was about to happen before suffering an agonising death. No one claimed responsibility for sending the Albanians running for the hills and they never ventured north again. Their annihilation became engrained in underworld folklore. Of course, retaliation was considered but the Koresh family couldn't be sure who to retaliate against and they couldn't fight everyone north of Watford. Len never heard the name Koresh spoken again. Until now.

Len could see the resemblance between Andi and Samiri. It was easy to identify them as relations. He watched young Koresh with interest. Samiri was positioned front of house, wearing something akin to a traditional vampire costume, white shirt, black cloak and fangs. The rest of the staff appeared to be dressed as killer clowns of varying shapes and sizes, most of which were terrifying. They were entertaining themselves by scaring the life out of people passing by and those in the queue. It was the most popular ride on the park. There was a queue snaking for a hundred yards or more. At five pounds a head, it was a goldmine. Len wondered if Leo had stood in that queue with Katrina before they died. He watched the riders climbing into the cars, getting comfortable, lowering the safety bars into place. The clowns checked the safety bars were locked into place before pushing the cars onto the drive chains, which propelled them through the doors and carried them through the ride. It made him think about what might have happened. Leo had been a tough young man; a keen martial artist and weightlifter. Attacking him and his girlfriend would have been a dangerous thing to do alone. Even with the help of others, he would have been a handful. There would have been easier targets to pick on.

Unless he was sitting down, locked into place by a safety bar.

That would have made him virtually helpless.

It was all clicking into place.

Len watched Samiri working the crowd. He had a patter which appealed to passers-by, especially the females. He seemed to be particularly attracted to groups of teenage females. The younger the better from what he could see. Len felt a creeping uneasiness seeping through him. The young girls giggled and flirted with the handsome vamp and his frightening friends. He had taken three mobile phone numbers in the space of time it had taken Len to eat his hotdog. Len watched how he interacted with his co-workers. They were completely focused on the young females, sneering, pointing and teasing them, regardless of the fact some were accompanied by boyfriends or husbands. They acted with impunity. Some of their prey were responsive, some of them clearly weren't interested but it didn't matter either way. They were relentless in their pursuit of young girls. Len felt his blood boiling. He was no nearer to identifying his son's killer for certain but the scenario playing out in his mind was plausible. Leo was fastened into a fairground car and couldn't fight back. It was more plausible than anything he had heard from the police in the last five years. Whatever the case, he instantly disliked Samiri and he became the focus of his attention.

Len walked through the fair and skirted the queue. The ghost train was set up at the far edge of the fairground, close to the river. Len was parked on the nearby car park a stone's throw away. Behind the ghost train were the trucks and vans which transported it and the people who worked on it. He slipped between two smaller stalls that were ladened with giant teddy bears and headed to the river, using the path next to it to bring him behind the Koresh ride. He noticed a flatbed truck which had a diesel tank mounted on the back. It was obviously the maintenance truck, which kept the noisy generators running. A metal toolbox was bolted to the bulkhead and acetylene tanks were laid on their sides; a welding torch attached. Next to the truck on the grass was a metal barrel. It was blue. He couldn't make out the lettering without his glasses. He walked closer and read the labels. He took a picture of it on his phone. It was Super red grease made by Miles lubricants. The same brand the detectives had been searching for. The same type of drum his son had been stuffed into. Len scrolled through his contacts and found a number he hadn't used for many years. Detective inspector Gill Robinson. He was about to send her the picture, not sure why, when he heard voices approaching. A young girl was giggling nervously as Samiri led her into the shadows behind the ride.

'You said you were going to let me on for nothing,' she complained. 'It's dark back here. I want to go back to my friends.'

'Shut up, you little prick teaser,' Samiri said. 'You're going to do as you're told before I let you go anywhere.'

'I'm not doing that. Get off me!'

Len waited behind the truck for them to pass. Samiri bundled her unwillingly into the darkness beyond the generators.

Chapter 32

Carlos had a shower and washed his hair. He was waiting for David to pick him up. When his phone had charged, he'd finally got through to him. He was in a state of panic rambling on about Russians who were going to rape and murder his mother and sister and a stash of class-A's in the lining of the trailer. It was a surreal conversation and he wasn't sure what the fuck he was talking about. He had to calm him down to get any sense from him and convince him that he needed to pick him up. Carlos wasn't sure exactly where he was. He had read the address from Martha's post. Luckily, the pickup had a sat nav built in because neither of them could pronounce the address. While he waited, he made himself a lamb sandwich with mint sauce on it and drank all the milk from the fridge to wash it down. There was a packet of dark chocolate Hobnobs in the cupboard, so he made a coffee and took them into the living room waiting for his lift to arrive. He munched on them while he waited. David was about twenty miles away. It wouldn't take long for him to get there.

The news was still replaying the same reels. Rhosneiger, organised crime, Newry Beach, rape and murder. Over and over. It was as if there was nothing else going on in the world. There was no way around the fact that they were in the middle of the shit show. Right smack bang in the middle of it and he couldn't see any way back. He tried to fathom a way of taking something from the situation and moving on to another place, where they could begin again. There may have been a chance if the woman had lived. But she hadn't and so there would be a murder investigation and that was unavoidable. Claus was in custody, which was a bummer but not the end of the world. David told him Benaim had sent a good lawyer to represent him. He might get bail. That would very much depend on what the forensic scientists recovered. He couldn't believe the woman was dead. That was going to bring down the law like a ton of bricks onto their heads. His phone vibrated and disturbed his thoughts.

'Carlos?' the voice asked. It was Benaim. He sounded surprised that he had answered. 'Carlos. Is that you, Carlos?'

'Yes. Who do you think it is?'

'I didn't expect you to answer your phone but you did.'

'Yes, Ben,' Carlos said. 'Who else would answer my phone?'

'You have a smart mouth,' Ben said.

'I didn't hear you complaining when it was around your cock,' Carlos said.

'Always the smart mouth.'

Their encounters had started soon after Benaim spotted them in Germany and gave them a job. Ben had a thing for Carlos and Carlos liked sex with anyone who wanted it, regardless of gender. Carlos had used it to manipulate Ben at every opportunity. He and Claus worked directly for Ben, supplying the fairgrounds and repairing vehicles and equipment. They became familiar with most of the rides and the mechanics behind them. Eventually, Ben set them up in business for themselves. It worked perfectly for all concerned. The money was good, the work was guaranteed and they answered only to their customers. They were good mechanics, so it worked. Their relationship continued over the years but their clandestine encounters clouded Benaim's judgement. Benaim thought it endeared Carlos to him but Carlos thought otherwise. The sex was quick and dirty and was a means to an end. There was no emotional attachment for Carlos. He kept his walks on the wild side a secret from Claus and David. They would never believe what he did for Ben nor would they understand. Ben played both sides too but he kept Carlos a secret that he would never have admitted to. His macho image would have been tarnished if it become common knowledge.

'Pity you don't have a smart brain to match it,' Ben said. 'If you were half as smart as you think you are, we wouldn't be in this shit.' Carlos snorted laughter. 'What are you laughing at, you think this is funny?'

'You have to laugh or cry,' Carlos said. 'You make me laugh. You're a joke.'

'I'm not laughing and neither is your brother,' Ben said. 'You ran away and left him, didn't you?'

'Fuck you, Ben,' Carlos said. 'I haven't got time for your shit. What is your problem?'

'You are my problem,' Ben said. 'A woman is dead. The police are all over you like shit on a blanket. You are not going to shake them off. What were you thinking? Drugging women for sex, idiot. You had it all given to you on a plate but you're so stupid, you've ruined everything.'

'I've ruined everything?' Carlos said. 'That's rich coming from the big people trafficker himself.'

'I can fix my problems,' Ben said. 'You can't.'

'I don't see it that way, to be honest,' Carlos said. 'You're calling me an idiot. Killing a bunch of pensioners and tossing your girlfriend from a balcony is right up there in the idiot category. I think you need to go and have a little look in the mirror before you start dishing out your advice to me.'

'You need to be incredibly careful what you're saying to me,' Ben fumed.

'Really?' Carlos asked. 'Why is that, exactly?'

'Don't push your luck,' Ben said. 'Just because you're not in front of me doesn't mean you can disrespect me.' Carlos remained silent. 'We have to keep our cool and work together. We're all in the crap together.'

'You're in the people trafficking and murdering people type of crap,' Carlos said. 'I'm not quite in your category yet. I'm not sure we're all in this together at all.' Carlos grinned at the silence. Benaim was clearly steaming on the other end of the call but he needed something, so he was keeping a lid on it. He must be desperate, Carlos thought. Really, really desperate. 'Anyway, I'm not arguing with you. I really can't be bothered. I'm glad you've called because I need to speak to you about what you've told David.'

'What do you mean?'

'David called me waffling on about a consignment of drugs hidden in the walls of our trailer.'

'We need to remove it, Carlos.'

'It's not as easy as you're making it sound,' Carlos said. 'The police have the trailer and you're putting it on him to recover your shipment. David is terribly upset about it.'

'That consignment is our way out of this,' Ben said. 'We have to recover it.'

'Just like that. You make it sound easy. David said you ordered him to cut them out of the trailer?'

'Yes. I will find out where the police have taken it. The compounds are guarded by security, not police. It will be easy to get in there.'

'Let me get this straight,' Carlos said. 'You want him to break into a police compound and steal back a consignment of drugs that he knew nothing about until an hour ago?' Ben didn't answer. 'A consignment of drugs that we were not going to earn any money from because you think we're stupid?'

'Yes. Don't complicate this. Or we're all dead.'

'He's not going to do it,' Carlos said.

'What?'

'You heard me. He's not doing it,' Carlos said. 'Do it yourself.'

'I have other shit that needs to be dealt with,' Ben argued. 'He is going to do it and there's nothing you can do about it,' Ben said, simmering. His voice was edgy. Carlos could picture his face and it made him smile. 'I met him earlier and he knows what he has to do. I don't want you sticking your oar in, making him have second thoughts. Leave him be. It needs to be done.'

'He's frightened,' Carlos said.

'He needs to man up and get it done.'

'Man up,' Carlos said. 'That sounds like fun.'

'Carlos, you're pushing me to the limit. I have the police searching for me and my operation is falling apart at the seams. There's no time for fucking about.'

'Man up, yourself, Ben. Do it yourself. We're all finished with you.'

'What are you taking about?' Ben asked, angrily. 'You don't finish with me. No one finishes with me. You don't just walk away.'

'Watch this space. David isn't working for you anymore. I've told him not to worry about it,' Carlos said. 'He's on his way to pick me up now and we're out of here. You can whistle.'

'Out of here, just like that. What are you talking about?'

'You heard me the first time. We're not playing your game anymore. We're leaving.'

'You can't just run away.'

'We can. And we will.'

'Look at this calmly. This doesn't need to be so hard. I told him to stay low until I call him,' Ben said, frustration in is voice. 'He shouldn't be going to pick you up. The police will be looking for his truck. Where are you?'

'I can't tell you that,' Carlos said. 'You're not a genuinely nice man and I don't trust you.'

'Listen to me,' Ben said, lowering his tone. 'We need those packages from that trailer. It's not open to debate. We need them.'

'You need them,' Carlos said. 'You are smuggling them for the Karpovs. You told me that yourself. It's your problem.'

'They were in your trailer,' Ben shouted. He was losing his calm. 'Don't you understand what that means?'

'It means, I don't want anything to do with drugs that belong to the Karpovs and neither does David.' Carlos sighed. 'Your drugs, your problem.'

'Don't make it sound like you don't know anything about this, idiot,' Ben said, angrily. 'You put them in there.'

'I put packages in there at your instruction. I thought it was insulation. At no point did I think they were full of anything illegal,' Carlos said. 'If I get arrested, I'll do a deal. That's what I'll say in court for the Karpovs to hear. Benaim asked me to put these packages into the lining of the trailer and I only did as he asked because we've been fucking for years, so I did as he asked. I always do as he asks.'

'Do not say anything like that,' Ben snapped. 'Don't even think about saying anything about us!'

'I will tell the world Benaim has been my lover for years and we're very much in love.'

'Shut up. You little idiot.' Ben grimaced at the thought of being outed. 'Don't be an idiot all your life.'

'I suppose I am an idiot for having anything to do with your smuggling enterprises. I must have been mad.'

'It's too late to pretend you're not part of it. They are there in your trailer and we can't change that,' Ben said. 'You put them in there and you can't deny it, so you are a part of this, like it or not.'

'You're right. I did,' Carlos said. He paused. There was a pregnant pause. 'I put the packages in to the trailer, and I took them out of there too.'

'What?'

'I wasn't comfortable with them in my trailer, so I took them out as soon as you'd gone.' Carlos waited for a reaction but none was forthcoming. 'They would have been picked up by the x-ray machines at the first port and I didn't want to be driving when they were discovered, so I moved them somewhere safe.'

'You're lying,' Ben said, losing it.

'Nope. I put them where you'll never find them. I was hoping we would get to Ireland before you knew they were gone, by which time, I would have been on my way to warmer climes and you would be having your fingers and toes cut off by a big hairy Russian mafioso.'

'What are you saying to me?'

'You heard me,' Carlos said. 'Your drugs are gone. Who is the idiot now?'

'You wouldn't dare do that,' Ben said.

'It's already done,' Carlos said. 'We're not being your puppets any longer. I'm calling the shots now.'

'Carlos. I don't know what you're playing at but this is an extremely dangerous game to play with me,' Ben said. 'Whatever you're thinking, think again. Think very carefully indeed.'

'Look on the bright side,' Carlos said. 'The consignment is not in the trailer and the police have the trailer. They will be taking it apart right now but they won't find any drugs in there because I took them out and put them safe. That must be a good thing, right?'

'Where are they?'

'Fuck you, Ben,' Carlos said. 'I wish I could be there when you have to explain to the Karpovs that you've lost their consignment. I think those burns on your head will pale into insignificance to what they will do to you. I heard they put people into barrels of acid?' Ben was quiet. 'That might improve your complexion.'

'Carlos, we need to stop fucking around here,' Ben said. 'If you have the drugs, that's great.' Ben tried to cool things down. 'Tell me where they are.'

'They are up my arse,' Carlos said.

'Stop this, Carlos,' Ben said. 'I'll buy them from you. Whatever you want to do, I'll do it. I must have that consignment in Ireland on Friday night.' Carlos didn't answer. 'I did you and your brother a lot of favours. I looked after you when you had nothing. Don't forget that.'

'I seem to remember returning those favours, mostly on my knees, so I don't feel like I owe you anything. Still, I haven't got time to chat, so thanks for everything and good luck for the future.'

'Carlos,' Ben said. 'I'm going to find you and when I do, you're going to wish you had never been born.'

'Blah, blah, blah,' Carlos said, laughing. 'You're so boring. Take care of yourself.'

Carlos hung up. David Prost pulled onto the driveway. He looked very worried. Carlos grabbed his coat and took the charger from the wall. He left through the front door and locked it. The street was quiet and he looked up at the bedroom window. Poor old Martha, he thought. Nice lady.

****

Richard Lewis checked his watch. The detective he was talking to had just come back from his lunch break. He was keen to find out what Richard had about females being drugged with Flunitrazepam. Richard had sent a request for information about similar incidents involving females being attacked while visiting travelling fairgrounds. The reaction had been instant and revealing. This was the fourth detective to contact him since nine o'clock that morning.

'This is DS Wakeford, GMP,' he said. 'I'm calling about the fairground incidents. Am I talking to the right detective?'

'Yes. I'm DS Lewis,' Richard said. 'Call me Richard. Thanks for getting back to me. I believe you have a recent Rohypnol case at a fairground?'

'I do,' Wakeford said. 'What's the background on your request?'

'We have a rape murder case in Holyhead. A young woman called Michelle Branning,' Richard said. 'The victim and her sister were drugged with Flunitrazepam in a local pub on their way to the fairground. The elder sister was pulled out of the sea last night. We have CCTV footage of the women being spiked and one of the men in custody but we were certain this isn't the first time they've done this, hence the communication to other forces. The suspects are all related. Brothers and their cousin. They're travelling mechanics attached to the circus. Wherever it goes, they travel with it.'

'I see, that's very interesting,' Wakeford said. 'I have sisters here too. They were drugged on their way to the circus.'

'What are the details?'

'They went to their local. Which was opposite the fairground and had a few drinks before the show. They were big fans of it online,' Wakeford said. 'I just want to confirm we're talking about the same show. Is it the Circus of Nightmares?'

'Yes. That's the one,' Richard said.

'It must be the same guys,' Wakeford said. 'The sisters are twenty-five and thirty. They remember being chatted up by two men with foreign accents. They said they were German.'

'Carlos and Claus Vincentia,' Richard said.

'No. My victims remember a man called David?'

'David Prost?'

'I don't think they got a second name,' Wakeford said. 'Anyway, they had a few drinks with them. They bought them shots and then they went to the fair. They remember feeling unwell almost immediately. The men turned up as if they'd been waiting for them to take ill. They remember the men saying they were taking them for a taxi but they were taken to a big caravan. One of the victims remembers being taken into a bedroom where she was assaulted by two men who looked alike. They had sex with her against her will but she couldn't resist.'

'Carlos and Claus are half brothers and they look alike,' Richard said. 'I'm going to email you their images for your victims to take a look at.'

'Thank you. The second victim doesn't remember anything about her attacker but knows she had sex against her will but couldn't resist. She remembers the man called David putting her clothes on in a hurry and bundling her into a taxi with her sister. They didn't make the compliant until over forty-eight hours later, by which time the drug has gone, as you know but their hair samples show they were drugged. The circus had moved on and we're short on suspects until now.'

'We have DNA now. That changes the game.'

'It does. That's amazing news.'

'Are they willing to press charges?' Richard asked.

'I'm confident the older sister will,' Wakeford said. 'The younger one is married and has a young baby. Her husband isn't dealing with it very well. He's left her. She doesn't want to ruin any chance of them getting back together by raking it all up in court.'

'That's understandable, poor girl,' Richard said. 'We've got one of them in custody. If you want to come up here and ask him a few questions, be our guest. I have a feeling there will be quite a queue of detectives wanting to speak to him.'

'I'll call you back when I've spoken to my gaffer,' Wakeford said. 'Thanks again for the heads up. I want to put this one to bed and if we can nail the bastards, all the better.'

'No problem,' Richard said. He hung up. Kim was looking at him. 'That's two more women drugged and raped.'

'Where were they?'

'Brighton,' Richard said. 'These boys have been busy. The slippery bastards think they can get away with this indefinitely.'

'Not now we have DNA,' Kim said. 'They can't slip out of that one. There will be plenty to compare it to from the other forces that want to speak to them.'

'Yes. There are seven rape kits so far and a three-month-old baby girl in Plymouth,' Richard said.

'What?' Kim said, open mouthed.

'The young woman found out she was pregnant following the attack. She hadn't had sex with anyone else and doesn't believe in abortion. If one of them fathered the unfortunate little darling, a judge will hopefully throw away the key. I'd cut their testicles off.'

'Run for Prime Minister,' Kim said. 'You've got my vote.'

****

Carlos got into the pickup and slapped David on the back. David hugged him and grabbed his hand.

'I've never been so glad to see you in my life,' David said. 'This has turned into a nightmare. It's all got way out of hand. What the fuck are we going to do?'

'Calm down,' Carlos said. 'We need to stay calm. Everything will be okay. We need to get as far away from this island as we can, right now.'

'Do you want me to drive to the port?'

'No.'

'Are we going to Ireland?' David asked.

'No.' Carlos checked his watch. 'The police will be looking for the truck. Forget the circus and Ireland. We can't go back there now. That chapter is finished. We'll have to start a new one. We have money, so the world is our lobster,' he said, smiling. 'Onwards and upwards.'

'What about Claus?'

'He can catch us up when he gets out,' Carlos said. Not really believing he would get out at all. 'He will contact us when he can. We need to turn our phones off for a few days until we get to wherever we're going and we can worry about Claus when we're safe and sound.'

'Okay,' David said. 'What about Benaim?'

'Fuck him.'

'He was so mad with us,' David said. 'I can't believe he wanted me to break into a police compound. He's nuts thinking I would do that.'

'He's a dickhead,' Carlos said. 'Not all the drugs are in the trailer.' David looked confused. 'I took a few kilos out. They're under the truck,' Carlos said smiling. 'I made a compartment where the spare wheel is. We should be able to sell them easily enough. We'll have enough money to disappear for good. Benaim can go fuck himself.' David was shaking his head. 'Close your mouth. You look retarded.'

'You took some of them?'

'Yes.'

A van pulled onto the driveway behind them and a BMW X5 mounted the pavement behind that. They blocked their exit.

'What the fuck is going on?' Carlos muttered. 'They don't look like police to me.' Two men got out of the van, carrying baseball bats. Three more got out of the BMW, carrying weapons. 'I think we're in the shit.'

'What are we going to do?' David asked. The men opened the doors, angry faces glared at them.

'I'm Martha's son,' one of the men growled. He punched Carlos in the face. Carlos spat blood onto the seat. 'She just phoned me and told me she'd been locked in her bedroom by the man from the telly.' He punched Carlos again. 'I'm glad I bought her that mobile phone,' the man said, dragging Carlos out of the truck. Carlos could hear David squealing like a child. He looked up at the bedroom window and saw Martha standing there holding her mobile to her ear. There was a moment of regret he hadn't checked where she kept her phone or tied her up. Blows rained down on him. He tried to cover his face and head. A bat connected with his head in a sickening thud. The world began to spin and unconsciousness descended.

Chapter 33

Wednesday

Len drove towards the lockup and stopped at Costa for a large latte on the way. He pulled onto an aging industrial estate, which looked like the place businesses went to die. To let and for sale signs adorned every other building. Most of the gates were fastened with rusted chains and encrusted padlocks. The rusting hulks of abandoned vehicles were scattered on forecourts, stripped of anything valuable and left on bricks. It was the land that time forgot without the dinosaurs. Len pulled onto his unit and used the remote to open the metal shutters. They clunked and rattled as they rolled up. The neighbouring units were in varying states of decay. He had rented the unit many years ago when Andi Koresh first ventured north. It was the last place Koresh had seen before he left this world for another. Fitting that his scumbag relation was here now. Maybe it was fate. It was certainly ironic.

Len closed the shutters behind him and turned off the engine. It was cold and he could see his breath. Samiri would have had an uncomfortable night naked and alone in the dark. He had been easy to disable and bundle into his vehicle. His mind was on assaulting the teenage girl he'd duped into going round the back of the ghost train. He hadn't heard Len approaching. The young girl had been frightened, grateful and relieved when Samiri collapsed in the dirt. Len told her not to be so stupid again and to run and not to stop running until she got home. She took off like a whippet chasing a hare. He could only hope she may have learned something from the experience.

Len climbed out of the truck and switched on the lights and the radio. Samiri was strapped to a chair, wearing nothing but a bag over his head. The smell of urine and excrement filled the air. He fidgeted as Len approached. Len could hear him trying to speak, the gag muffling his efforts to a series of desperate grunts. He removed the hood and the gag and opened a bottle of sparkling water from Costa. He put it to Samiri's lips and let him drink. The man was thirsty, almost emptying the bottle before he stopped gulping.

'Who are you, man?' he gasped. 'Why are you doing this to me?'

'I need to ask you some questions,' Len said, matter of factly.

'This is a bit extreme, isn't it?' Samiri said, shaking his head.

'You have no idea what extreme is,' Len said.

'Do you know who I am?'

'Yes,' Len said. 'You're Samiri Koresh, which means absolutely nothing to me or anyone else of any standing. You're the second cousin, once removed of a long dead psychopath who liked scaring women and children. It would appear, you have the same traits. You prey on weak young girls, which means I don't like you.' Len shrugged and drank his coffee. 'What happens to you today is in the balance. The fact that I don't like you doesn't help me or you but it might influence how this ends up.'

'I haven't got a fucking clue what you're talking about,' Samiri said, shaking his head. 'My dad will have you carved up, man. You're a dead man walking.'

'Do you think you're an OG, Samiri?'

'Fuck you. Let me go.'

'Big tough original Gangsta man. This is not a rap song. This situation is very real for you,' Len said, shaking his head. 'Your relatives were the real deal but apart from some genetic similarities, you're not in their league. Neither is your father. Please don't threaten me again or I'll cut off your penis and let you bleed to death, sitting in your own shit.' Len picked up a nasty looking curved

237

blade from a workbench. Samiri tried to back away but could move. He closed his legs to protect his genitals. 'No one will hear you screaming and no one will ever find your body.' Samiri began to shake. 'Are we understanding the situation?' Samiri nodded. 'Good.'

'Can I have some more water?' Samiri asked. Len let him finish the water. 'Just tell me what the fuck you want.'

'I need you to cast your mind back five years ago,' Len said.

'Are you joking, man?'

'No joke.' Len took out a taser. He pressed the button and a blue light crackled between the prongs. 'This is fifty thousand volts of electricity. If I touch your bollocks with it, your muscles will spasm so hard, you could bite off your tongue. After a couple of times, your testicles will explode and that will hurt. They will quickly become infected inside your sack and cause sepsis. It's an incredibly painful process to go through and could take days to die.' Samiri sat stoic, eyes wide, filling with tears. 'I haven't got time to play cat and mouse, do you understand?'

'Yes, man,' Samiri said, tears flowing. 'Ask me what you want to know for fucks sake, man. I'll tell you whatever you want to know.'

'Good. Five years ago, you were working on the fairground attached to the Circus of Nightmares,' Len said.

'Yes. We travelled with them for a few years. That's where all the clown shit comes from,' Samiri said. 'What about it?'

'You were pitched on a site near Speke airport, Liverpool,' Len said. 'Next to a retail park.' Len could see Samiri thinking. He could almost smell the wood burning is his mind. 'The police came to see you a few times because a young couple went missing.' Len showed him a photograph on his phone. 'Katrina Watkins and Leo Jobson. Do you recognise them?'

'Yes,' Samiri said, nodding. His eyes were darting everywhere. His brain was processing the information and forming answers. Answers that might keep him attached to his penis. 'I remember them because the police came to see us a couple of times and we told them the same thing each time. They just wouldn't listen.'

'What did you tell them?' Len asked, frowning. His interest peaked.

'That we weren't there that weekend,' Samiri said. He shook his head vehemently. 'We were in London. My uncle died and we were at his funeral,' Samiri said. 'We told them to check but our family in London don't talk to the police. They came back again and we told them the same thing. We weren't there that weekend.'

'Are you lying to me?' Len asked. He made the taser crackle.

'It's the truth. I swear it is.'

'So, who was working your ghost train?'

'I don't know,' Samiri said. Len looked angry. Anger flashed in his eyes. 'My dad would have made all the arrangements. He will know who was looking after it for us. I swear we weren't there.' He shrugged. 'Ask my dad. I have his number in my phone. Call him and ask him. He will remember who was there.'

'You told the police this at the time?'

'Yes. That was years ago,' Samiri said. He looked confused. 'Why are you asking this now, man?'

'Because they found their bodies stuffed in a barrel,' Len said. 'A barrel of grease like you use on your ride.'

'Who were they?' Samiri asked.

'Leo was my son,' Len said.

'I'm sorry about your son,' Samiri said, shaking his head. 'I am really. Please. I wasn't there that weekend. I had nothing to do with your son dying. Call my dad. Ask him. He will tell you.'

Len walked away and took out his phone. He toyed with the idea of calling Tarek but it didn't sit right with him. He scrolled through his contacts and found DI Gill Robinson. He pressed dial and listened to it ring. He wondered if she still had his number programmed into her contacts. She answered after a couple of rings.

'Hello Len,' Gill said. 'Are your ears burning?'

'Nope, why?'

'I was just talking about you to the superintendent,' Gill said. Len waited for her to expand. 'A young man by the name of Samiri Koresh went missing from a fairground in Chester yesterday. You wouldn't know anything about that would you?'

'What was the name again?'

'Samiri Koresh.'

'Doesn't ring a bell but I was going to ask you about the people who owned the ghost train when Leo went missing,' Len said.

'Tarek Koresh,' Gill said. 'Father of Samiri Koresh.'

'It's a small world, sometimes,' Len said. 'Were they ruled out of the original investigation?'

'The family being Koresh?' Gill asked, fishing. 'As in Samiri Koresh, the man who is missing from the very same ghost train we're talking about?'

'Yes. Doesn't sound good does it?' Len said, grimacing. 'He'll turn up somewhere unharmed. I'm certain of that.'

'Are you?'

'Yes. Certain,' Len said. 'Were they ruled out of the initial investigation?'

'No one was ruled out,' Gill said. 'They never are. But some information was never logged. Information we now have.'

'Information that they weren't there that weekend?' Len asked.

'Yes.'

'Fucking hell,' Len said.

'Now, you listen to me, Len Jobson,' Gill said. 'I know what you're trying to do and I understand why but that man isn't involved in what happened to Leo. Do you hear me?'

'Yes. Loud and clear,' Len said. 'Like I said, he'll turn up somewhere.'

'You're crossing the line, Len.'

'If they weren't there, do you know who was running it?'

'We have a couple of names,' Gill said. 'And better than that, we have DNA.'

'What do you mean, DNA?' Len said.

'Katrina had hair in her hand,' Gill said. 'We think she pulled it from her attackers head.'

'You're kidding me?'

'No. And she has skin under her nails,' Gill said. 'She put up a fight. It's degraded but alongside the hair samples, it could help us to nail their killer.'

'Have you had a hit on the database?' Len asked.

'For the last time, leave this to us, Len or I will have you banged up,' Gill said. 'Samiri Koresh had better turn up unharmed and he'd better turn up soon.'

'I'm sure he will,' Len said. Gill hung up, leaving Len with more questions than answers.

Chapter 34

Wayne Best was sitting in an interview room waiting for a detective to speak to him. It smelled of disinfectant and Old Spice aftershave. Detective Sergeant Chod Hall came into the room with his laptop and a young female DC. He smiled and sat down opposite him. Wayne felt anxious. The whole episode had shaken anyone who knew the family. Chod scrolled to the app he needed and looked up.

'This won't take long, Wayne,' Chod said. 'I'm DS Hall and this is DC Thorpe. Thanks for coming in to talk to me.'

'No problem,' Wayne said. 'Have you found them?'

'Found who?' Chod asked, smiling.

'The bastards who killed Michelle,' Wayne said.

'What makes you think there's more than one person responsible?' Chod asked, frowning.

'Everyone knows those three blokes from the fair drugged Chelle and Tiff,' Wayne said. 'It's common knowledge around town.'

'I can't comment on an ongoing investigation,' Chod said. 'But I can tell you we've recovered DNA and it won't be long before we can make an announcement. Until then, we need to rule everyone out of the investigation and because you were with Tiffany Branning when we arrived, we have to speak to you formally. I'm sure you'll understand.'

'Of course,' Wayne said. 'I'll help in any way I can.'

'Okay. How long have you known Michelle Branning?'

'Since we were teenagers,' Wayne said.

'You're thirty years old?'

'Yes. Nearly thirty-one.'

'So, there's ten years between you, roughly?'

'Roughly, yes,' Wayne said, nodding. 'I can't believe she's dead. It still hasn't sunk in properly.' He shook his head. 'Mind blowing to think she's gone just like that.'

'These things take some time to adjust to,' Chod said. He paused. 'You dated for a while, quite recently?'

'Yes. Last year,' Wayne said. 'For about three months.'

'Was it a serious relationship?' Chod asked.

'I don't think you would call it serious,' Wayne said. He shrugged. 'We weren't planning to get married or anything. What is serious?'

'Serious is being a couple in a relationship. Saying, we're going out together exclusively,' Chod said. 'Let's not be coy about it. You were dating as a couple, weren't you?'

'Yes. If you put it like that,' Wayne said.

'She ended the relationship?' Chod asked. There was a flicker of something in Wayne's eye. What was it? Resentment? Regret? Remorse?

'Yes. She dumped me by text. The new easy way of finishing with someone without having to look them in the eyes. Long distance dumping. Send the text and turn your phone off,' Wayne said, shrugging. 'There's nothing you can do about it when someone has made up their mind. I can't say I didn't see it coming.'

'Really. She finished it because she found out you were cheating on her, yes?' Chod asked, looking him in the eye to gauge his reaction. Another flicker in the right eye. Anger maybe.

'I wouldn't say I was cheating,' Wayne said. 'I made a mistake on a night out after too much beer. It was just the once. We've all done it, haven't we?'

'I haven't personally,' Chod said. 'I've been married to my missus Sandra for a hundred and ten years and if she ever caught me cheating, she'd cut my nuts off while I'm sleeping. Best not to, in my opinion.' Wayne blushed. 'So, Michelle caught you cheating and finished the relationship?'

'Yes,' Wayne, agreed reluctantly.

'Were you upset about it?'

'Not really,' Wayne said. He blushed again. 'We weren't deadly serious or anything.'

'Obviously, we have her phone records. Some of the text messages you sent to her sound like you were very upset about it,' Chod said. 'In fact, they sound a little desperate.' He looked at Wayne and he shifted uncomfortably in his chair. Chod turned the laptop so Wayne could read some of the messages they'd taken from her phone. 'A couple sound suicidal and then they get increasingly aggressive. Then she changed her number.'

'I was annoyed with myself, not Chelle. It wasn't her fault it was mine and I was angry. I don't recall sending those messages. Probably after a few drinks,' Wayne said. 'Don't text or go on Facebook after a few sherbets. That's the law,' Wayne Joked.

'A few threats were made?' Chod said, not smiling.

'There was nothing malicious in what I said. I was drinking every day and sometimes I was drinking heavily,' Wayne said, blushing. 'I don't recall every message I sent to her but they weren't to be taken seriously. We can say stupid things when we're pissed, can't we?'

'I don't know, do you?'

'Not always but I obviously did back then. I was a bit confused how I felt about the breakup,' Wayne said. 'I might have been a bit of a dick but I didn't do anything wrong. I'm not a bad man for being upset. I didn't mean any harm.'

'No one is saying you did but we need to have everything in its place,' Chod said. 'This conversation will be irrelevant when we have the DNA results.

Whatever happened between you and Hayley Barnes will be the stuff of legend and no one will care if it's true or not. You understand my point.' Wayne nodded, confused.

'How do you know her name?' Wayne asked, frowning.

'Hayley Barnes?'

'Yes.'

'We're the police,' Chod said, shrugging. 'We have to know things. Sometimes we have to know shit that doesn't matter, like you cheating with Hayley Barnes, not once but on six different occasions?' Chod read from the screen.

'You've spoken to Hayley about us?' Wayne asked, shocked.

'Yes,' Chod said, nodding. 'I'm not sure why you're so surprised. Obviously, we've spoken to her family at length about her previous relationships and yours ended acrimoniously.' Chod watched Wayne. He looked frightened. Frightened and angry. 'Hayley told us you stayed at her house when her husband was working nights and that this went on for a number of weeks.'

'Did she?' Wayne muttered. 'I might have on the odd occasion.'

'Odd occasion being six,' Chod said. He sat back and folded his arms. 'This is all very uninteresting but we have to know it because it might be relevant.' Wayne nodded. He looked baffled. 'Can you tell me your movements on the day Michelle went missing.'

'What, all day?'

'Yes. From the time you opened your eyes until you went to bed,' Chod said, smiling again. 'You can leave out anything illegal.'

'I didn't do anything illegal,' Wayne looked shocked and embarrassed.

'I don't care what you did one way or the other but we need it on the record,' Chod said. 'Start from leaving the house.'

'Okay. I got up and made a few calls. I have a few jobs on the go at the moment,' Wayne said. 'I wanted to make sure everything was organised for next week.'

'You're a heating engineer?' Chod asked. 'Central heating, boilers and the like?'

'Yes. I made my calls and then went to Tesco to do a bit of shopping. That was about eleven o'clock,' Wayne said. 'I went to Kentucky for my lunch, then I went to see my parents. They live in Valley. I stayed there until about half three and then made my way to the Newry.'

'So, you got to the fairground at what time?'

'About six o'clock. I parked on Porth-y-felin hill and popped into the Vic for a pint and then drove down to the Newry and had one in the Boathouse,' Wayne said. 'I went up to the fairground and had a walk around and spoke to a few people I know.'

'Which people?' Chod asked.

'Pardon?' Wayne looked confused.

'Which people did you speak to?'

'Just people I know from town,' Wayne said.

'Which people from town?' Chod asked. 'I'll need their names.'

'What for?'

'To verify you were where you said you were,' Chod said, shrugging. 'It's not a difficult concept to grasp. I ask you where you were, you tell me and we check you're telling the truth. It's called police work.'

'Why would I lie to you?'

'Who said you are lying?'

'You're insinuating I am,' Wayne said.

'I'm not insinuating anything,' Chod said. 'I'm asking you a perfectly simple question.'

'Do I need a solicitor?' Wayne asked, becoming agitated.

'I don't know, do you?' Chod asked. 'I'm asking you questions about your whereabouts. If you think you need legal advice to tell us who you spoke to at the fairground, we can stop the interview right now and get you a brief.' Chod looked sternly at Wayne. Wayne withered in his chair. 'Is there a problem, Wayne?'

'No. I don't have a problem but I think you have one,' Wayne said. 'I helped Tiffany to find Michelle and I came here to help you. I didn't expect this kind of scrutiny. I feel like a suspect.'

'You are a suspect,' Chod said. He sat back and folded his arms again. He shrugged and smiled. 'You must understand that. Every man on this island is a suspect until the DNA proves you aren't. This is not personal, Wayne. You seem to be making a big deal out of a few bog-standard questions.'

'Sorry. I'm tired and emotionally drained. If I'm being a dick, I apologise,' Wayne said, rubbing his eyes. He looked up at the ceiling to refocus. 'Can we go back to where you asked me who I spoke to?'

'That's fine by me. Let's do that,' Chod said. He smiled to put Wayne at ease but wasn't smiling on the inside. 'Can you tell me who you spoke to?'

'George Mud. Ian McDonald. Sian Smith,' Wayne said, counting them on his fingers. 'I was talking to George for a while. Anything to do with music or motorbikes and we can talk for hours.'

'Okay. We can check that easily enough. Then what did you do?' Chod asked.

'I had a burger and walked around for a bit, then I fancied a pint, so I went into the beer tent,' Wayne said. 'That's when I saw Tiffany asleep with her head on the table. I recognised the tattoo on her arm. There was no one with her, so I went over to check if she was alright. She was bladdered and acting oddly.'

'What time was that?'

'Seven o'clock,' Wayne said.

'You sound sure about that.'

'I am because Tiff asked me the time when she woke up,' Wayne said. 'She was shocked because Chelle had gone for food at half four. That's why I remember.'

'Okay. To summarise, you got to the fair about six o'clock, walked around for a bit until seven when you saw Tiffany?'

'Yes.'

'Then you were with Tiffany until what time?'

'Until the police sent her and her mum home. I gave them a lift,' Wayne said.

'You had your car there. You said earlier.' Chod said.

'Yes. My work van.'

'What make is it?'

'Ford Transit.'

'Where did you park it when you arrived?'

'At the bottom of the Newry, opposite the Boathouse.'

'Overlooking the boatyard?' Chod said.

'Yes. That's the place.'

'And you got there about six? Chod asked. He studied Wayne's face.

'Yes.'

'Which side of the road did you park?'

'The boatyard side.'

'So, you walked up the Newry along the pavement overlooking the boatyard at about six o'clock?'

'Yes.'

'Michelle was assaulted sometime after four-thirty at the boatyard,' Chod said. 'You didn't see anything suspicious?'

'No. Nothing.' Wayne shrugged. 'It's unnerving to think she might have been there when I walked past.'

'She may have been,' Chod said, nodding.

'I didn't pay the boatyard any attention. When you've walked past it once, you've seen it a million times. It never changes.'

'And after you dropped off Tiffany and her mother?'

'I went home. Tiff called me to tell me they'd found Chelle dead in the marina. I was stunned and had half a bottle of whisky,' Wayne said. 'I fell asleep on the couch. I still couldn't believe it the next day.'

'Like I said earlier, it takes time,' Chod said. 'I think we have everything we need. Except a swab.' He studied Wayne's expression. 'You're okay giving us a DNA sample?'

'Yes. Of course,' Wayne said. Chod and the DC stood up and gathered their things. 'We may need to talk to you again. Don't make any plans to travel.'

'No problem.'

'I'll send an officer to take the swabs,' Chod said. 'Thanks again for your time.'

They walked out of the room and headed upstairs towards operations. Alan Williams was talking to Kim at the top of the stairs. They turned as he approached.

'We've got Carlos Vincentia and David Prost,' Kim said. 'Unfortunately, they've had a good kicking and are on their way to Ysbyty Gwynedd.'

'That's great news. What happened?' Chod asked, laughing.

'Carlos tricked his way into an old lady's house and she recognised him and called her son. David Prost arrived to pick Carlos up just as the son arrived with some friends, all tooled up. They've given them a bit of pasting but they'll survive.' Chod laughed again. 'We've also found a shitload of cocaine welded into their trailer. Pamela Stone just called.'

'That's a bonus,' Chod said.

'How did it go with Wayne Best?'

'There's something not right with him,' Chod said, shaking his head. 'He's squirrelly. He's lying about something but I can't put my finger on it. I'm not comfortable with his version of events.'

'Why?' Alan asked. 'What did he say?'

'He was reluctant to answer some pretty basic questions about who he spoke to at the fairground. I got the impression he was making it up as he went along,' Chod said. 'Listen to this. He drove to the Vic, had a pint then drove down the hill onto the Newry and parked his car down the bottom opposite the Boathouse pub.'

'Overlooking the boatyard,' Alan said.

'Yes.'

'What time does he say he arrived?'

'Six o'clock,' Chod said. 'But I don't believe him.'

'Why?'

'I have no idea,' Chod said. 'Trust issues,' he joked.

'Excuse me, Chod,' a voice called from the bottom of the stairs. 'Which room did you say your interviewee is in?'

'He's in three,' Chod said.

250

'There's no one in there,' the uniformed officer said, shaking her head. 'He's gone.'

Chapter 35

Kelly and her family checked into a bed and breakfast. They dumped their meagre belongings in their rooms and headed out to explore. Sheree and Steve had been there many times in their youth before Kelly and her sister Amy arrived. When they met, they lived with Steve's parents, Mike and Angela for a while. Mike and Angela had a caravan at the Dwygyfylchi and they went there for a little space on their own at the weekends. Eventually, Sheree got a job at the big orange, B&Q and Steve became a delivery driver. They went to Barmouth on occasion for a change from the caravan. It had been a while but Sheree was keen to show off her knowledge of the resort. She fastened her jacket to the neck and marched up the path.

'Let's go this way,' Sheree said, pointing.

'Why are we going that way?' Elle asked.

'The sea is this way,' Sheree said, smiling.

'I know the sea is that way,' Steve said. 'There's a bloody big mountain in the other direction. It can only be one way.'

'Now then, children,' Elle said, teasing her grandparents. 'No arguing or you're not having an ice cream.'

'That's us told,' Steve said. He began singing, morning has broken to himself.

'Will you please stop singing that bloody tune,' Sheree said. 'I'll have it in my head all day.'

'Do you remember that café we used to go to on the front?' Steve asked.

'It was the milk bar,' Sheree said. 'They used to make the best strawberry milkshakes on the planet.'

'And the best fry-ups,' Steve said. 'I wonder if it's still there.'

'The last time we had breakfast in there, we'd just finished making Amy,' Sheree said.

'Don't be disgusting,' Kelly said, trying not to laugh. 'That's an image, I don't need in my head.'

'Are they talking about you know what?' Elle asked.

'You don't need to know anything about you know what just yet. Ignore them,' Kelly said, giggling. It felt good to be there, safe and anonymous. They walked down the road and reached a tee junction, where they waited at the zebra crossing. The traffic was light but persistent. The lights changed and they crossed the road. The sound of the funfair reached them and the smell of candy floss touched the air. A crowd of people crossed with them. They reached the opposite side and Sheree stopped at the doors of an old church. Its dark brown bricks were huge and crusted with exhaust fumes. The place of worship was now a pound-shop. Luminous green and pink signs enticed visitors in with the promise of everything being a pound. It was a mecca for tourists on a budget. They could buy sticks of rock for loved ones at home.

'Come on,' Sheree said. 'I want to go in there. Let's see what we can buy for a pound.'

'Oh, for god's sake. I should have stayed in Holyhead and took my chances with the criminals,' Steve said, moaning. 'It would be less painful than being dragged around a pound-shop.'

'Shut up,' Sheree said, glaring at him. 'There are no criminals.'

'What criminals?' Elle said.

'Criminals in the government,' Steve said. 'Stealing all my money in tax.'

'You mean Boris,' Elle said.

'Yes. I do,' Steve said. 'He's a tatty-headed-bumbling-bandit.' Elle chuckled.

'Well recovered, dad,' Kelly said nudging him in the ribs. 'Come on. We need stuff for the rooms anyway. They'll sell crisps and pop.'

'How much will they be?' Steve asked.

'A pound,' Elle answered.

They walked inside and followed the other shoppers, who were milling around the vast array of products. Sheree and Kelly carried baskets, which were soon half full of bargains. Steve spotted a young girl, stocking the shelves. He picked up an electric plug.

'Excuse me, how much is this?' he asked. Elle frowned.

'A pound,' the girl said, without turning around. She continued to stack phone cases.

'How much for two?' Steve asked.

'Grandad,' Elle said, punching his leg. 'You're so embarrassing.'

'If I had a pound for every time someone thought that was funny, I could buy everything in this shop and still have change.' The girl finished stacking the box and walked away.

'Some people have no sense of humour,' Steve said.

'She probably has a sense of humour but it's not the same as yours,' Sheree said. 'Yours is unique.'

'I'll take that as a compliment,' Steve said.

'Please don't,' Sheree said. 'Take it as constructive criticism.'

'What does that mean?' Elle asked.

'It means your grandad is a numpty,' Sheree said. Elle laughed.

Kelly took her hand and guided her through a throng of customers who were sifting through baskets of socks.

'Now then, there's a question for you,' Steve said. 'Is it a pound for a pair of socks or fifty-pence each?' Elle thought about it for a second. Steve stopped smiling and stood still. Kelly caught his expression. 'Don't turn around,' Steve said. Kelly froze. 'Look in that mirror,' he whispered. The mirror was part of a display on the wall, printed with the logo of an imaginary beer. Kelly looked in it. She saw the looming figure in the doorway of the church. He was scanning the crowd, looking for someone. 'He has burns on the other side of his face,' Steve said. 'Is that him?' Kelly nodded. She pulled Elle closer to her.

'Is it who?' Elle asked, confused.

'Call nine, nine, nine,' Sheree said.

Chapter 36

Carlos winced as another stitch was put into his scalp. He was handcuffed to the trolley. His right eye was nearly closed shut. The swelling was painful. He could taste blood in his mouth and his front teeth felt loose. There was a sickly twisted feeling in his guts. He felt like a rat in a trap. His mind was racing looking for a way out but he couldn't find one. There were police everywhere he looked and they weren't there for his benefit. He could sense the animosity towards him. The police would question him soon and there was nothing he could say to muddy the waters. He contemplated blaming everything on Claus and David and chucking Benaim into the mix. That might confuse things. If he could spread the blame, he would. A detective opened the curtain.

'Can we have five minutes with him?' Kim asked. The doctor frowned and shook his head. 'He's the main suspect in the Michelle Branning murder,' she added.

'Take as long as you need,' the doctor said, changing his tune. 'He's had a few stitches and has a bump on the head but there's no reason he can't be interviewed. Arsehole,' he added, looking at Carlos.

'We can't interview him here,' Kim said. 'I just need a word.'

'Be my guest.'

Kim closed the curtain. She approached the trolley. Carlos tried to sit up but only managed to slump against the pillow.

'You're going to be moved to the interview suite at St Asaph,' Kim said. 'We're moving you because the entire town wants to skin you alive.' Carlos grinned. 'Funny?' Kim asked, frowning. 'Any minute now, we'll have the DNA results back from the lab and when we do, I'm going to wipe the smile from your face. There are six different police forces waiting on those results and another three on Europol showing an interest because of historic sex crimes involving a travelling fairground and Rohypnol. I reckon you and your pals are going to be identified as the perpetrators in a lot of those cases.' Carlos frowned and shrugged. He pretended not to be phased but his eyes said something different. 'Flunitrazepam. You've been ordering it from the internet. It's a very specific drug and you haven't covered your tracks,' Kim said. 'We recovered some from your bedroom in your trailer and one of our detectives recovered some more from the marsh near Porth-y-felin. Right next to one of your footprints,' Kim said. Carlos blinked and looked uncomfortable for a second. 'Have a good think about it, Carlos,' she whispered. 'Serial rapists get life. That's what you and your scumbag relatives are. Serial rapists.' He stopped grinning. 'Life in jail. Does that make you laugh? If we can put you at the murder scene for Michelle Branning, you're never getting out.' His eyes glazed over as if he didn't want to hear it. 'They'll carry your dead body out of jail in a metal box.' She smiled. 'How funny is that?' Kim opened the curtain and walked out, closing it behind her.

Chapter 37

Kelly switched on her phone and waited for the signal to appear. The structure of the church was blocking the reception. She kept her eye on the big man in the mirror and tried to keep Elle from sensing her fear. Her mother was holding her arm, shielding the phone from view. Steve was standing the other side of her. He looked around for a weapon but could only see plastic swords and water pistols. There was nothing heavy in a pound-shop. Kelly made the call and explained to the operator what their emergency was. The fact the male was possibly the main suspect in the Rhosneiger murders meant her call was escalated. Armed units were despatched and her call was patched through to Alan Williams. He told her to stay where she was, surrounded by people. She hung up.

'He must have followed us,' Steve said.

'I thought we were safe,' Sheree said.

'Take the mirror off the wall, dad,' Kelly said. 'The police are on the way out I want to be as far away from him as I can be.' She checked where Benaim was. He was standing inside the doors, trying on a baseball cap. It was black with a red NY logo on it. 'Let's move up to the far end,' she said.

'What's going on?' Elle asked. 'Why are we whispering?'

'There's a man over there, who is wanted by the police,' Kelly said. 'I've called them and they're coming to arrest him but we don't want him to know it was me that called them. It's like a game of hide and seek.'

'I'm not a kid, you know,' Elle said. She tutted and tried to move away from Kelly.

'Stay right were you are, young lady,' Kelly said. She tightened her grip on her daughter. 'This is not the time to be stubborn. Do as you're told.'

'He's moving away from the door,' Steve said.

'Where's he going?' Kelly asked.

'He's paying for the hat.'

'There's a fire exit there,' Sheree said. 'Shall we go out that way?'

'See if it's open,' Kelly said. Steve pushed the bar and the alarms sounded, blaring. They were deafening. The door opened slightly and then jammed on a security chain. 'It's locked!'

'Armed police!' a voice shouted. Then another joined the cacophony, and another and another. Benaim Bronski was surrounded, forced to kneel, cuffed and marched out of the building. Several senior officers made their way through the frightened shoppers.

'Kelly Williams?' one of them called. 'We're looking for Kelly Williams?'

'I'm over here,' Kelly said.

'You called this in?' the officer said.

'Yes.' Kelly nodded. 'How did you get here so quickly?'

'A traffic cop spotted him near Bala. They've been following him.' The policeman called in that they'd identified Kelly and her family. 'We need to get you away from here,' the officer said.

'We're booked into a bed and breakfast around the corner,' Steve said.

'You're no longer safe here,' the officer said. 'Men like that rarely work alone. If he followed you here, they know where you're staying. We'll get you out of here and arrange to pick up your things from your digs. Follow us please.'

'Are we under arrest?' Elle asked.

'No,' Kelly said. 'We haven't done anything wrong. We need to go with these officers to somewhere safe. That man is a criminal and knows I called the police.'

'Are you going to be a witness again, mummy?'

'Yes, darling. I think I am,' Kelly said.

259

'Here we go again,' Steve said, rolling his eyes.

Chapter 38

Pamela Stone walked into Alan's office. There was an air of expectation in the operations room. Alan had called a briefing for as many detectives as were available. They were gathering and chatting, swapping information. The atmosphere was taut. The Vincentia brothers were both in custody alongside David Prost and Benaim Bronski. They had been moved to St Asaph to avoid any public unrest outside the station at Holyhead. It had been a whirlwind investigation. It needed the science to identify the actual culprit for the murder of Michelle Branning. Alan could hardly contain himself. He wanted to know what the DNA results had revealed but Pamela insisted she relay it personally. Kim brought a tray of coffee into his office and put it down on the desk. Pamela took out her laptop and fired it up. She appeared to be unusually quiet. Alan looked forward to seeing her but she was subdued. He liked her dark humour but today, she hadn't cracked any funnies, inappropriate or otherwise, which worried him. Alan closed the door and they all sat down.

'I want to run through the findings before we hold the briefing,' Alan said.

'That's why I wanted to go through it with you,' Pamela said. The results are complicated.

'I don't like complicated,' Alan said. 'Please tell me we have a hit.'

'We have several,' Pamela said.

'Several is good,' Alan said. 'It is good, isn't it?'

'Let me start with the boat.' Pamela wouldn't be drawn.

'Okay,' Alan said. 'Please do.' He smiled at Kim. It was a nervous smile. He was anxious. Cases were won and lost on the strength of the forensic evidence found. This one had to be one hundred percent, no doubt about it, nailed. He had a personal desire to finish the case, lock them up and never think about the bastards ever again, although that would be difficult. They were a special level of serial predator. Total scumbag level.

'We found traces of blood, which belong to the victim, so we can confirm she was in the boat. We also have her hair and vaginal fluid on the sheets,' Pamela said. 'When we examined her at the mortuary, her body didn't yield anything we can use genetically. The seawater destroyed most of the evidence but we do have a set of teeth marks taken from her right breast. Your suspects have all refused to let us take an imprint of their teeth. We're waiting on dental records from Germany,' she explained. 'None of your suspects have used a dentist here, which is frustrating but shouldn't affect the outcome. They have been in the UK for years, which means their records from Germany are probably obsolete now. The teeth will have changed as they aged.'

'Tell Chod Hall to pull the dental records for Wayne Best,' Alan said to Kim. Kim typed the order into her phone and sent it.

'Who is he?' Pamela asked.

'He's an ex-boyfriend who was at the fairground with the victim's sister,' Alan said. 'He wasn't on our radar until he did a vanishing act when we asked for a swab test. Then he left the building in a hurry.'

'Ah,' Pamela said. 'That's bad news but I have good news. The good news is we found traces of semen on the mattress.' She paused. 'And we have a hit.'

'Carlos Vincentia?' Alan asked. 'Or his brother Claus?'

'Both,' Pamela said. 'They clearly attack as a team. We also have saliva on the pillow from both men and hair on the sheets from both men.'

'Superb,' Alan said. He punched the air. Kim high fived him. 'We've got the bastards.'

'I thought you would be pleased,' Pamela said. 'To back the findings up, we also have a clear footprint on the deck belonging to Carlos Vincentia. I think you have him hook, line and sinker.' She frowned and held up her hands. 'This is all very clear but we have some other findings which aren't so clear.'

'What other findings?' Alan asked, confused.

'We dismantled most of the boat at the warehouse as you know,' Pamela said. 'The galley toilet has a chemical tank beneath it, which usually processes the initial breakdown of waste. It had been used. Normally the chemicals in the tank would render everything useless to us but in this case, there are several different hits on urine samples,' she explained. 'There are no chemicals in the tank because the boat is out of the water and it had been drained, so it was easy to identify that three different men used the toilet.'

'Three different men?' Alan asked.

'Yes. And we found a used condom, which had been flushed,' Pamela said. Alan shook his head and looked at Kim. She went pale. 'The semen doesn't match either of the Vincentia brothers and the DNA isn't in the system.'

'A third attacker?' Kim asked. 'Obviously, not David Prost.' Pamela shook her head. 'Who hasn't given us a sample?' she asked, looking at Alan.

'Wayne Best,' Alan said. 'I want that little scrote dragged in here and swabbed. Have we located him?'

'His parents said he's gone fishing,' Kim said.

'This is amazing work, Pamela,' Alan said. 'There are a list of forces waiting for those results. It will be enough to put them away for good.'

'Several forces have been in touch directly,' Pamela said. 'Are you okay with me sharing the results with them?'

'Yes,' Alan said. 'If it gives closure to other cases, it's fine by me. These three men make my stomach turn. I don't want them getting out ever.'

'I think all the other forces agree with your sentiment.' Pamela shook her head. 'The other cases are shocking but they all have a similar pattern. Women being drugged and assaulted. I think this is the tip of the iceberg. A lot of their victims won't have come forward, some won't even know they've been assaulted. But the most interesting conversation I've had this afternoon was with a detective inspector from Merseyside. Regarding a double murder.'

'Gill Robinson?' Alan asked, interested. Pamela nodded. He was keen to get to the troops with the news but he wanted to hear what the Merseyside detective inspector had to do with it. 'What has this got to do with them?'

'They came to Anglesey to speak to the owner of the circus a few days ago,' Pamela said. 'Regarding a couple who disappeared five years ago. Leo Jobson and his partner Katrina Watkins vanished and were found in a metal drum on a construction site, last week.'

'They were dumped in a pond and the pond was drained, right?' Alan asked. He was still baffled.

'Yes. That's the case. When I examined the bodies, we found Katrina Watkins had hair in her hand and skin under her nails. She put up a fight by the looks of things.'

'Bloody hell. That's incredible,' Alan said, shaking his head. 'And you're going to tell me you have a match?'

'Yes. The hair belongs to Carlos Vincentia,' Pamela said. 'It seems that the owners of the ghost train were away for the week and Benaim Bronski offered to staff it for them while they were away,' she explained. 'The Vincentia brothers and Prost were working for Bronski and were familiar with the machinery. Bad news for Leo Jobson and Katrina Watkins. It appears they've been stalking females since way back.'

'That is the icing on the cake. They were at it for years,' Alan said. 'Not anymore. They're finished.'

'You know what they say about leopards,' Pamela said. 'I did wonder about their decision to kill her.' Alan frowned. 'Michelle Branning, I mean.'

'I don't follow,' Alan said.

'Initially, I thought they have been doing this for years but haven't killed anyone. They assault them and leave them to recover in their own homes or they put them into a taxi and send them away,' Pamela said.

'You're suggesting they might not have killed Michelle?' Kim asked, shaking her head.

'I'm not suggesting anything,' Pamela said. 'I'm saying that since the Liverpool couple, they haven't killed anyone.'

'Until now,' Kim said.

'Pamela may be right,' Alan said. 'The used condom suggests there was another male there this time around. Someone we can't identify yet.'

'But the Liverpool murders show they actually have killed,' Kim said. 'Five years ago, to be exact.'

'They're killers for sure,' Alan said. 'And this evidence will see them locked away for the remainder of their shitty lives but we need to make sure the evidence backs us up.' A knock on the door interrupted them. 'Come in,' Alan said.

'Wayne Best has just used his debit card in a hotel in Keswick,' Richard said. 'Long way to go fishing. Shall I send the locals to pick him up?'

'Oh yes,' Alan said. 'I want to have a conversation with that man.'

Chapter 39

Fred Garret was stressed. He was always stressed. The insurance company were still digging their heels in about rebuilding the workshop. The clean-up of sunken yachts from the storms a few years back was still ongoing, causing all kinds of problems, not least yacht owners refusing to pay for their berths. He was getting to the point of telling them all to come and get their fucking boats and stick them where the sun doesn't shine. He would take them all out of the water if he could and knock a fucking big hole in the keel of each one. Pretentious buggers, some of them. More money than sense until it's time to pay the bill. Now the murder in the boatyard had the flat owners jumping ship. Three of them had been put up for sale and another one was insisting he wasn't paying the service charge. There were more empty flats than occupied ones and it was beginning to bite financially. Fred was doing the rounds of the empty flats, checking for maintenance issues. A burst pipe the month before wasn't spotted until the ceiling of the shop below collapsed. That was another costly fuckup.

Fred walked into number eight and switched on the lights. The beige carpets were worn and stained. One of the downsides of renting the flats out on short lease. The tenants didn't give a shit. He checked the bedrooms, all good. The bathroom and kitchen were in good order too. It was warm and quiet and empty. There wasn't a stick of furniture in the place. The view from the living room was stunning, overlooking the marina, breakwater and mountain. He opened the balcony door and looked out over the boatyard. The security camera which covered the balcony blinked. A red light flickered as he moved. He looked at the camera and a light came on in his mind. He took out his phone and looked for Alan's number.

Chapter 40

Lottie was standing on the viewing deck of the Ulysses as it sailed out of the port of Holyhead, heading for Dublin. She lit her cigarette and inhaled deeply. The woman next to her rolled her eyes and tutted. Lottie ignored her and blew her smoke into the wind. It blew back into the face of the offended woman.

'Do you mind?' she moaned.

'Nope,' Lottie said. The woman walked away in a huff. Liz came and stood next to her. 'Are you okay?' Lottie asked. She put her arm around her shoulder.

'I'm okay,' Liz said. 'I don't think we'll forget that stop for a while.'

'We certainly didn't make any friends,' Lottie agreed. 'Tomorrow is another day. New town, new country, new start.' She flicked her cigarette into the foaming wake and watched it vanish into the bubbles. 'I think I'm going to take some time away,' Lottie said.

'Really?' Liz said. 'You're due a holiday,' she agreed. 'I could stand in for you as the ringmaster for a while.'

'Do you think you could?'

'Yes. I've been wanting to try those boots on forever.'

'Get your own boots,' Lottie laughed.

'Where will you go?'

'Sri Lanka,' Lottie said. 'I didn't get to finish my trip. Maybe it's time I did.' Lottie watched Anglesey become smaller as they sailed away. 'I need to sort dad out first,' she added. 'I think the twins told him about that bloody nuisance Malcolm Orange and I think he went out in the night.'

'Not up to his old tricks again.'

'I know. He worries me.'

'You could always take him with you.'

'I want a rest,' Lottie said. 'I really want a rest.'

Chapter 41

Alan and Kim walked into the interview room. Wayne Best was sitting next to his brief, a middle-aged woman called Doreen. Alan had met her a few times. She was from a decent practice in Bangor and was a no-nonsense type of brief. If she thought her client was being obstructive to their own detriment, she would have no problems telling them so. Likewise, she wouldn't have any inappropriate behaviour from the officers conducting the interview. Her client was looking very sheepish and sorry for himself. Kim went through the legal process and they sat down to begin the interview. Kim had her laptop set up so they could all see it.

'How was your trip to the lakes?' Alan asked. Wayne shrugged but didn't answer. 'Can you tell me why you went on the run?'

'It was all getting on top of me,' Wayne said. 'I just flipped out and needed some space.'

'Plenty of space in Keswick,' Alan said, frowning. 'It was nothing to do with being asked for a DNA sample?'

'Nope. I've given you one.'

'You consented to giving one since we arrested you,' Alan said. 'That's not quite the same as volunteering one.'

'Whatever. It's done now,' Wayne said. 'It's not a big deal, is it?'

'It might be,' Alan said. 'The first thing we're going to do is compare the sample you gave against the semen found in a used condom we found at the boatyard.' Wayne flushed red. 'Do you know anything about a used condom in the toilet aboard the Wave Rider?'

'No,' Wayne said. He was lying. Alan could taste the lie it was so obvious.

'I think you do,' Alan said. 'You know a bit about boats, don't you?'

'A bit.'

'You're a plumber, so you know a bit about how the toilets work?'

'I'm a heating engineer,' Wayne said.

'Same thing,' Alan said. Wayne shook his head. 'You work with pipes full of water, just like a plumber except yours are hot.'

'If you say so,' Wayne said.

'Is there a question here?' Doreen asked.

'I'm getting to it,' Alan said. 'My point is the toilets on a boat like the Wave Rider have a waste tank which is usually full of powerful chemicals.' Alan paused and waited for Wayne to react. He was uncomfortable. 'The chemicals would usually destroy any evidence flushed down the toilet.' He paused. 'You know that don't you?'

'I suppose so.'

'But the tank had been drained,' Alan said. 'Because it was out of the water. It was used by three men to urinate and someone flushed a used condom down there too. Of course, we've tested the DNA because everything is still intact. Luckily for us, the chemicals weren't in the tank.' Alan watched Wayne struggling. His face said he was panicking inside. 'You've done some work at the boatyard recently, haven't you?'

'I've done the odd job there,' Wayne said. 'Fitting boilers and radiators in boats.'

'But not on the Wave Rider,' Alan said.

'No.'

'I want you to understand completely what I'm saying,' Alan said. 'Because the Wave Rider was being repaired, the system was drained. The waste tank was dry.' Alan waited for a reaction. 'So, we know three men took a piss onboard the boat. Carlos Vincentia and Claus Vincentia were two of them. I think the other man was you.' Alan stared at Wayne. He couldn't hold eye contact. 'Anything to tell us?'

'No. I don't know what you're talking about.'

'I'm talking about the condom you used to rape Michelle Branning,' Alan said. 'The DNA will tell us the semen is yours and the vaginal cells on the latex belong to Michelle Branning.' Doreen took off her glasses and stared at Wayne. She looked horrified. 'You raped her, discarded the condom and took a piss, thinking the chemicals would destroy any evidence.'

'I'm going to advise my client to say nothing further at this point,' Doreen said. 'And I would request a break so, I can advise him further.'

'Have you got anything to add?' Alan asked.

'No comment.'

Chapter 42

Len Jobson waited patiently in the visitor's block. They were searched and processed before being shown into the visiting area. He filed in and waited until he was shown to his seat. The prisoners were brought in, greeted their visitors and were seated. Len didn't know the man he was visiting but they pretended they were old friends. Reggie Quinn had arranged it. Len shook his hand and smiled thinly. His name was Tommy Doyle. He was serving fifteen years for a nasty armed robbery in which a security guard was shot. Tommy was an old friend of the Quinns. They had used him several times on bank jobs. Len wanted to see the man who had murdered his son. He wanted to see his face. Cutting his face would have been better but he was in the hands of the law now in the relative safety of the penal system. It was bittersweet. The police had caught him using DNA evidence. The best type of evidence there was. Evidence that couldn't be tampered with or made to lie. There was hair in Katrina's hand and it belonged to Carlos Vincentia. A German. A German fairground worker. Len had to see him for himself. It was a morbid curiosity.

'Len Jobson,' Tommy said. 'An absolute pleasure to meet you.'

'Likewise,' Len said. His eyes were focused on Carlos Vincentia. The German was being visited by a skinny woman with bad teeth. Probably an ex with fuck all better to do. How any woman could visit a nonce was beyond Len. 'That's Vincentia over there,' Len said. 'His brother isn't in here.'

'He hasn't got a visit today,' Tommy said. 'Don't worry. I know who they are. They stick together on the wing but they're not popular. No one has any time for beasts in here. Fucking nonces will get their prison stripes when we have the chance.'

'Beasts never were liked inside, even when I was a lad,' Len said. 'You know what needs to be done?'

'Yes.'

'I'll take the money in cash to your missus at your house as soon as I get the word it's been done, okay?' Len asked. Tommy nodded. 'And I'll stick a little bonus in there for your kids if I get photographs. I need to know they suffered. You know what I mean.'

'Leave it with me,' Tommy said. 'I won't let you down.'

Chapter 43

Carlos went back to his cell and jumped onto his bunk. His visit had killed an hour and delivered a small block of weed. Skunk. The good stuff. Diane had smuggled it in wrapped in clingfilm to mask the smell and stuffed it up her tush. Clever girl Diane. Nice tush too. She wasn't too bright but she could suck for England. Always handy to have a girl like that in your contact list. Especially when everyone else has fucked you off because you've been charged with rape and murder. That's when you see who your true friends are. As it turned out, Carlos had none. His cellmate Donny walked in and climbed onto the top bunk. Donny was a fat nonce from Deeside, in for grooming children online. Fucking pervert. Messing with kids was wrong, Carlos thought.

'How was your visit?' Donny asked, opening a bag of crisps.

'Great. I was sitting there with a massive hard on and couldn't go near her. It's cruel in here,' Carlos moaned.

'That's what you get in here. Fuck all,' Donny said. 'There are a lot of rumours about you. You're the talk of the north out there on the landings.'

'Why are they talking about me?'

'Because they have fuck all else to do,' Donny said. 'They say you killed three people?'

'Who says that?' Carlos asked.

'They. They say. Everyone. They.' Donny went quiet. 'The whispers on the landings. You know how it is.'

'Not really but I'll take your word for it,' Carlos said.

'They say you killed two women and a guy?'

'What else do they say?'

'They say you stuffed a guy and his woman in an oil drum and dumped them in a pond. They say you would have got away with it but someone drained the water out of it?' Donny asked.

'They know too much in here. How do they know that when I haven't told them?'

'The screws love to gossip. They are the ones in the know,' Donny said. 'If you want to know anything about another con, ask a screw. They can't help themselves.'

'I'll bear that in mind.'

'Is that true?'

'No. I'm innocent,' Carlos said.

'We're all innocent but is that true?' Donny asked. 'Did they drain the pond?'

'Yes. They drained the fucking pond.' Carlos shook his head in disbelief. 'Can you actually believe that?'

'That is sick, man,' Donny said.

'Sick,' Carlos agreed.

'Who was the other woman you killed?'

'That one isn't on me,' Carlos said.

'They said you raped the woman and threw her into the sea?'

'I fucked her but I didn't kill anyone,' Carlos said. 'My brother had her too but she was alive when we left. She was on another planet but she was breathing fresh air. And that is the truth.'

'Sounds like bullshit to me, man,' Donny said, munching. 'I'll tell you another thing too.'

'I'm all ears,' Carlos said.

'They say the guy you killed and stuffed in the barrel was connected,' Donny said. He lowered his voice.

'Connected to who?' Carlos asked.

'The heavy mob,' Donny said, laughing. 'You picked on the wrong dude.'

'What are you talking about?'

'They say his father is a hitman for an outfit in Liverpool.' Carlos got off his bunk and stood up. He looked Donny in the eye.

'Are you shitting me?' Carlos asked.

'Nope. They are saying there's a hit on you, man.'

'Is that what they're saying?' Carlos asked, shaking his head. 'Sounds like bullshit to me.'

'I'm just telling you what they're saying,' Donny said. 'You better watch your back, man.'

Chapter 44

Claus was lying on his bunk, reading a book about Fred West. He was impressed by just how fucked up the guy was and his missus was even worse than he was. It was comforting to know there were some really evil people out there. Torturing their own kids and burying them in their garden. That is sick, crazy sick. Not right in the head sick. Claus had sometimes questioned his own sanity. When they were much younger, he had wondered if Carlos and he were sick but as time went by, he decided they were probably less sick than most other people. They were different but acted with clarity. It was a personal preference. They chose to do what they did and they were good at it. Yes, they drugged women for sex but don't all men do that? The drug they used was flunitrazepam whereas the rest of society used alcohol and money to woo their targets. He had seen nightclubs many times and watched the interaction with interest. Females dress to attract males and then moan when they get attention from males they don't like. Tell a woman she looks sexy and you'll get a positive response if she likes you. If she doesn't, you're a pervert. A sex pest. Not every man can have a sixpack stomach and great cheekbones. Flunitrazepam levelled the playing field.

The first time they used roofies, the girl was nineteen and fit as fuck. She was way out of their league, prancing around wiggling her arse like a show pony. All the guys on the fairground were staring at her with their tongues hanging out. Under normal circumstances, she wouldn't look twice at Carlos or him. He remembered watching the drug take effect, seeing her eyes roll. They got her back to their caravan and undressed her. It was like unwrapping a Christmas present that breathed. She was amazing. Claus remembered thinking it was the most exciting thing he had ever done and they talked about her for weeks. He still had her pictures on his phone. The police would be looking at them on his phone and hundreds of others but they would never find out who he was. Some guys spent weeks courting a woman and spent a fortune and still didn't get laid. Carlos and Claus had sex with them anyway they wanted and they didn't have all the hassle of dating them. Who was crazy?

The cell door opened and three prisoners slipped inside, closing it behind them. Claus opened his mouth to scream for help but they shoved a pair of socks in and taped his mouth shut. He gagged and felt burning bile in the back of his throat. He began to choke. Strings of vomit spurted from his nostrils. One of the men showed him the picture of a young man he vaguely remembered.

'Remember him?' the man said. 'Leo Jobson. His father sends his regards.'

They threw boiling liquid into his face. It scalded him. The pain was intense but didn't subside. It was homemade napalm. The water was laced with sugar and ketchup, which clung to the skin like napalm, burning it deep. His eyes were stinging. He saw one of them loading tins of beans into a towel. His vision was blurred but he saw the towel swung high in the air. The tins impacted with his face, splitting the skin and shattering bones. He felt it impact over and over until his skull was mush and more of his brains were on the pillow than in his cranium.

Chapter 45

Alan and Kim went back into the interview room. Wayne had his head in his hands. Doreen was scribbling onto her tablet with an iPen. She looked stressed. Kim ran through the necessaries and they began again.

'I take it you've been advised by your solicitor. Is there anything you want to say?' Alan asked.

'My client is willing to read a statement but will not answer any more questions,' Doreen said.

'Are you sure you want to do that before we present our questions?' Alan asked. 'I wouldn't advise doing it that way.'

'He won't answer any more questions. If what you told me is the truth, read the statement,' she snapped at Wayne. He looked at it like a moody teenager, deciding what to do. 'If it isn't the truth, don't say anything,' she added. Alan didn't think Wayne had told her the truth. He hoped he hadn't told the truth. Liars always trip up. They waited a few minutes before he spoke. Wayne read from a sheet of paper.

'Last Sunday about five o'clock, I was walking from my car near the boatyard on Newry Beach, when I noticed my ex-girlfriend, Michelle Branning with two men. I hadn't seen either of them before. They were walking either side of her, holding her by the elbows. She appeared to be drunk. They went into a boatyard and climbed up some steps onto the back of a cruiser, opened the hatch and went inside. I was intrigued and waited a while to see what would happen. After about twenty-minutes, the men came out of the boat, closed the hatch and left. They walked up the Newry towards the fairground. I was curious and went down to the boat to speak to Michelle. I knocked on the door and then opened it. Michelle was on the bed, drunk but conscious.'

Alan exchange glances with Kim. They knew what was coming next.

278

'I chatted with her and then we kissed. One thing led to another and we had sex. Consensual sex. After we had sex, I used the toilet, disposed of the condom and left. Michelle was asleep and in good health when I left the boat.' He looked up. 'That's all I have to say.'

'So, that's the best you can do?' Alan said, shaking his head. 'You expect us to believe she had sex with you and then you left and that's it?'

'No comment.'

'Are you sure that's your best version of events?' Alan asked.

'No comment.'

'I suggest you watch this CCTV footage which was brought to our attention yesterday.' Wayne went white. Doreen took off her glasses again and sat back, resigned to the fact they were about to be blindsided. 'It's taken by a security camera. The marina flats suffered from a spate of break-ins a few years ago and the balcony was the point of entry in each case. This camera was placed to monitor the balcony of flat number eight in case of burglary. It covers the Wave Rider and the area around that part of the dock. Play the footage.'

The images were clear. Carlos Vincentia and Claus left the boat, smiling and laughing. They walked towards the Newry and quickly went out of shot. The figure of Wayne Best appeared. He was acting suspiciously, hands in his pockets, peering in the portholes of the boat. Then he climbed up the steps and went inside, closing the hatch behind him. Alan fast forwarded the footage. Half an hour went by. Wayne opens the hatch and walks out of the cabin, holding Michelle by the arm. She was naked from the waist down and looked unsteady on her feet. He frogmarched her towards the dock wall. It was no more than ten yards from the boat. Michelle tried to resist as he turned her around and pushed her over the edge. She fell ten feet into the sea and went under. The camera showed Wayne standing on the dock for a minute before he walked away, hands in his pockets, head down. Michelle didn't resurface. They stopped the footage and waited for Wayne to comment. Doreen was sitting in silence white as a sheet.

'I didn't mean to kill her. I was trying to sober her up,' Wayne said. Doreen shook her head and closed her eyes. 'She went under and didn't come up. I thought she would come straight back up and climb up the ladder.'

'Wayne Best, I'm charging you with the rape and murder of Michelle Branning,' Alan said.

Chapter 46

Donny was escorted by the librarian to the far side of the library. Tommy Doyle was sitting at a desk with two of his cronies. They didn't have a straight nose between them. All three men looked like they had sprinted full speed into an oncoming bus. They were very frightening men and they didn't like nonces. Donny was particularly disliked because he wasn't just a sex offender, he favoured children. He was at the bottom of the food chain, the lowest of the low and he knew it. Life inside was terrifying for a paedophile like Donny. He had a target on his back and was fair game for anyone with the inclination to kick his face in on a whim. Paedos were the prison punchbags. He was constantly looking over his shoulder.

'Here he is. Donny-dirty-dick,' Tommy said, as he approached the table. The men stared at Donny with hatred and disgust in their eyes. 'Sit down you horrible cretin.' Tommy said, pointing to a chair.

'I'm okay standing,' Donny said. The librarian punched him in the testicles and Donny dropped to his knees. He was bent double by the pain.

'If I say sit down, then you sit down.' The men picked him up and sat him opposite Tommy. 'Do you know why you're here?'

'I can take a guess it is to do with my cellmate,' Donny said, quietly. He didn't want to provoke another attack. 'What do you want?'

'Your cellmate smokes a bit of weed, doesn't he?' Tommy asked. Donny nodded, still unable to breathe properly. Tommy held out a readymade spliff. 'Take this with you. When you get back to the cell, light this up and take one drag.' Tommy held up his finger. 'One drag, understand?' Donny nodded. 'Then give it to Carlos.'

'Okay,' Donny said. 'I can do that. What's in it?'

'If you take more than one drag, you'll find out,' Tommy said, a twisted mile on his face. 'Do as you're told and then go to the showers.'

'Okay.'

'One more thing. I need you to put this under your pillow,' Tommy said. 'You sleep on the top bunk, right?'

'Yes,' Donny said. He took what looked like a toothbrush from him. The brushes had been removed and three razorblades melted into the plastic head. 'I don't want anything to do with this,' Donny complained, shaking his head.

'Fine, then I'll get the boys to hold you down while I cut your cock off with this.'

'No. There's no need for that.' Donny took the evil looking blade and put it in his pocket. 'I'll do it.'

'I thought you would,' Tommy said. 'Do as I've told you, and I'll make sure no one in here touches you while you serve your sentence.'

'Okay.'

'Go on then,' Tommy said. 'Fuck off.'

****

Chod Hall walked into the Victoria Inn with Richard Lewis. They checked the vault to see who was in. A couple of the locals were leaning at the bar chatting. Chod recognised two of them as local painters. They said hello and the detectives went into the bar. The barmaid spotted them immediately.

'They're over there,' she said, pointing to the pool table. 'George said to call you if they came in.'

'Thanks Anne,' Chod said. They walked over to the pool table. The three men standing there looked flustered. 'Barry Coop,' Chod said. 'Just the man I'm looking for.'

'I haven't done anything,' Barry said.

'You lost your wallet,' Chod said.

'How do you know that?'

'Because I found it in the marsh,' Chod said. 'You dropped it when you were running away from the quarry road after dropping a block onto Trevor Branning's head,' Chod said, holding up the wallet in an evidence bag.

'We didn't do that,' Wilf Jones said, taking his shot.

'Who mentioned you?' Chod asked.

'I'm just saying,' Wilf said.

'We didn't know it was Trevor,' Barry said. The others looked at him horrified.

'You fucking idiot,' Wilf said.

'I think we should take a look in the boot of your vehicles,' Chod said. 'And before you think about bullshitting me, George has given us the CCTV footage from the pub. It shows, you three idiots going to your vehicles to arm yourselves with a couple of baseball bats and a tyre iron, before you jump the stile into the fields. Now, one of you couldn't move that block and I'm quite sure, two of you would struggle, so when the forensics come back, I'm putting my money on it saying the three of you moved that block and pushed it onto Trevor.'

'I told you it was a shit idea,' Barry said, to Wilf. 'Why do I listen to you?'

'You're all under arrest,' Richard said.

'What's the charge?' Wilf asked.

'Being a fucking idiot will do for a start,' Chod said. 'Come on.'

Chapter 47

Donny checked the landing for screws and walked into the cell. He pushed the door closed. His heart was beating like a drum. Carlos was lying on his bunk reading. Donny wanted to tell him what was about to happen but was too frightened.

'I'm going for a shower,' Donny said. 'Do you want a puff before I go?'

'What have you got?'

'Fuck knows,' Donny said. 'I got it from one of the Wrexham blokes They always have good weed.'

'Why did they give you a smoke?'

'I paid for it,' Donny lied. He lit it and took a drag. 'Here get your lips around this.'

Carlos took the joint and inhaled deeply. He held the smoke in his lungs for a few seconds before exhaling. Donny took the shank from his pocket and hid it under his pillow. Carlos took three long pulls on the joint. He wasn't in a rush to give it back to Donny. Donny grabbed his towel and shampoo.

'Don't you want any more?' Carlos asked, inhaling again.

'No. It's too strong for me. I'm off to the showers. See you in a bit, Donny said, Heading towards the door in a hurry.

Carlos coughed and grabbed his chest. His eyes widened as if they would pop out of his head. His hands began to shake and then his entire body went into spasm. Donny couldn't move. White foam dribbled from the corner of his cellmate's mouth, flecked with blood. A gurgling sound came from his throat. The door opened and two cons walked in. One of them retrieved the shank from beneath Donny's pillow, the other took out a phone and began to take pictures. The con with the blade striped Carlos across the face. Three bloody lines appeared and his nose hung from a piece of cartilage. The man repeatedly drew the razorblades across his flesh until he was no longer recognisable. His skin was sliced to ribbons. All the time his body was jerking like a fish out of water. Donny couldn't watch anymore. He grabbed his towel and ran out of the door.

Chapter 48

12 months later

Alan was sitting at his desk when an email from Interpol arrived. It was an update from Sri Lanka. The year before, his communication about the bar owner Nok, had been received and a courteous reply sent back to him, basically saying thank you and mind your own business. This was the first time he had heard anything from them since. The message read that the bar owner had vanished many years ago and a brief investigation revealed he was a conman with many enemies. They assumed he had taken off for his own safety or been murdered. The bar had been sold to pay the taxes he owed the government and was being run by a local couple and was very popular with tourists, none of whom had gone missing. The subject was closed. Alan wondered what had happened to him for a few seconds and then it was gone. He didn't have time to speculate. His phone rang.

'DI Williams,' he answered.

'Alan it's Del from HMP Manchester,' Del said. He was originally from Valley and was the assistant warden. Manchester was the closest category-A prison to North Wales. 'I have news about your man Benaim Bronski.'

'Ah,' Alan said. 'Is it good news?'

'Depends on your standpoint,' Del said. 'He's been found hanging in the laundry. They cut him down early this morning. He went to the infirmary but he'd been gone too long for them to do anything other than confirm his death.'

'Did he jump or was he pushed?' Alan asked.

'Too early to say, to be honest,' Del said. 'It's been no secret certain fellow Russians wanted him silenced. My money is on him being pushed but no one saw anything. He's a big lump of a man and the sheets were plaited together to hold his weight. I'm not sure he had time to do that without someone seeing him do it. I don't suppose we'll ever know. There were nine other cons in the laundry but none of them saw anything.'

'Of course, they didn't',' Alan said. 'It's a cat-A prison. Seeing anything in there comes with a public health warning, doesn't it?'

'We try our best but if the residents want to kill each other, they can be pretty inventive and determined. That's why they're in here in the first place. They're naughty.' Del laughed, hoarsely. 'On a positive note, it's saved the public an absolute fortune in legal and custodial bills. Bronski would have gone through all the appeal process protesting his innocence and still been in here until he was dribbling in his soup. Whatever happened, it's done us all a favour. If you ask me.'

'Say it as it is, Del,' Alan said. 'Don't beat around the bush.'

'I'll call you if we find anything interesting.'

'I won't hold my breath,' Alan said, 'Or lose any sleep over it. Take care, Del.'

Alan sat back in his chair and took a half bottle of single malt from his desk. He poured a nip into a crystal glass that he kept in his bottom drawer and raised it to those who died at the hands of Bronski and his poisonous network. The whisky burned and soothed simultaneously. It would take a few more to relax him enough to sleep that night. Or any night.

288

Chapter 49

Reggie Quinn lit a cigar and puffed it until the end glowed red. He inhaled the smoke and let it fill his lungs. It was a Montecristo. Reggie and Len had been partial to the odd Montecristo. It was cigar smoking which had done the damage to Len's lungs. Reggie took out a silver hipflask and opened it. He swigged the Haig malt and let it burn his tongue before he swallowed it.

'Cheers Len,' he said to the headstone. Len had been buried in a family plot, three months after he'd finally laid Leo to rest. His deterioration following the discovery of Leo's body and his subsequent burial, was dramatic. It was as if he'd given up fighting. 'I hope you're at the bar with your Leo, raising a glass together. We miss you down here. It's not the same without you around. Reggie sucked on the cigar and took another slug of whisky. 'Sorry this one took so long but they put the bastard into solitary after we hit the Vincentia scum. He took out his phone and scrolled through some pictures. 'There he is. The last of the bunch. David Prost. They cut off his head with a spade on gardening detail.' Reggie smiled and raised a toast. 'They stuck his head on a bamboo stake, which was holding up broad beans. Look at that,' he laughed and showed the image to the headstone. 'Now that shows imagination.' Reggie shook his head. 'I'm sure you're laughing wherever you are. Rest in peace my old friend I'll see you on the other side.'

The End

Circus of Nightmares
Amazon USA; https://www.amazon.com/dp/B08SXPGKWQ

Printed in Great Britain
by Amazon